T0329980

Welfare Measurement, Sustainability and Green National Accounting

NEW HORIZONS IN ENVIRONMENTAL ECONOMICS

General Editor: Wallace E. Oates, *Professor of Economics, University of Maryland*

This important series is designed to make a significant contribution to the development of the principles and practices of environmental economics. It includes both theoretical and empirical work. International in scope, it addresses issues of current and future concern in both East and West and in developed and developing countries.

The main purpose of the series is to create a forum for the publication of high quality work and to show how economic analysis can make a contribution to understanding and resolving the environmental problems confronting the world in the late twentieth century.

Recent titles in the series include:

Models of Sustainable Development
Edited by Sylvie Faucheux, David Pearce and John Proops

Contingent Valuation and Endangered Species
Methodological Issues and Applications
Kristin M. Jakobsson and Andrew K. Dragun

Acid Rain and Environmental Degradation
The Economics of Emission Trading
Ger Klaassen

The Economics of Pollution Control in the Asia Pacific
Robert Mendelsohn and Daigee Shaw

Economic Policy for the Environment and Natural Resources
Techniques for the Management and Control of Pollution
Edited by Anastasios Xepapadeas

Environmental Policy and Technical Change
A Comparison of the Technological Impact of Policy Instruments
René Kemp

Welfare Measurement, Sustainability and Green National Accounting
A Growth Theoretical Approach
Thomas Aronsson, Per-Olov Johansson and Karl-Gustaf Löfgren

The Economics of Environmental Protection
Theory and Demand Revelation
Peter Bohm

The International Yearbook of Environmental and Resource Economics
1997/1998
A Survey of Current Issues
Edited by Henk Folmer and Tom Tietenberg

The Economic Theory of Environmental Policy in a Federal System
Edited by John B. Braden and Stef Proost

Economics of Ecological Resources
Selected Essays
Charles Perrings

Welfare Measurement, Sustainability and Green National Accounting

A Growth Theoretical Approach

Thomas Aronsson

Department of Economics, University of Umeå, Sweden

Per-Olov Johansson

Department of Economics, Stockholm School of Economics, Sweden

Karl-Gustaf Löfgren

Department of Economics, University of Umeå, Sweden

NEW HORIZONS IN ENVIRONMENTAL ECONOMICS

Edward Elgar

Cheltenham, UK • Brookfield, US

Published by
Edward Elgar Publishing Limited
8 Lansdown Place
Cheltenham
Glos GL50 2HU
UK

Edward Elgar Publishing Company
Old Post Road
Brookfield
Vermont 05036
US

A catalogue record for this book is available from the British Library

Library of Congress Cataloging in Publication Data
Aronsson, Thomas, 1963–
    Welfare measurement, sustainability, and green national accounting:
a growth theoretical approach/Thomas Aronsson, Per-Olov Johansson,
Karl-Gustaf Löfgren.
(New horizons in environmental economics)
    Includes bibliographical references.
    1. Economic development—Environmental aspects—Econometric
models. 2. Welfare economics—Econometric models. 3. Environmental
auditing. 4. Social accounting. I. Johansson, Per-Olov, 1949–
II. Löfgren, Karl-Gustaf. III. Title. IV. Series.
HD75.6.A764   1996
363.7—dc20   96–23170
                                                                         CIP

ISBN 978-1-85898-485-8

Printed and bound by CPI Group (UK) Ltd, Croydon, CR0 4YY

Contents

Figures

Foreword

Writing a book is not a one-man job; not even a three-man job. Many people have been involved in the process. Some of them have contributed to a considerable extent. Kenneth Backlund, Umeå University, not only co-authored a paper on which parts of Chapter 7 are based, he also provided us with the computations and graphs in Chapter 5. Bengt Kriström, Swedish University of Agricultural Sciences, and Eva Polbring, Umeå University, have also been involved as co-authors. Bengt has, in addition, played an essential role as organizer of the Ulvö meetings, where much of the final material in the book has matured. Karl-Göran Mäler, Stockholm School of Economics, has probably been the single most important discussion partner during these meetings. We have been told that some of the discussions were memorable.

Marie Hammarstedt, Umeå University, has been the most important person in the editing process. She not only did the lion's share of the typing, but she was also the 'link' between both sides of the Atlantic, in the last stages of the journey. Some of the final work was done at the Department of Economics, University of Wisconsin, Madison. We owe much to their hospitality, and competent personnel, who helped us to find our way in the jungle of the foreign word processing equipment, fax machines and e-mail. In particular, Bonnie Rieder and Katrin Johnson at Faculty Services, and Alisienne Sumwalt at the Social System Research Institute were very helpful. At the Stockholm School of Economics, Pirjo Furtenbach has always been ready to help us with references and other details. She is also one of the organisers of the Ulvö meetings. Finally, Chris Hudson at the Department of Political Science in Umeå has made the manuscript readable, also to English-speaking people.

The mathematical pyrotechnics are probably, here and there, infected by errors and unclear thinking. We have, however, benefited from the generosity of Atle Seierstad, Oslo University, who provided us with a theorem on the differentiability of the value function in an infinite horizon optimal control problem. His book, written jointly with Knut Sydsæter, on optimal control theory, is like an American Express card: 'Don't leave home without it'. The mathematics in Chapter 8 have been improved by Sara Sjöstedt at the Department of Mathematical Statistics, Umeå University. It was an easy task.

Marty Weitzman at Harvard University is one of the intellectual fathers of our thinking, and we have been able to discuss some of the material in Chapter

3 directly with him. Rob Mendelsohn and Bill Nordhaus at Yale University invited one of the authors to present some of the material at their joint seminar. Dick Brazee at the University of Illinois, Urbana-Champagne, was kind enough to ask the same author to give a short graduate course on the main content of the book in February 1995. Another of the authors was invited to present Chapter 5 at the meeting of the Finnish Society for Economic Research in Tallin, Estonia, 1995. No doubt these events provided fresh inputs into the manuscript.

The Swedish Research Council of Agriculture and Forestry (SJFR) financed parts of the research agenda from which the book has emerged.

We thank you all.

Thomas Aronsson
Per-Olov Johansson
Karl-Gustaf Löfgren
Madison and Stockholm, March 1996

1. Introduction

1.1 SCOPE OF THE STUDY

Since their first course in macroeconomics, students are taught that the NNP (net national product) may not be a suitable measure of welfare. This is so for a variety of reasons. One is related to the definition of net investments: the only information about net investments in the conventional NNP refers to physical, man-made capital. This means that changes in other important stocks, such as natural resource stocks, environmental stocks and the stock of human capital, are not taken into account. Another – although related – example refers to external effects. If these effects are present, the market data on which NNP is based do not reflect socially optimal decisions. In other words, the *observed* resource allocation does not maximize social welfare and is, therefore, insufficient as a basis for welfare analysis. A third example is that the NNP does not reveal how consumption possibilities are distributed across individuals, households or generations.

There is a rapidly growing literature on what is sometimes called 'social accounting', where one of the purposes is to augment, or extend, the conventional NNP measure so as to obtain a better indicator of welfare. Such a measure may be called *a national product related welfare measure*. This type of welfare measure is interesting for several reasons. One is, of course, that it provides understanding of the informational content of the national accounts, as well as showing what that content could have been if certain key variables had been measured in a more appropriate way. This knowledge is also, for obvious reasons, valuable in empirical research. However, equally important is the practical convenience of national product related welfare measurement. Much would be gained if it were possible to augment the NNP by observables so that the augmented NNP measure reflects future utility. The idea of making the national accounts a better indicator of welfare has been recognized in several areas of economic research. One example is the discussion of how to 'green' the national accounts. The basic issue here is that production depletes natural resources and causes environmental damage. Changes in these stocks of 'natural' capital are part of the investment policy undertaken by society and should, therefore, be included in a more correct NNP measure. Another example is the recent attempts to measure the value of investments in human capital and to augment the NNP with these investments.

Welfare measurement is also connected to sustainability. The concern here is intergenerational equity, which can be interpreted to mean that resources are allocated so that the present generation can meet its needs without compromising the ability of future generations to meet theirs. This involves planning over very long time horizons and may require that greater weight be placed on the well-being of future generations than is often the case in the utilitarian framework, where the utilities of future generations are subject to discounting. The importance put on sustainability by policy makers was emphasized by the formation of the 'Brundtland Commission', whose primary concern was that the present generation is depleting the stocks of natural capital too fast, thereby reducing the consumption possibilities of future generations. The discussion about sustainable development is, to a large extent, ethical; the economist's task is primarily to provide 'a formula' for allocating the resources so that the outcome reflects these ethical values. From a neoclassical point of view, one may expect this resource allocation to be such that the capital asset is kept intact, so as to maintain the possibility to produce in the future. Other requirements may reflect biological concern by imposing lower bounds for certain environmental assets. In line with the emphasis on sustainable development, one would also like to have an indicator of sustainability, preferably an easily observed static measure. Intuitively, an augmented NNP measure may seem to be a suitable choice, since NNP is sometimes interpreted as the maximum consumption we can afford without reducing the capital stock. However, as we shall see below, this idea is not, in general, valid when there are several types of capital, which means that an NNP measure is less suitable as an indicator of sustainability in all but special cases.

1.2   IMPORTANT ISSUES IN PREVIOUS RESEARCH

There is now a large (and growing) literature dealing with welfare measurement, sustainability and related topics. References to these studies will be given throughout the book. Here, for the reader's convenience, we give a brief review of how the research has developed in these areas. The welfare interpretation of the NNP comes originally from an influential paper by Martin Weitzman (1976), where the NNP is shown to be an exact indicator of welfare under certain conditions. More precisely, in an economy with a stationary technology, no externalities and in which agents have perfect foresight, Weitzman was able to show that the NNP (or the utility value thereof) is proportional to the value function, by which we mean the maximized intertemporal objective function of the representative consumer. One important aspect of Weitzman's result is, therefore, the interpretation of the NNP as a *static equivalent to future utility*, i.e. the national accounts provide information about the present value of future utility along the optimal path.

The NNP concept in Weitzman's paper may (and should) be interpreted in a broader sense than has become the convention in actual systems for national accounts. This follows from Weitzman's definition of the capital stock, where he argued that, in addition to physical, man-made capital, 'pools of exhaustible natural resources ought to qualify as capital, and so should stocks of knowledge resulting from learning or research activities'. This possible extension of the conventional NNP (into what we have called a national product related measure) has inspired much of the more recent research on social accounting and welfare measurement. Hartwick (1990), Dasgupta and Mäler (1991) and Mäler (1991) study the situation where, in addition to physical capital, natural and environmental resources are also important factors in the economic system. Following Weitzman, these papers argue that a national product related welfare measure should include the value of changes in these resource stocks in addition to net investments in physical, man-made capital. The multiple use character of certain types of resources and the resulting consequences for welfare measurement are also discussed.

Another direction of recent research concerns complications for welfare measurement following disembodied technological change and externalities; see, for example, Kemp and Long (1982), Löfgren (1992), Aronsson and Löfgren (1993, 1995a, 1995b). The basic concern here is welfare analysis in a non-autonomous economic system, by which we mean that time itself has a *direct* effect on utility and/or production (in addition to its influence via the equilibrium variables and via the discount factor). If utility and/or production are explicit functions of time, so is welfare, implying that there is no simple relationship between a static, observable NNP measure and the social welfare function. However, there is also a fundamental difference between exogenous technological progress and external effects. If the non-autonomous time dependence originates from external effects, it would, in principle, be possible to create an autonomous economic system by internalizing these externalities. The latter also indicates some of the practical challenges and difficulties involved in applying the ideas behind 'green' accounting, since the informational requirements that need to be met are enormous (to say the very least).

The analysis of sustainable development has a long history and goes back to economists such as Irving Fisher, John Hicks and Erik Lindahl, who were all concerned with measuring income: see Fisher (1906), Hicks (1939) and Lindahl (1933). Hicks's definition of income as 'the maximum amount of money which the individual can spend this week, and still be able to spend the same amount in real terms each ensuing week' is appealing, because of its close connection to sustainable consumption. Probably influenced by the earlier studies, some economists have (until very recently) argued that a 'complete' NNP concept should reflect the maximum sustainable consumption level, since it measures what we can consume at present without reducing the capital stock. However, although intuitively appealing, this interpretation of the NNP is not as general as it may seem. As Asheim (1994a) points out, in an economy with heterogeneous capital, the value of the net investments *at a given point in time* is no indicator of sustainability. The reason is that, in the multiple capital goods case, it is not clear which capital stock should remain intact. As a consequence, even if the value of the net investments (defined as the sum of the value of net investments in different capital goods) is greater than or equal to zero at a given point in time, consumption may actually exceed its maximum sustainable level.

An important question is, therefore, under what conditions is consumption constant along the optimal path in the multiple capital goods case? One answer was provided in a paper by John Hartwick (1977). Hartwick showed that if the value of the net investments is zero *along the optimal path*, then consumption is constant along the optimal path. The particular example given by Hartwick refers to a specific investment rule in an economy where the capital concept involves both a non-renewable natural resource and physical, man-made capital. The constant consumption path follows, in this case, if the proceeds from harvesting this natural resource are invested in man-made capital, so as to keep the value of net investments zero. This is often referred to as Hartwick's rule. Dixit et al. (1980) proved the converse proposition, namely that if consumption is constant along the optimal path, then the value of the net investments must be zero along the optimal path.

In general, however, the optimal consumption path derived on the basis of a utilitarian objective function does not meet the requirements for intergenerational equity, since the utility of future generations is subject to discounting. At the same time, given the requirement that the utility is to be constant across generations, we would certainly like to give each generation as much utility as possible, and may ask what resource allocation (among the feasible paths) maximizes the sustainable utility level. Such a resource allocation is sometimes referred to as 'the green golden rule' and is in sharp contrast to the utilitarian – usually single peaked – consumption/utility paths; see Chichilnisky (1993) and Heal (1995). A compromise between these two cases is discussed by Chichilnisky (1993), who uses the term 'dictatorship of the present' when discussing the utilitarian social welfare function, while the maximand implicit in the green golden rule path – which is defined as the limit of the instantaneous utility when time goes to infinity – is called 'dictatorship of the future'. She then suggests an objective function which excludes these two extremes. This results in a resource allocation that is more oriented towards future generations than the allocation implicit in the utilitarian approach, but less 'conservative' than the green golden rule.

1.3 PLAN OF THE BOOK

The purpose of this book is to integrate the existing research on welfare measurement discussed above. The content essentially coincides with the issues outlined in the previous two subsections. In a number of cases, this involves pushing the theory forwards in new directions, as well as applying the analysis to topics neglected in previous research. Some parts of the analysis are also related to recent empirical work within the field of growth accounting.

Chapter 2 introduces some concepts of importance in the analysis to follow such as Hamiltonians, control variables, state variables and costate variables. This is accomplished within a simple discrete time model, where we relate the necessary conditions of the Lagrange method to their counterparts in optimal control theory. The chapter also provides some foundations for the welfare interpretation of the NNP in a dynamic economy. Chapter 3 concerns welfare analysis in the Ramsey growth model, which is a continuous-time, infinite horizon model. In this simple benchmark model, the (utility value of the) NNP is the appropriate welfare indicator. We also show that, given the assumptions on which the Ramsey model is based, the decentralized market solution supports a command optimum, which means that market data contain all the relevant information for measuring welfare. The chapter also examines the effects of previously unanticipated shocks to the economy, both in terms of effects on consumption and capital formation and in terms of welfare effects.

Chapter 4 extends the benchmark model by introducing technological change and external effects. The analysis is based on a model originally developed by Brock (1977), where firms' release of emissions gives rise to a consumption externality. We have also augmented this model with disembodied technological change, which makes production an explicit function of time. We start by showing that disembodied technological change expected by agents introduces a non-autonomous time dependence in the economic system, which makes welfare an explicit function of time. In this case, there is no observable, static equivalent to future utility. We also show that the decentralized economy does not support a command optimum because of the consumption externality. This means that, even in the absence of disembodied technological change, observable market data (i.e. a national product related measure) would be insufficient as a basis for welfare measurement. The chapter also contains cost–benefit rules for evaluating the welfare effects of policy changes designed to affect the quality of the environment.

Chapter 5 presents an application to a specific topic: the complications for welfare measurement arising from investments in human capital. This is motivated by the concern for human capital in several recent empirical papers on growth accounting, where one of the main issues has been to measure the value of these investments. The analysis is based on a Ramsey type growth model, where consumers choose consumption of goods, time in market work and time in education. Our approach to modelling the production side of the economy relates to endogenous growth theory in the sense that human capital gives rise to a positive production externality. In addition to deriving welfare measures – and comparing these with the augmented NNP measures suggested in some of the empirical papers – the chapter is also concerned to design a tax and transfer system such that the external effect becomes internalized. We also discuss the situation when the government is not able to fully internalize the external effect, and we derive the welfare effects of policy changes designed to affect the consumers' valuation of the stock of human capital.

Sustainability and related topics are analysed in Chapter 6. We start by discussing optimal consumption paths following from a Rawlsian social welfare function. This type of function reflects concern for intergenerational equity in the sense of maximizing utility for the generation with the lowest utility level. Another part of the chapter deals with the informational content of the net investments in the multiple capital goods case. As mentioned above, the value of the investments at a given point in time is no indicator of sustainability in such an economy. To facilitate the interpretation of this result, we derive an exact relationship between the value of the net investments at a given point in time and future consumption preferences. If the value of the net investments happens to be zero at a given point in time, this only means that the preferences are such that a weighted average of future changes in consumption is zero along the optimal path. It also turns out that this result relates, in a natural way, to Hartwick's rule. The chapter ends with a comparison between the utilitarian case and the green golden rule.

Chapter 7 analyses a variety of issues neglected in the previous chapters such as open economies, non-constant rates of time preference and stochastic time horizons. Section 7.1 relates to Chapter 6 – by focusing on sustainability – but extends the analysis to an open economy. One important result is that, if we want to keep the national wealth constant over time, then the maximum allowable consumption will be an NNP measure augmented by capital gains. We also discuss the seemingly conflicting result that, if we were to add all countries into a world economy and keep the aggregate consumption constant, consumption would equal a measure of NNP that does not include capital gains. Sections 7.2 and 7.3 continue by addressing two recent topics in social accounting: the complications for welfare measurement arising from a non-constant rate of time preference (Section 7.2) and the treatment of household defensive expenditures in 'green' NNP measures (Section 7.3).

Welfare measurement under stochastic time horizons originates from the health economic literature (see Aronsson et al., 1994). However, the application in Section 7.4 relates to the global warming problem. The most important complication, in comparison with the previous chapters, is that we here relax the assumption that the economy will continue forever with perfect certainty. The global warming problem is, in a fundamental way, related to uncertainty, and depends on the impact of greenhouse gases on the climate. It seems indisputable that high concentrations of greenhouse gases in the atmosphere will lead to substantial changes in the environment that could severely affect the living conditions of mankind. We shall incorporate this uncertainty into the model by introducing what we call 'the probability of doomsday'. This means that, if the catastrophe scenario implicit in the global warming problem becomes reality, the instantaneous utility level will drop to zero and stay so ever after. In Section 7.4 we show how to incorporate this assumption into an optimal control model, as well as analysing its implications from the points of view of resource allocation and welfare measurement.

Chapter 8 extends the basic models of Chapters 3 and 4 in order to analyse complications for welfare measurement arising from uncertainty. The aspects of uncertainty dealt with here refer to the aggregate level of the economy, and are very different from the analysis of stochastic time horizons in Chapter 7. Naturally, uncertainty can occur in all parts of the economy, and it would not be feasible to try to capture all possible sources of uncertainty. Our approach is to examine the welfare properties of a well known growth model introduced in its basic form by Merton (1975), where the growth rate of the labour force is stochastic from 'the social planner's' point of view. Welfare measurement under uncertainty in a dynamic model requires other mathematical tools than those used in previous chapters, which justifies a brief introduction to stochastic control theory. With these tools at our disposal, we are able to show that national product related welfare measurement requires that the NNP is augmented by a term reflecting attitudes to risk. Moreover, the welfare measures derived under perfect certainty appear as nested special cases in this more general model, which closes the circle in a natural way.

2. Introducing dynamic models and welfare indices

This book focuses on continuous time dynamic growth models and their welfare implications. The solution technique we use is optimal control theory. One of the purposes of this short chapter is to introduce certain concepts which are important in the remaining chapters such as Hamiltonians, control variables, state variables and costate variables. We shall do this by formulating a discrete time optimization problem, which makes it easy to relate the familiar necessary conditions of the Lagrange method to the necessary conditions in optimal control theory. To simplify the analysis, we shall use a two-period model. Another purpose of the chapter is to provide some foundations for the welfare interpretation of the net national product (or a measure related to the net national product). Accordingly, it is primarily directed at readers who are not very familiar with optimal control theory and it should, we hope, make it easier for them to follow the analyses in later chapters. Readers familiar with control theory can, without loss of notational convention, go directly to Chapter 3. At the same time, the chapter also serves as an introduction to some of the problems and models which come later. This is valuable, at least, for teaching purposes.

The chapter is structured as follows. Section 2.1 introduces a simple two-period model and relates the outcome of the familiar Lagrange method to the necessary conditions in optimal control theory. We also give a graphical interpretation of the net national product (NNP), which is based on the relationship between the NNP and the social welfare function. Section 2.2 adds a pollution stock to the optimization problem. The purpose is to broaden the capital concept and, therefore, the definition of 'net investments', which is important in obtaining a national product measure suitable for welfare analysis (and in understanding the recent literature on social accounting). The section ends with a cost–benefit rule aimed at capturing the costs and benefits of pollution control.

2.1 A TWO-PERIOD MODEL

In this section, we consider a very simple decision problem, where the economy consists of a single individual who lives for two periods, interpreted as representing today and the future, respectively. What happens after the second period is ignored, i.e. there are no bequest motives for carrying over resources to periods beyond the second period. The individual derives utility from consuming a single homogeneous commodity. We assume that utility is intertemporally separable, which means that the intertemporal utility function can be written

$$U = u(c(0)) + \Lambda(1)u(c(1)) \tag{2.1}$$

where $u(c)$ is an increasing and strictly concave instantaneous utility function and $c(t)$ is consumption in period t. The utility discount factor is defined by $\Lambda(t) = (1+\theta)^{-t}$, where θ is the rate of time preference. The assumption of a separable utility function is used in the continuous time models set out in the remaining chapters, which makes it natural to use this assumption here as well.

One purpose of this section is to introduce, in the simplest possible way, a number of tools – such as Hamiltonians, control variables, state variables and costate variables – which are important in the analysis to follow. Another purpose is to discuss briefly the welfare foundation of national product (income) measures. We shall neglect production and examine what may be thought of as 'a consumption economy'. Ignoring production also means that we can disregard the difference between the social planner's optimal solution (i.e. the socially optimal allocation of the resources) and the decentralized equilibrium. This implies, among other things, that we are here neglecting externalities (and their implications for welfare measurement in the decentralized economy), an issue discussed at some length in later chapters.

Let $k(t)$ denote the individual's asset position (which we may interpret as physical capital) in the beginning of period t, i.e. the asset carried over from period $t-1$ to period t. The individual also receives an exogenous income, y, which for simplicity is assumed to be constant over time. This means that, at the end of period t, the individual will decide how to allocate his/her income, $y + \theta k(t)$, between consumption, $c(t)$, and 'investments', $k(t+1) - k(t)$. Given the choice of time horizon, the economy's budget constraint or resource constraint takes the form

$$y + k(0) + \theta k(0) = c(0) + k(1) \tag{2.2}$$

$$y + k(1) + \theta k(1) = c(1) + k(2) \tag{2.3}$$

where $k(0)$ is the predetermined or fixed asset in period zero. The nominal price of the consumption good is constant over time (and equal to unity) for notational convenience. Equations (2.2) and (2.3) are based on the assumption that the interest rate, i.e. the marginal product of capital, equals the rate of time preference. As we shall show in Chapter 3, this is precisely the steady state (or dynamic equilibrium) condition obeyed by the physical capital stock in a more general version of the model, which involves production. Obviously, to solve the utility maximization problem, some kind of constraint must be placed on $k(2)$ in order to prevent the individual from unlimited borrowing. A reasonable constraint is that $k(2) \geq 0$, which effectively implies that $k(2) = 0$, as there are no incentives in this model for the individual to carry over resources beyond period one. We shall use $k(2) = 0$ as part of the conditions obeyed by the optimal solution and refer to it as a terminal condition, since it relates to the terminal point of the planning period.

Lagrangeans and Hamiltonians

To maximize the utility function in (2.1) subject to (2.2) and (2.3), we formulate the Lagrangean

$$L = \sum_{t=0}^{1} L(t) = \sum_{t=0}^{1} \left\{ \Lambda(t)u(c(t)) + \lambda^{L}(t)[y + k(t) + \theta k(t) - k(t+1) - c(t)] \right\} \quad (2.4)$$

where $\lambda^{L}(t)$ is the Lagrange multiplier associated with the period t budget constraint. As mentioned above, we would like to formulate the optimization problem so that its solution resembles the outcome of the optimal control problems analysed in the remaining chapters. Therefore, we shall here follow Leonard and van Long (1992) and introduce a discrete analogue to the Hamiltonian function. The idea is to express the within-period budget constraints as difference equations, since we are using a discrete time model; a continuous time model uses differential equations. Rearranging (2.2) and (2.3), by solving for the change in the capital stock, i.e. $k(t + 1) - k(t)$, the discrete analogue to the present value Hamiltonian is written

$$H(t) = \Lambda(t)\, u(c(t)) + \lambda(t)\, [k(t + 1) - k(t)] = \Lambda(t)u(c(t))$$
$$+ \lambda(t)\, [y + \theta k(t) - c(t)] \quad (2.5)$$

where $t = 0, 1$. The variable $\lambda(t)$ is interpreted as the present (period zero) utility value of additional capital in period t. Substituting Equation (2.5) into (2.4) and using the fact that $\lambda(t) = \lambda^{L}(t)$, we obtain

$$L = \sum_{t=0}^{1} \left[H(t) - \lambda(t)(k(t+1) - k(t)) \right] \quad (2.4a)$$

where $H(t)$ is defined as suggested by the term after the second equality in Equation (2.5). Maximizing (2.4a) with respect to $c(0)$, $c(1)$, $k(1)$, $\lambda(0)$ and $\lambda(1)$, the necessary conditions are written

$$\frac{\partial L}{\partial c(t)} = \frac{\partial H(t)}{\partial c(t)} = \Lambda(t)u_c\big(c(t)\big) - \lambda(t) = 0, \quad t = 0,1 \qquad (2.6a)$$

$$\frac{\partial L}{\partial k(t)} = \frac{\partial H(t)}{\partial k(t)} + \lambda(t) - \lambda(t-1) = 0, \quad t = 1 \qquad (2.6b)$$

$$\frac{\partial L}{\partial \lambda(t)} = y + k(t) + \theta k(t) - c(t) - k(t+1) = 0, \quad t = 0,1 \qquad (2.6c)$$

where a subindex denotes a partial derivative, e.g. $u_c(c) = \partial u(c)/\partial c$, while $\partial H(t)$ $/ \partial k(t) = \lambda(t)\theta$. Note that Equations (2.6) constitute, together, only part of the necessary conditions. In addition, we require that $k(0)$ takes its predetermined value, which is an initial condition, and that the solution obeys the terminal condition $k(2) = 0$.

It is interesting to observe that the necessary conditions for maximizing the Lagrangean can be interpreted in terms of the Hamiltonian. In an optimal control problem, consumption (which is a flow variable) would be termed 'control variable', and the interpretation of (2.6a) is that *the Hamiltonian should be maximized with respect to the control variable at each point in time*. Similarly, a stock variable such as k is called 'state variable', and Equation (2.6b) relates the impact of the state variable on the Hamiltonian (which measures the marginal product of capital) to *the development over time of the shadow price of this state variable*. Since capital is a state variable, we use the term 'costate variable' for its shadow price. Finally, (2.6c) simply restates the accumulation equations for the capital stock, i.e. the within-period budget constraints in (2.2) and (2.3). Together with the initial and terminal conditions, Equations (2.6) completely characterize the solution to the optimization problem. Given the resource constraint, Equation (2.6a) defines consumption conditional on the marginal value of physical capital. The latter variable is obtained by solving the difference equation (2.6b). The reader will recognize the continuous time counterparts of these conditions once he/she arrives at Chapter 3.

A Graphical Interpretation of 'NNP'

It is desirable to be able to define an indicator of aggregate economic welfare related to an observable measure such as the NNP. One of the main purposes of this book is to derive such welfare indicators and to examine how the conventional NNP should be augmented so as to become a better measure of welfare. How to accomplish this task, and how to prove formally the welfare equivalence of the national product related measure, under certain conditions, is left for later chapters. What we shall do here is to provide a graphical interpretation of the NNP using the simple model set out above. Consider Figure 2.1, which gives a graphical illustration of the optimal resource allocation in period t. In the figure, A – A' represents the frontier of the 'utility production set', while the term $i(t)$ is a short notation for net investments in period t, i.e. $i(t) = k(t + 1) - k(t)$. To make the welfare interpretation of NNP explicit, we define 'the utility NNP' as

$$NNP = u(c^*(t)) + \lambda^{c^*}(t)[k^*(t + 1) - k^*(t)] \qquad (2.7)$$

where $\lambda^{c^*}(t) = \lambda^*(t)\Lambda(t)^{-1}$ is the current value shadow price of capital measured in utility units, while the superindex * is used to indicate the optimal solution. Graphically, we represent the (negative of the) current value shadow price of capital by the straight line connecting the two axes. Using the linear

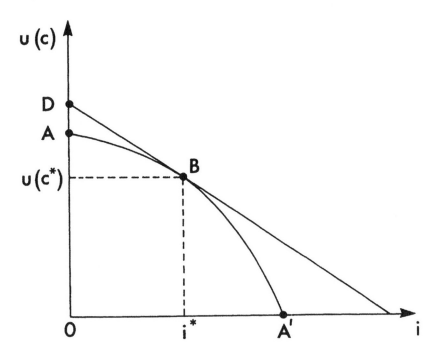

Figure 2.1   The utility NNP

approximation $u_c(c^*(t))c^*(t) = \lambda^{c^*}(t)c^*(t) \approx u(c^*(t))$, we can define (a local approximation of) the real NNP by dividing Equation (2.7) by the marginal utility of consumption, $\lambda^{c^*}(t)$. The optimal solution occurs at point B, where the 'marginal rate of transformation' is equal to the relative price of investments in terms of the price of utility. Now, since the figure depicts the socially optimal resource allocation in period t, there is a close connection between the welfare level and the utility NNP. This is so because the utility NNP involves both the current welfare level – measured along the vertical axis in the figure – and the future welfare effects caused by present actions (i.e. saving).

Using Figure 2.1, we can measure the utility NNP as the vertical distance $0 - D$. This is a strictly hypothetical instantaneous utility level in period t, since the linear relationship between the instantaneous utility and the net investment only holds locally. The maximum instantaneous utility level that is actually attainable in period t is given by the distance $0 - A$ on the vertical axis. However, it also turns out that the maximum utility obtained along the optimal path, i.e. $u(c^*(0)) + \Lambda(1)u(c^*(1))$, is the same as would be obtained if we were to 'consume' the utility NNP in every period, which makes utility NNP a static equivalent of welfare. To illustrate, let us once again use the linear approximation $\lambda^{c^*}(t)c^*(t) \approx u(c^*(t))$, which makes it possible to define utility NNP in period zero as

$$\lambda^{c^*}(0)(c^*(0) + i^*(0)) = \lambda^{c^*}(0)(y + \theta k(0))$$

Using the welfare function in Equation (2.1), the first-order condition $\theta\lambda^*(1) + \lambda^*(1) - \lambda^*(0) = 0$ in Equation (2.6b) and the terminal condition that $k(2) = 0$, we find that[1]

$$\lambda^*(0)c^*(0) + \lambda^*(1)c^*(1) = \lambda^*(0)(y + \theta k(0)) + \lambda^*(0)\frac{(y + \theta k(0))}{(1 + \theta)} + \lambda^*(0)\frac{k(0)}{(1 + \theta)}$$

which means that the utility from consuming $c^*(0)$ and $c^*(1)$ in the first and second period, respectively, is the same as would be obtained by consuming the NNP for period zero in both periods plus consuming the capital stock when arriving at the time horizon. The present value of the latter term would go to zero, when the number of periods go to infinity. So far, the welfare interpretation of the NNP (or, more generally, a measure related to the NNP) is just a claim within a very simple model, but in Chapter 3 we shall formally prove this result, which was originally derived by Weitzman in his classic 1976 paper. We shall also show, in later chapters, that the interpretation of the (utility) NNP as a welfare measure is closely related to the socially optimal resource allocation: if the resources are not allocated in an optimal way, the NNP has no welfare interpretation along the lines suggested above.

2.2   TOWARDS A BROADER INVESTMENT CONCEPT

Part of the problem of using the traditional NNP measure as a welfare indicator is its inability to correctly account for the value of changes in the capital stocks. In actual national accounting, the term 'net investment' means changes in the stock of physical capital. Changes in other capital stocks relevant for the production of output, such as natural resources, the human capital stock and pollution stocks, are not accounted for. An important part of constructing a national product related welfare measure is, therefore, to measure the value of the additions (positive or negative) to these stocks. In other words, the analysis requires a broader investment concept. This also means that the term 'NNP' can be interpreted in a broader sense than is commonly the case. To give the reader an idea of what we mean by the broader investment (or NNP) concept, we would like to broaden the capital stock in a very simple way by assuming that, in addition to the stock of physical capital, there is also a pollution stock that affects the welfare level.

At this stage of the analysis, our concern is not to analyse the sources of pollution, but to capture how pollution affects the welfare level and the definition of 'NNP'. To accomplish this task in the simplest possible way, we shall continue to neglect production by assuming that the output of final goods and services is exogenous. Since there is no production side in the model, we also assume that human activities produce a constant per period flow of emissions. These emissions are assumed to exceed the environment's assimilative capacity. As the individual's welfare is negatively affected by the stock of pollution, he (or implicitly the public sector) is, therefore, carrying out pollution treatment measures. The individual derives utility from consuming a single commodity, and is damaged by the stock of pollution. Denoting the stock of pollution at the beginning of period t by $z(t)$, the intertemporal utility function is written

$$U = u(c(0), z(0)) + \Lambda(1)u(c(1), z(1)) \tag{2.8}$$

By taking the costs of pollution treatment activities into account, the resource constraint takes the form

$$y + k(0) + \theta k(0) = c(0) + I(\alpha(0)) + k(1) \tag{2.9a}$$

$$y + k(1) + \theta k(1) = c(1) + I(\alpha(1)) + k(2) \tag{2.9b}$$

where the function $I(\alpha)$ denotes the expenditures aimed at reducing pollution, and α is an intensity parameter, i.e. $\partial I(\cdot)/\partial \alpha > 0$. The stock of pollution evolves according to the following equations:

$$z(1) = e(\alpha(0)) + (1 - \gamma)z(0) \qquad (2.9c)$$

$$z(2) = e(\alpha(1)) + (1 - \gamma)z(1) \qquad (2.9d)$$

where $e(\cdot)$ denotes the flow of emissions as a function of the public sector's pollution treatment activities, $z(0)$ the initial (predetermined) stock of pollution, $z(2)$ the stock of pollution carried over to period two, and γ the environment's exogenously given assimilative capacity ($0 < \gamma < 1$). We assume that the emission production function has the property $e_\alpha (\cdot) < 0$.

The optimization problem can now be formulated such as to maximize (2.8) subject to (2.9a)–(2.9d), as well as to initial and terminal conditions for the physical capital stock and the stock of pollution. The most obvious way to solve this problem is to form a Lagrangean. By proceeding in the same way as in the previous section, we can also in this case write the Lagrangean in terms of the Hamiltonian function. This enables us once again to relate the the necessary conditions of this optimization problem to those in optimal control theory. The (discrete analogue to the) present value Hamiltonian takes the form

$$H(t) = \Lambda(t)u(c(t),z(t)) + \lambda(t)[k(t + 1) - k(t)] + \mu(t)[z(t + 1) - z(t)] \qquad (2.10)$$

or, by using the expressions for $k(t + 1) - k(t)$ and $z(t + 1) - z(t)$,

$$H(t) = \Lambda(t)u(c(t),z(t)) + \lambda(t)[y + \theta k(t) - c(t) - I(\alpha(t))]$$
$$+ \mu(t)[e(\alpha(t)) - \gamma z(t)] \qquad (2.11)$$

where $t = 0,1$ and $\mu(t)$ is the costate variable associated with the difference equation for the evolution of the stock of pollution, and is interpreted as the (presumably negative) utility value in period zero of an addition to the stock of pollution in period t. Using the definition of the present value Hamiltonian in Equation (2.11), it is easily verified that the Lagrangean can be written as

$$L = \sum_{t=0}^{1} \left\{ H(t) - \lambda(t)\left[k(t + 1) - k(t)\right] - \mu(t)\left[z(t + 1) - z(t)\right] \right\} \qquad (2.12)$$

By maximizing the Lagrangean with respect to $c(0)$, $c(1)$, $\alpha(0)$, $\alpha(1)$, $k(1)$, $z(1)$, $\lambda(0)$, $\lambda(1)$, $\mu(0)$ and $\mu(1)$, the necessary conditions become

$$\frac{\partial L}{\partial c(t)} = \frac{\partial H(t)}{\partial c(t)} = \Lambda(t)u_c\big(c(t)\big) - \lambda(t) = 0, \quad t = 0,1 \qquad (2.13a)$$

$$\frac{\partial L}{\partial \alpha(t)} = \frac{\partial H(t)}{\partial \alpha(t)} = \mu(t)e_\alpha(\alpha(t)) - \lambda(t)I_\alpha(\alpha(t)) = 0, \quad t = 0,1 \qquad (2.13b)$$

$$\frac{\partial L}{\partial k(t)} = \frac{\partial H(t)}{\partial k(t)} + \lambda(t) - \lambda(t-1) = 0, \quad t = 1 \qquad (2.13c)$$

$$\frac{\partial L}{\partial z(t)} = \frac{\partial H(t)}{\partial z(t)} + \mu(t) - \mu(t-1) = 0, \quad t = 1 \qquad (2.13d)$$

$$\frac{\partial L}{\partial \lambda(t)} = y + \theta k(t) - c(t) - I(\alpha(t)) + k(t) - k(t+1) = 0, \quad t = 0,1 \qquad (2.13e)$$

$$\frac{\partial L}{\partial \mu(t)} = e(\alpha(t)) - \gamma z(t) + z(t) - z(t+1) = 0, \quad t = 0,1 \qquad (2.13f)$$

In arriving at the necessary conditions, we have imposed the terminal condition that $z(2)$ is fixed or predetermined. We also require the initial condition that $z(0)$ takes its fixed and predetermined value as well as the initial and terminal condition for the physical capital stock discussed in Section 2.1. The necessary conditions (2.13) can be interpreted in a way similar to their counterparts in Section 2.1. The control variables are, in this case, consumption and pollution treatment in periods zero and one. For example, Equation (2.13b) means that the Hamiltonian is to be maximized with respect to $\alpha(0)$ and $\alpha(1)$, i.e. the pollution treatment is optimally chosen at each point in time. Similarly, this problem involves an additional state variable, z, and an additional costate variable μ, and we see from (2.13d) that the development over time of μ depends on the impact of z on the Hamiltonian. Finally, (2.13e) and (2.13f) restate the accumulation equations for the state variables.

We mentioned previously that broadening the net investment concept also implies a broader definition of the NNP than the one used in actual national accounting. In this economy, where the stock of pollution affects the social welfare function, changes in the stock of pollution will also have an impact on the utility NNP. The reason is that such changes are examples of present activities that will affect future well-being. The utility NNP in period t is written

$$u(c^*(t), z^*(t)) + \lambda^c(t)[k^*(t+1) - k^*(t)] + \mu^c(t)[z^*(t+1) - z^*(t)] \qquad (2.14)$$

where the superindex ^{c} indicates current (period t) value. We are also in this case able to interpret the utility NNP as the sum of the current welfare level and the future welfare effects of the present investment actions. However, in an economy where the optimal resource allocation obeys Equations (2.9) and (2.13), this interpretation cannot be given to the standard NNP measure of the previous section. The reason is that the former measure neglects the value of the changes in the stock of pollution. Therefore, if changes in stocks other than the physical capital stock – such as resource stocks, the stock of human capital and stocks of pollution – affect the welfare function (either directly or indirectly), a national product related welfare measure should value these changes (and possibly value the stocks) appropriately in order to capture all the welfare effects of present actions.

2.3   THE BENEFITS AND COSTS OF POLLUTION CONTROL

In this section, we shall consider the benefits and costs of pollution treatment. The analysis serves as a brief introduction to cost–benefit analysis in intertemporal models. To begin, let us redefine $\alpha(0)$ and $\alpha(1)$ as parameters, which are exogenous in the initial optimization conducted by the individual. If pollution treatment is not a control variable, the stock of pollution will be exogenous in the (initial) optimization problem, meaning that the set of necessary conditions reduces to Equations (2.13a), (2.13c) and (2.13e). Suppose that, for a given initial scale of operation of the pollution treatment activities, the individual (or the government) has to decide whether or not to change the scale of operations, i.e. to increase or decrease $\alpha(0)$ and $\alpha(1)$. Increasing the scale of operation of the pollution control means reducing consumption at present, while enjoying the benefits of reduced pollution in the future. It is obvious that there are no benefits associated with period one pollution treatment measures. The 'benefits' occur in period two which is beyond the time horizon of the individual (or society) under consideration. The optimal scale of period one pollution treatment is hence $\alpha(1) = 0$. Let us, therefore, consider pollution treatment in period zero, which means reducing consumption in period zero in order to be able to reduce the stock of pollution in period one. Differentiating the social welfare function in Equation (2.8) with respect to $\alpha(0)$, and using the necessary condition for optimal consumption, we obtain a general version of the cost benefit rule:

$$\frac{dU}{d\alpha(0)} = \lambda(0)\frac{\partial c(0)}{\partial \alpha(0)} + \Lambda(1)u_z\big(c(1),z(1)\big)\frac{\partial z(1)}{\partial \alpha(0)} \qquad (2.15)$$

The optimal period zero pollution treatment level must be such that $dU / d\alpha(0)$ = 0. Multiplying all terms in Equation (2.15) by $1/\lambda(0)$, we find that the optimal scale of period zero pollution treatment is such that the period zero marginal cost in terms of real consumption is equal to the present value marginal willingness to pay for a reduction of the period one stock of pollution. Note also that, to design the current period (i.e. period zero) pollution treatment activity in an optimal way, we would require knowledge of the future marginal utility of a reduction in the stock of pollution. This shows, in a simple way, that cost–benefit analysis may require information about the future path taken by the economy.

Using Equations (2.9a) and (2.9c), Equation (2.15) can be rewritten as

$$\frac{dU}{d\alpha(0)} = -\lambda(0)I_\alpha(\alpha(0)) + \Lambda(1)u_z(c(1), z(1))e_\alpha(\alpha(0)) \qquad (2.16)$$

It is interesting to observe a relationship between the cost-benefit rule in Equation (2.16) and derivatives of the present value Hamiltonian. When $\alpha(0)$ is a parameter (rather than a control variable), the present value Hamiltonian in Equation (2.11) reduces to

$$H(t) = \Lambda(t)u(c(t), z(t)) + \lambda(t)[y(t) + \theta k(t) - c(t) - I(\alpha(t))] \qquad (2.17)$$

where $t = 0,1$. By using (2.17), the Lagrangean implicit in the individual's optimization problem takes the form

$$L = \sum_{t=0}^{1}\left[H(t) - \lambda(t)(k(t+1) - k(t))\right] \qquad (2.18)$$

Using the derivatives of (2.17) or (2.18), Equation (2.16) can be written as

$$\frac{dU}{d\alpha(0)} = \frac{\partial H(0)}{\partial\alpha(0)} + \frac{\partial H(1)}{\partial\alpha(0)} = \frac{\partial L}{\partial\alpha(0)} \qquad (2.19)$$

which means that the welfare effect of a change in a parameter is obtained by differentiating the present value Hamiltonians partially and summing these partial derivatives over the planning horizon. Note also that we have only to take the partial derivatives of the Hamiltonians with respect to the policy parameter; the indirect effects of this parameter via the control, state and costate variables vanish as a consequence of optimization.[2] In fact, Equation (2.19) is a straightforward application of the envelope theorem.[3] Although the computational simplification suggested by Equation (2.19) may not seem to be of much help in the simple model set out here, the reader will find it very useful in the more complicated models to come later.

NOTES

1. To derive this result, use Equation (2.6b) to obtain

$$\lambda^*(0)c^*(0)+\lambda^*(1)c^*(1)=\lambda^*(0)c^*(0)+\frac{\lambda^*(0)}{1+\theta}c^*(1)$$

Substituting the resource constraint into this equation gives

$$\lambda^*(0)c^*(0)+\frac{\lambda^*(0)}{1+\theta}c^*(1)=\lambda^*(0)\big(y+\theta k(0)+k(0)-k^*(1)\big)+\frac{\lambda^*(0)}{1+\theta}\big(y+\theta k^*(1)+k^*(1)-k^*(2)\big)$$

By rearranging and using the terminal condition, we obtain the result.
2. Note that the effect of α on the stock of pollution remains, as the stock of pollution is not a state variable in this case.
3. See, e.g., Varian (1992).

3. A dynamic general equilibrium model

This chapter presents a simple dynamic general equilibrium model sometimes referred to as 'The Ramsey Growth Model'. This model was first introduced by Frank Ramsey in 1928, but appears here in a modified form known to a macroeconomic audience from the work of Blanchard and Fisher (1989) and Barro and Sala-I-Martin (1995).[1] Here, the model will serve as a benchmark from which further elaborations are made in later chapters. Agents are assumed to have infinite horizons and to operate in competitive markets. In the simplest version of the model, neither technological change nor externalities are present. As we shall show in Section 3.1, these assumptions mean that the resource allocation in the decentralized economy coincides with the resource allocation that would be chosen by a utilitarian social planner.[2] Such a result also has obvious implications for welfare measurement, since it means that the optimal path is the path we *observe* in the decentralized economy.

Two important issues are raised in Section 3.2. The first concerns the information required to measure economic welfare, and the second whether the necessary information is available in current market data. Given the assumptions on which the benchmark model is based, we show that a national product related measure is the appropriate indicator of economic welfare. This measure is sometimes referred to as 'a static equivalent of welfare', and the convenience with the benchmark model is that this information *is* available in current market data. Section 3.3, finally, deals with the dynamic properties of the model in terms of behavioural and welfare effects of previously unexpected changes in technological parameters. To discuss behavioural effects, we derive 'comparative dynamic' results, measuring how these parametric changes affect the optimal paths for consumption and the capital stock. We also show that the resulting welfare effects are – as a general rule – not measurable by 'a static equivalent'. The reason is that shocks to the technology or the environment affect future consumption possibilities, and these are not captured by a static measure based on current prices.

3.1 THE CENTRAL PLANNER VERSUS THE DECENTRALIZED ECONOMY

As mentioned previously, agents are assumed to be identical and have infinite horizons. To simplify the analysis, we follow the convention in the literature on welfare measurement and disregard population growth and normalize the population to equal one.[3] The individual's utility function (which in this case is identical to the social welfare function) is written as

$$U(0) = \int_0^\infty u\big(c(t)\big)e^{-\theta t} dt \qquad (3.1)$$

where $c(t)$ is consumption at time t and θ is the constant rate of time preference. The instantaneous utility function, $u(c)$, is assumed to have the conventional properties of being increasing and strictly concave in its argument. This means that the utility function is 'well behaved' in the sense that utility maximization, subject to a convex feasibility set, results in a unique global solution. The individual supplies one unit of labour inelastically at each point in time, which explains why leisure is not included in the utility function.[4]

Turning to the supply side of the economy, output is determined by capital, k, and labour, which are the only production factors. Output is defined by the equation

$$y(t) = F\big(k(t), 1\big) = f\big(k(t)\big) = c(t) + \frac{dk(t)}{dt} \qquad (3.2)$$

where $y(t)$ is output at time t, which can either be used for consumption, $c(t)$, or investments, $dk(t)\,/\,dt$. The latter refers to net investments, meaning that depreciation has been accounted for. The production technology is assumed to exhibit constant returns to scale. This means that the production function $F(k, 1)$ is homogeneous of degree one in capital and labour, where the labour force (which is assumed to coincide with the population) is normalized to equal one. Therefore, a more convenient notation for the production function is $f(k)$, which is assumed to be strictly concave in its argument.

The Social Planner

Let us start with the resource allocation that would be chosen by a social planner. The social planner's problem is to maximize (3.1) subject to (3.2) and an initial condition for the capital stock. Formally, we can write the optimization problem as

$$\text{Max} \int_0^\infty u(c(t))e^{-\theta t}\,dt$$
$$c(t)$$

$$\text{s.t.}\,\frac{dk(t)}{dt} = f(k(t)) - c(t)$$

$$k(0) = k_0$$

where the second restriction is the initial condition, which means that the social planner starts with an exogenously given capital stock at time zero. The current value Hamiltonian is written

$$H^c(t) = u(c(t)) + \lambda^c(t)[f(k(t)) - c(t)] \tag{3.3}$$

where, as a matter of notational convention, the superindex ^{c} refers to current value. The utility maximization problem discussed here is a standard optimal control problem, where c is a control variable, k a state variable and λ^c a costate variable. The interpretation of $\lambda^c(t)$ is that it measures the marginal value in utility terms at time t of an additional unit of capital at time t. In addition to Equation (3.2) and the initial condition, the necessary conditions are:

$$\frac{\partial H^c(t)}{\partial c(t)} = u_c(c(t)) - \lambda^c(t) = 0 \tag{3.4a}$$

$$\frac{d\lambda^c(t)}{dt} - \theta\lambda^c(t) = -\frac{\partial H^c(t)}{\partial k(t)} = -\lambda^c(t)f_k(k(t)) \tag{3.4b}$$

$$\lim_{t \to \infty} \lambda^c(t)k(t)e^{-\theta t} = 0 \tag{3.4c}$$

where $u_c(\cdot) = du(\cdot)\,/\,dc$, $f_k(\cdot) = df(\cdot)\,/\,dk$.

Let us start by interpreting the first-order conditions. Equation (3.4a) – which resembles the type of necessary conditions often found in static models – follows because $\partial H^c\,/\,\partial c$ must equal zero for all t along the optimal path. This is the continuous-time counterpart to Equations (2.6a) in Chapter 2. It means that the marginal utility of consumption equals the marginal value (in current value terms) of one additional unit of capital. This is a very intuitive condition; if the marginal utility of consumption exceeds, or falls short of, the marginal utility value of capital, it would be possible to increase the utility by changing the consumption and investment behaviour. Equation (3.4b) relates the change over time of the costate variable to the rate of time preference and the marginal product of capital. It is the continuous time counterpart to Equation (2.6b) in Chapter 2. An interpretation is that the 'interest rate', θ, required by the consumer to postpone consumption over a short time interval along the optimal path must equal the rate of capital gains, $(d\lambda^c(t) / dt) / \lambda^c(t)$, plus the market interest rate, $f_k(k(t))$. To see more clearly what these conditions reveal about the optimal paths for the variables involved, we differentiate (3.4a) with respect to time to find that

$$u_{cc}\left(c(t)\right)\frac{dc(t)}{dt} = \frac{d\lambda^c(t)}{dt} \qquad (3.4d)$$

where $u_{cc}(\cdot) = d^2u(\cdot) / dc^2 < 0$. The interaction between the paths for c, k and λ^c may be understood from (3.2), (3.4b) and (3.4d). If $\theta > (<) f_k(k(t))$, which would imply that $d\lambda^c(t) / dt > (<) 0$, consumption will decrease (increase) at time t according to (3.4d). In the steady state, where λ^c is constant, (3.4b) uniquely determines the capital stock from the equality between the rate of time preference and the marginal product of capital. We shall return to the properties of the steady state below.

The condition represented by (3.4c) is the transversality condition and reflects the optimal behaviour at the terminal point (which the economy only reaches asymptotically in this case). To interpret the transversality condition, consider for the moment the case with a finite horizon, T, and write $\lambda^c(T)k(T) \exp(-\theta T) = 0$. An interpretation is that, if the capital stock is positive at time T, then the marginal utility of consumption at time T must be equal to zero. Otherwise it would be possible to increase the utility at time T by increasing consumption. On the other hand, if the capital stock at time T is equal to zero, there is no restriction on the marginal utility of consumption. We may then think of Equation (3.4c) as the limit when T goes to infinity.[5]

Given knowledge of the functional forms for preferences and the technology, how can we use the necessary conditions to derive the optimal paths for c, k and λ^c? Equation (3.4a) implicitly defines consumption as a function of λ^c, i.e. $c(t) = c(\lambda^c(t))$, which is sometimes called 'the lambda constant' demand, as it is defined *conditional on the marginal utility value of capital*.[6] Replacing $c(t)$ in (3.2) by the lambda constant demand function and solving the system of simultaneous differential equations (3.2) and (3.4b), the solutions for $k(t)$ and $\lambda^c(t)$ follow. Finally, substituting the utility maximizing $\lambda^c(t)$ back into Equation (3.4a), we can determine the optimal path for consumption. The properties of the optimal solution will be discussed later in this section as well as in Section 3.3, where we solve a linearized version of the necessary conditions. The reason for doing so is that the comparative dynamic analysis previously mentioned requires formal expressions for c and k along the optimal path.

The Decentralized Economy

Before we continue by examining the properties of the model in more detail, it is important to observe that Equations (3.2) and (3.4a)–(3.4c) would also be the outcome in a decentralized economy. In the decentralized economy, the consumer's accumulation of capital is determined by the equation

$$\frac{dk(t)}{dt} = r(t)k(t) + w(t) - c(t) \tag{3.5}$$

where r is the market interest rate and w is the payment per unit of labour. Although Equation (3.5) is sometimes referred to as 'a dynamic budget constraint', it is not an intertemporal budget constraint. It only describes how the capital stock evolves through the individual's decision to save at each point in time. As has been pointed out by, for example, Blanchard and Fisher (1989), utility maximization subject to (3.5) has a trivial solution – the consumer would borrow until the marginal utility of consumption is zero (or an infinite amount if the marginal utility of consumption is always positive). To derive the intertemporal budget constraint, subject to which the consumer maximizes the utility, we would also require a restriction on the consumer's possibility to borrow and lend. Suppose that we require that the debt does not grow too fast by imposing the condition

$$\lim_{t \to \infty} k(t) \exp\left(-\int_0^t r(s)ds \right) \geq 0 \tag{3.6}$$

which is usually referred to as the No Ponzi Game (NPG) condition. The NPG condition means that debt should not grow faster than the interest rate. Since it would not be optimal for the consumer to hold a capital stock with a positive value at the terminal point, Equation (3.6) will hold as a strict equality. To see the usefulness of (3.6) in deriving the intertemporal budget constraint, we solve the differential Equation (3.5) to obtain

$$k(T) = k(t) \exp\left(\int_t^T r(s)ds \right) + \int_t^T \left(w(s) - c(s) \right) \exp\left(\int_s^T r(\tau)d\tau \right) ds$$

If we multiply each term by

$$\exp\left(-\int_t^T r(s)ds\right),$$

let T go to infinity and use (3.6) we have

$$\int_t^\infty c(s)\exp\left(-\int_t^s r(\tau)d\tau\right)ds = k(t) + \int_t^\infty w(s)\exp\left(-\int_t^s r(\tau)d\tau\right)ds \qquad (3.7)$$

which is the intertemporal budget constraint. The interpretation of Equation (3.7) is that the present value of consumption (the left hand side) equals the sum of non-human and human wealth. This means that (3.5) and (3.6), together, are equivalent to the intertemporal budget constraint given by (3.7). The consumer maximizes the utility function (3.1) subject to the intertemporal budget constraint – or, equivalently, subject to (3.5) and (3.6) – and the initial condition for capital. The utility maximization problem is formally written as

$$\underset{c(t)}{\text{Max}} \int_0^\infty u(c(t))e^{-\theta t} dt$$

$$\text{s.t. } \frac{dk(t)}{dt} = r(r)k(t) + w(t) - c(t)$$

$$\lim_{t\to\infty} k(t)\exp\left(-\int_0^t r(s)ds\right) \geq 0$$

$$k(0) = k_0$$

The current value Hamiltonian corresponding to this problem is

$$H^c(t) = u(c(t)) + \varphi^c(t)[r(t)k(t) + w(t) - c(t)] \qquad (3.8)$$

where $\varphi^c(t)$ reflects the consumer's valuation in current value terms of an additional unit of capital at time t. In addition to (3.5), (3.6) and the initial condition for the capital stock, the necessary conditions for an optimal path become

$$\frac{\partial H^c(t)}{\partial c(t)} = u_c(c(t)) - \varphi^c(t) = 0 \tag{3.9a}$$

$$\frac{d\varphi^c(t)}{dt} - \theta\varphi^c(t) = -\frac{\partial H^c(t)}{\partial k(t)} = -\varphi^c(t)r(t) \tag{3.9b}$$

$$\lim_{t \to \infty} k(t)\varphi^c(t)e^{-\theta t} = 0 \tag{3.9c}$$

Although these conditions look similar to (3.4), they are only partial equilibrium conditions in the sense that the consumer regards the return to capital as independent of the choice of capital stock (i.e. the consumer optimizes subject to an exogenously given path for the market interest rate). Turning to the producer side of the economy, firms are assumed to be identical, act competitively and face the constant returns technology described earlier. The representative firm chooses capital such as to maximize the present value of profit, i.e.

$$\max_{k(t)} \int_0^\infty \left[f(k(t)) - w(t) - r(r)k(t)\right] \exp\left(-\int_0^t r(s)ds\right) dt$$

and behaves (at all t) according to the conditions

$$f_k(k(t)) - r(t) = 0 \tag{3.10}$$

$$f(k(t)) - r(t)k(t) - w(t) = 0 \tag{3.11}$$

Equation (3.10) means that the firm chooses capital such that the marginal product of capital equals the interest rate, and Equation (3.11) follows from the assumption of constant returns to scale, which means that pure profits are zero. An interpretation of Equation (3.11) is obtained if we replace r by $f_k(\cdot)$, in which case we find the well known condition that the marginal product of labour should equal the market wage rate. Substituting (3.10) and (3.11) into Equations (3.5) and (3.9a)–(3.9c), we obtain the general equilibrium solution for the decentralized economy:

$$\frac{dk(t)}{dt} = f(k(t)) - c(t) \tag{3.12a}$$

$$u_c(c(t)) - \varphi^c(t) = 0 \tag{3.12b}$$

$$\frac{d\varphi^c(t)}{dt} - \theta\varphi^c(t) = -\varphi^c(t)f_k\big(k(t)\big) \quad (3.12c)$$

$$\lim_{t\to\infty} \varphi^c(t)k(t)e^{-\theta t} = 0 \quad (3.12d)$$

and $k(0) = k_0$. A comparison between (3.12b) and (3.4b) reveals that that these two differential equations are identical and, consequently, have the same solution. Replacing φ^c by λ^c in (3.12a)–(3.12d) we find that (3.5), (3.9a)–(3.9c), (3.10) and (3.11) are, together, equivalent to (3.2) and (3.4a)–(3.4c). This means that the resource allocation in the decentralized economy is the same as would be chosen by a social planner. Therefore, in this simple benchmark model, the decentralized economy solves society's optimization problem. One reason for this to occur is that the social planner and the consumer in the decentralized economy have the same objective function. The conclusion also depends on the assumption of perfect competition in the decentralized economy which, for example, means that no external effects are present. In the presence of external effects, the decentralized economy will not, by itself, solve society's optimization problem. Instead, in order for the decentralized resource allocation to be a social optimum, we would have to design a policy – for example, an optimal tax and transfer system – such that the external effects would be fully internalized. We return to this question in Chapters 4 and 5.

Steady State and Local Stability Analysis

This subsection concerns two related issues: (1) the existence of a unique steady state in the model set out previously; and (2) the idea that the economy moves along the optimal path towards that steady state. This is important both for a full understanding of the welfare analysis in the next section and the comparative dynamic analysis in Section 3.3. To examine the steady state, it is convenient to rewrite the necessary conditions in terms of differential equations for consumption and capital. The differential equation for k is given by (3.2), while the differential equation for c is derived by substituting (3.4b) into (3.4d). Hence, the system of simultaneous differential equations that we are looking for is given by

$$\dot{c} = \frac{u_c(\theta - f_k)}{u_{cc}} = \dot{c}(c,k) \quad (3.13a)$$

$$\dot{k} = f(k) - c = \dot{k}(c,k) \quad (3.13b)$$

where we use the short-hand notations $\dot{c} = dc \,/\, dt$ and $\dot{k} = dk \,/\, dt$, and the time indicator has been dropped for notational convenience.

In the steady state $dc \,/\, dt = dk \,/\, dt = 0$, meaning that Equations (3.13) reduce to read

$$f_k(\tilde{k}) - \theta = 0 \tag{3.14a}$$

$$f(\tilde{k}) - \tilde{c} = 0 \tag{3.14b}$$

where $\sim$ refers to a steady state value. The existence of a unique steady state is equivalent to the existence of a unique solution to Equations (3.14). Given the assumptions made earlier about the properties of the production function, we can uniquely determine the steady state values of consumption, $\tilde{c}$, and capital, $\tilde{k}$. Note that Equations (3.14) form a recursive system; (3.14a) uniquely determines the capital stock in the steady state, and (3.14b) uniquely determines consumption given the capital stock.

In order to conduct a local stability analysis, we linearize (3.13) around the steady state:

$$\begin{bmatrix} \dot{c} \\ \dot{k} \end{bmatrix} = \begin{bmatrix} \dfrac{\partial \dot{c}}{\partial c} & \dfrac{\partial \dot{c}}{\partial k} \\ \dfrac{\partial \dot{k}}{\partial c} & \dfrac{\partial \dot{k}}{\partial k} \end{bmatrix} \begin{bmatrix} c - \tilde{c} \\ k - \tilde{k} \end{bmatrix} \tag{3.15}$$

where the matrix of partial derivatives on the right-hand side, called the dynamic Jacobian, is determined by differentiating (3.13) and evaluating the resulting derivatives at the steady state (note that this is not the same as differentiating (3.14)). The dynamic Jacobian matrix is given by

$$J = \begin{bmatrix} \dfrac{\partial \dot{c}}{\partial c} & \dfrac{\partial \dot{c}}{\partial k} \\ \dfrac{\partial \dot{k}}{\partial c} & \dfrac{\partial \dot{k}}{\partial k} \end{bmatrix} = \begin{bmatrix} 0 & -\dfrac{u_c}{u_{cc}} f_{kk} \\ -1 & f_k \end{bmatrix} \tag{3.16}$$

The local stability analysis is conducted by finding the characteristic roots corresponding to the system (3.15). Denote the roots by δ_1 and δ_2, respectively. A convenient result, in order to determine the sign of the roots, is that the sum of the diagonal elements of J – called the trace of J and denoted trJ – is equal to the sum of the roots, and the determinant of J is equal to the product of the roots. The reader can easily convince himself/herself about these results by using the characteristic equation $|J - \delta I| = \delta^2 - (trJ)\,\delta + |J| = 0$, where I is the identity matrix. The roots are given by

$$\delta_1, \delta_2 = \frac{trJ_-^+ \sqrt{(trJ)^2 - 4|J|}}{2}$$

In this case we have $\delta_1 + \delta_2 = f_k = \theta > 0$ and $|J| = \delta_1 \delta_2 = -(u_c/u_{cc})f_{kk} < 0$, where the latter means that one root is positive and the other negative. It follows that the steady state is a saddle point. The result that the steady state – the solution to (3.14) – is a saddle point means that only the saddle point path (the path that takes the economy to the steady state) obeys the necessary conditions represented by Equations (3.4). This is illustrated in Figure 3.1, which gives a graphical representation of Equations (3.14) and how their solutions, i.e. $\tilde{c}$ and $\tilde{k}$, are obtained. The dynamics are indicated by arrows in the figure and follow because above (below) the $dk(t)\,/\,dt = 0$ locus the capital stock falls (rises). Similarly, to the left (right) of the $dc(t)\,/\,dt = 0$ line, consumption rises (falls)

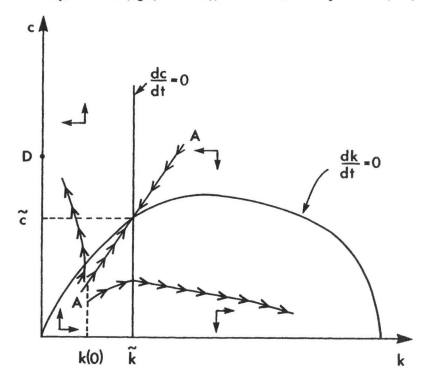

Figure 3.1   Steady state and dynamics

according to (3.13a). Given $k(0)$, the only path satisfying the necessary conditions in (3.4) is the saddle point path, A – A, which leads the economy to the steady state represented by the solution to (3.14). Any other path will either violate (3.4d), i.e. paths starting above A – A, or (3.4c), paths starting below A – A.

To see this, note from the figure that paths starting above the saddle point path will reduce the capital stock to zero, which occurs when the economy reaches some point, say D, on the vertical axis. This would require consumption to jump from a positive value to zero, which surely violates Equation (3.4d). Similarly, paths starting below the saddle point path converge asymptotically to the point where the $dk(t) / dt = 0$ locus crosses the horizontal axis in Figure 3.1. This means that the marginal product of capital will eventually become negative, whereas the capital stock becomes approximately constant close to the point where the $dk(t) / dt = 0$ locus crosses the horizontal axis. As a result, the costate variable will increase over time at a rate exceeding the rate of time preference – see Equation (3.4b). This means that Equation (3.4c), i.e. the transversality condition, is violated. Therefore, since these other paths do not fulfil the necessary conditions, they cannot represent the optimal solution to the social planner's utility maximization problem (or the resource allocation in the decentralized economy).

3.2   THE WELFARE EQUIVALENCE OF THE NET NATIONAL PRODUCT

The measurement of economic welfare is for obvious reasons both important and difficult. For practical purposes, the net national product in per capita terms has often been used as an indicator of the national welfare level. On the other hand, from a theoretical point of view, one may argue that welfare is more appropriately defined by a wealth-like measure such as the present value of future consumption.[7] However, although correct, such a measure may be very difficult to calculate in practice. An important question is, therefore, what information would be required to measure welfare correctly and, in particular, is the necessary information available in current market data? Originating from the influential paper by Martin Weitzman (1976), this question has been discussed by several authors. Weitzman's contribution was to show that the net national product is, under certain conditions, the appropriate measure of welfare. This does not mean that a measure such as the present value of future consumption is unimportant for welfare analyses. As we shall show below, the present value of future consumption and the net national product are in principle – to use Weitzman's own words – 'two sides of the same coin'. Much of the more recent research has focused on complications such as technological progress, externalities, investments in natural resources, etc., and the main concern among analysts has been how to augment 'the basic' welfare measure to capture the effects of these phenomena. However, in this chapter we concentrate on welfare measurement in the benchmark model and return to these complications in later chapters.

What do we mean by economic welfare? Given the model set out previously, the most natural definition would be the present value of future utility. Is it possible to find a static equivalent to the present value of future utility? As we are about to show, this static equivalent turns out to be the familiar expression $u(c^*(t)) + \lambda^{c^*}(t)dk^*(t) / dt$, where $c^*(t)$, $k^*(t)$, $\lambda^{c^*}(t)$ represent the optimal paths for consumption, the capital stock and the costate variable (where the latter has been interpreted as the marginal utility of consumption or the utility value of capital). These paths are optimal in the sense that they solve society's optimization problem and can, in this case, be the outcome either of the decision made by a utilitarian social planner or the behaviour in the decentralized economy.

Let us substitute $c^*(t)$, $k^*(t)$ and $\lambda^{c^*}(t)$ back into the current value Hamiltonian in Equation (3.3). The current value Hamiltonian along the optimal path is written

$$H^{c^*}(t) = H^c\left(c^*(t), k^*(t), \lambda^{c^*}(t)\right) = u\left(c^*(t)\right) + \lambda^{c^*}(t)\frac{dk^*(t)}{dt} \quad (3.17)$$

It is possible to relate the current value Hamiltonian along the optimal path to a 'national' welfare measure. To see this, we differentiate (3.17) totally with respect to time:

$$\frac{dH^{c^*}(t)}{dt} = \frac{\partial H^{c^*}(t)}{\partial c^*(t)}\frac{dc^*(t)}{dt} + \frac{\partial H^{c^*}(t)}{\partial k^*(t)}\frac{dk^*(t)}{dt} + \frac{\partial H^{c^*}(t)}{\partial \lambda^{c^*}(t)}\frac{d\lambda^{c^*}(t)}{dt} \quad (3.18)$$

Using the necessary conditions that $\partial H^{c^*} / \partial c^* = 0$ and $d\lambda^{c^*} / dt = \theta\lambda^{c^*} - \lambda^c f_k(k^*)$, from (3.4a) and (3.4b), as well as the facts that $\partial H^{c^*} / \partial k^* = \lambda^c f_k(k^*)$ and $\partial H^{c^*} / \partial \lambda^{c^*} = dk^* / dt$ from (3.17), we can rewrite (3.18) to read

$$\frac{dH^{c^*}(t)}{dt} = \theta\left[H^{c^*}(t) - u\left(c^*(t)\right)\right] \quad (3.18a)$$

which has the form of a Bernoulli equation. Solving for the current value Hamiltonian at time T gives

$$H^{c^*}(T) = H^{c^*}(t)e^{\theta(T-t)} - \theta\int_t^T u(c(s))e^{\theta(T-s)}ds.$$

If we multiply by $e^{-\theta(T-t)}$ and use the result that $H^{c^*}(T)e^{-\theta(T-t)}$ approaches zero when T goes to infinity (see Michel, 1982), we obtain the welfare measure

$$\theta\int_t^\infty u\left(c^*(s)\right)e^{-\theta(s-t)}ds = H^{c^*}(t) = u\left(c^*(t)\right) + \lambda^{c^*}(t)\frac{dk^*(t)}{dt} \qquad (3.19)$$

Equation (3.19) has important implications for welfare measurement, which are summarized by Proposition 3.1 below:

Proposition 3.1   *Given the model set out in Section 3.1 and the appropriate differentiability conditions, interest on the present value of future utility equals the current value Hamiltonian along the optimal path.*

By the term 'interest' in Proposition 3.1 we mean the rate of time preference, which is the rate at which future utility is discounted. It follows from the proposition that the current value Hamiltonian contains all information relevant for welfare measurement and is, therefore, a static equivalent of welfare. We may think of the current value Hamiltonian along the optimal path as a national product related welfare measure, since all information necessary to measure welfare at time t is available at that time. In other words, given that the economy follows the optimal path, welfare measurement does not require knowledge of what this path will look like in the future.

To facilitate the welfare interpretation in terms of the national product, it is instructive to use the linear approximation of the welfare measure suggested by, for example, Hartwick (1990) and Mäler (1991). Following the convention in these studies, let us, therefore, approximate $u(c^*)$ by the linear function $\lambda^{c^*}c^*$. Replacing $u(c^*(t))$ by $\lambda^{c^*}(t)c^*(t)$ in (3.19) we have what is usually referred to as the net welfare measure (*NWM*):

$$NWM = \lambda^{c^*}(t)c^*(t) + \lambda^{c^*}(t)\frac{dk^*(t)}{dt} \qquad (3.20)$$

Equation (3.20) measures the net national product in utility units or, put another way, the local approximation of the welfare measure is proportional to the net national product, where the factor of proportionality equals the marginal utility of consumption along the optimal path. Dividing (3.20) by the marginal utility of consumption gives the net welfare measure in real terms. Therefore, in the benchmark model, interest on the present value of future utility can be approximated by the net national product evaluated at the price $\lambda^{c^*}(t)$. For the national product to be 'an exact' measure of welfare, we would require the utility function to be linear in consumption, i.e. $u(c) = c$. Using such a linear utility function, Weitzman (1976) derives the welfare measure

$$\theta \int_t^\infty c^*(s)e^{-\theta(s-t)}ds = c^*(t) + \rho^*(t)\frac{dk^*(t)}{dt} \qquad (3.19a)$$

where ρ measures the market value of one unit of capital relative to the price of consumption goods. Although (3.19a) is only a special case of (3.19), and reflects a relation between the present value of future utility and the current value Hamiltonian along the optimal path, the linear utility function means that (3.19a) also describes a relation between the present value of consumption and the net national product. Hence, in the case of a linear utility function, the net national product and the present value of future consumption are, indeed, two sides of the same coin, since one is proportional to the other.

However, Equation (3.19a) is more difficult to derive than may seem to be the case at first glance because of the linear utility function. When the utility function is linear, the optimization problem is a bang-bang control problem, where the optimal path for the capital stock will be such as that depicted in Figure 3.2, based on the assumption that the initial capital stock, $k(0)$, is smaller than the steady state capital stock, $\bar{k}$. The bang-bang control problem then means that the economy will consume as little as possible, $c = 0$, and invest as much as possible, $dk/dt = f(k)$, until the capital stock becomes equal to $\tilde{k}$, which is assumed to occur at time t' when investments will drop to zero. Hence, the optimal path for the capital stock involves a kink-point, meaning that $dk(t)/dt$ is not continuous. This is why we need the reservation in Proposition 3.1 about the appropriate differentiability conditions. However, as is shown in Chapter 4, it is still possible to derive an equation with the same interpretation as (3.19a) for each of the subintervals $[0, t')$ and (t', ∞). Another complication is, of course, that a bang-bang control solution cannot easily be supported by a competitive equilibrium path, which makes the national product interpretation of Equation (3.19a) a little artificial.

It may have come as a surprise to the reader that the welfare measure in (3.19) appears to contain no information about the stock of wealth. Put differently, should not welfare depend on the value of accumulated investments? Following

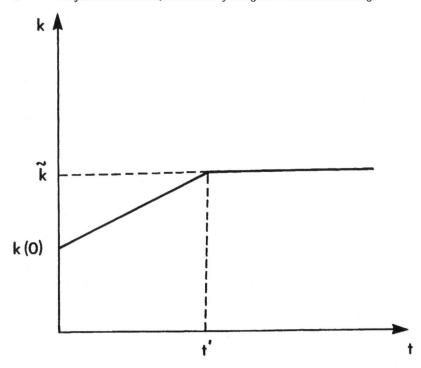

Figure 3.2   The capital stock in the bang-bang control problem

Hartwick (1994), let the present value of future utility along the optimal path
be given by

$$V^*(t) = \int_t^\infty u\big(c^*(s)\big) e^{-\theta(s-t)} ds$$

It follows from Equations (3.18a) and (3.19) that

$$\frac{dV^*(t)}{dt} = \frac{1}{\theta} \frac{dH^{c^\cdot}(t)}{dt} = \lambda^{c^\cdot}(t) \frac{dk^*(t)}{dt} \qquad (3.21)$$

Solving this equation we obtain a convenient relation between the present value
of future utility and the utility value of accumulated investments:

$$V^*(t) = V(0) + \int_0^t \lambda^{c^*}(s)\frac{dk^*(s)}{ds}\,ds \qquad (3.22)$$

To interpret (3.22), let us integrate the second term on the right-hand side by parts, i.e.

$$\int_0^t \lambda^{c^*}(s)\frac{dk^*(s)}{ds}\,ds = \lambda^{c^*}(s)k^*(s)\,|_0^t - \int_0^t \frac{d\lambda^{c^*}(s)}{ds}k^*(s)\,ds$$

which (in utility terms) means that the value of accumulated investments is equal to the wealth accumulated up to time t (the first term on the right-hand side) minus the value of accumulated capital gains (the second term on the right-hand side). Substituting (3.22) back into Equation (3.19) gives

$$\theta\left(V(0) + \int_0^t \lambda^{c^*}(s)\frac{dk^*(s)}{ds}\,ds\right) = H^{c^*}(t) = u\big(c^*(t)\big) + \lambda^{c^*}(t)\frac{dk^*(t)}{dt} \qquad (3.23)$$

Comparing Equations (3.19) and (3.23), we have a duality type of result. Along the optimal trajectory, the present value of future utility equals the utility value of investments accumulated up to time t (plus the utility level corresponding to the initial capital stock). Equation (3.23) can be interpreted such that the current value Hamiltonian along the optimal trajectory equals interest on the utility value of the capital stock. In the case of a linear utility function, $u(c) = c$, and if we disregard the problem with the discontinuity mentioned above, we would obtain the even more convenient result that the actual net national product (or income) equals the interest on the market value of accumulated investments. Hence the connection between welfare, net national product and wealth appears to be straightforward in this simple model.

The content of another interesting result, called Hartwick's rule (Hartwick, 1977), is easily recovered from (3.23). Let us interpret k as a vector of different types of capital. Suppose that some of the elements of k are non-renewable natural resources, and consider a specific investment policy such that, from time zero and on, the rents from these natural resources are invested in other productive capacity. We also assume that no other net investments take place. This particular investment policy, therefore, means that $\lambda^c dk/dt = 0$ for all t along the optimal path. Our concern here is the interpretation of Hartwick's rule. As mentioned by Solow (1986), the policy of investing resource rents in reproducible capital suggests that some 'stock' is being maintained intact, and that consumption is the interest on that stock. Deriving the analogue to Equation (3.23) when $\lambda^c dk / dt = 0$ for all t along the optimal path, we obtain the welfare measure

$$u(\bar{c}(t)) = \theta V(0)$$

implying that consumption, $\bar{c}$, is constant. Hence the policy suggested by Hartwick of investing resource rents in reproducible capital generates a constant consumption stream. It also means that current consumption leaves the 'capital stock' intact, which Hartwick in his (1994) paper refers to as 'a Hicks type of result', since it relates to Hicks's (1939) definition of income as the maximum consumption one can afford without reducing the capital stock.[8] We shall return to Hartwick's rule in Chapter 6.

3.3   BEHAVIOURAL AND WELFARE EFFECTS OF PREVIOUSLY UNEXPECTED SHOCKS

The first part of this section examines how the optimal paths for consumption and capital are affected by previously unexpected shocks to the technology or the environment, by which we mean parametric changes of the production possibility set. Since our concern here is the behavioural effects of these shocks along the entire optimal path, we use the term comparative dynamics – as opposed to comparative statics, which only concern the (long-run) movement between steady states.

We shall then continue with the welfare effects of these shocks. In the welfare analysis we are able to show, by using an envelope result, that only the direct effect of a small change in the relevant parameter matters for measuring the change in economic welfare – the indirect effects via the capital stock or consumption vanish from the welfare change measure as a consequence of optimization. The latter will, of course, make it much easier – at least from a technical point of view – to measure the welfare change. We shall also show that the welfare change following a change in a technological parameter is generally not recoverable from a static measure based on current prices. Furthermore, the measure of the welfare effect of a small change in a parameter of the production function bears a close resemblance to cost–benefit rules. If we think of the parametric change as 'the project' – the profitability of which we would like to evaluate – the relevant cost–benefit rule would coincide with the welfare change measure we are about to derive. Therefore, there is a close connection between the analysis conducted here and the discussion of cost–benefit rules in Chapter 4.[9]

Comparative Dynamics

The comparative dynamic analysis presented here draws heavily on Aronsson and Löfgren (1993), where the responses in consumption and the capital stock to technological shocks are formally worked out. Their paper uses results derived by Caputo (1989) who, in the context of a resource management model, relates comparative dynamics to comparative statics in the steady state. In order to study comparative dynamics we would need formal expressions for consumption and the capital stock along the optimal path. Naturally, such a formal solution would require knowledge about the functional form for the utility and production function. What we can do, given the general forms for preferences and the technology, is to solve a linear approximation of the system (3.13). Such a linear approximation is given by (3.15). Solving the system (3.15) not only requires knowledge of the characteristic roots – which were provided in Section 3.1 – but also of the characteristic vectors. The characteristic vectors (v_1^i, v_2^i) corresponding to the roots δ_i, $i = 1,2$, are the solutions to

$$
\begin{bmatrix}
\dfrac{\partial \dot{c}}{\partial c} - \delta_i & \dfrac{\partial \dot{c}}{\partial k} \\[2ex]
\dfrac{\partial \dot{k}}{\partial c} & \dfrac{\partial \dot{k}}{\partial k} - \delta_i
\end{bmatrix}
\begin{bmatrix}
v_1^i \\[1ex]
v_2^i
\end{bmatrix}
=
\begin{bmatrix}
0 \\[1ex]
0
\end{bmatrix}
\tag{3.24}
$$

If we choose $v_2^i \equiv 1$ as the normalization, we have

$$
\left(v_1^i, v_2^i \right) = \left[\frac{-\partial \dot{c} / \partial k}{\partial \dot{c} / \partial c - \delta_i}, 1 \right]
$$

Let us denote the stable root by δ_1. Note also that, since $\partial \dot{c} / \partial k < 0$ and $\partial \dot{c} / \partial c = 0$, we find that $v_1^1 > 0$. The solution to the system (3.15) along the saddle point path is easily recovered by standard methods. Given the initial condition for the capital stock we have

$$
c^*(t;k(0),\theta,\alpha,\beta) = \tilde{c}(\theta,\alpha,\beta) + (k(0) - \tilde{k}(\theta,\alpha,\beta))v_1^1 e^{\delta_1 t} \tag{3.25a}
$$

$$
k^*(t;k(0),\theta,\alpha,\beta) = \tilde{k}(\theta,\alpha,\beta) + (k(0) - \tilde{k}(\theta,\alpha,\beta))e^{\delta_1 t} \tag{3.25b}
$$

where we use the superindex * despite the fact that Equations (3.25) are only approximations of the optimal solution. Given knowledge of the 'optimal' paths for consumption and the capital stock provided by Equations (3.25), we shall now continue with the main subject of this subsection: the effects on the

paths for consumption and the capital stock of previously unexpected shocks
to the technology or the environment. At this point it is necessary to define the
technological parameters α and β in (3.25), which are assumed to affect the
production function. Suppose that the technological parameters enter in such a
way that the production function can be rewritten

$$f(k(t)) = \alpha + \beta q(k(t)) \tag{3.26}$$

From the properties of $f(\cdot)$ it follows that $q(\cdot)$ is increasing and strictly concave
in k. We see that α represents an additive shock, while β represents a
multiplicative shock. Another interpretation of β is in terms of 'a capital-
augmented technological change', which refers to the influence of β on the
marginal product of capital.

Let us start with the steady state analysis of previously unexpected
technological shocks. Using the above definition of $f(\cdot)$ and Equations (3.14),
we derive the comparative static results:

$$\frac{\partial \tilde{c}}{\partial \alpha} = 1 \tag{3.27a}$$

$$\frac{\partial \tilde{k}}{\partial \alpha} = 0 \tag{3.27b}$$

$$\frac{\partial \tilde{c}}{\partial \beta} = q(\tilde{k}) - \frac{q_k^2(\tilde{k})}{q_{kk}(\tilde{k})} \tag{3.27c}$$

$$\frac{\partial \tilde{k}}{\partial \beta} = \frac{-q_k(\tilde{k})}{\beta q_{kk}(\tilde{k})} \tag{3.27d}$$

We are now able to apply a method suggested by Caputo (1989) that links
comparative dynamics to comparative statics in the steady state. Suppose that
$\alpha = 0$ and $\beta = 1$ initially, and that the economy has reached a steady state. Our
concern is how changes in α and β will affect the paths for $c^*(t,\cdot)$ and $k^*(t,\cdot)$ for
$t \in [0,\infty)$. The comparative dynamic results are derived by differentiating
Equations (3.25) with respect to the relevant parameter and evaluating the
resulting derivative at the point where $k(0) = \tilde{k}$. The assumption that the
economy's initial optimum is the steady state is particularly convenient, since
it means that terms involving derivatives of the root with respect to the relevant

parameter will vanish (since $k(0) - \tilde{k} = 0$). Consider first the case with an additive technological shock. Differentiating (3.25) with respect to α we obtain

$$\frac{\partial c^*}{\partial \alpha} = \frac{\partial \tilde{c}}{\partial \alpha} - \frac{\partial \tilde{k}}{\partial \alpha} v_1^1 e^{\delta_1 t} = 1 \tag{3.28a}$$

$$\frac{\partial k^*}{\partial \alpha} = \left(1 - e^{\delta_1 t}\right)\frac{\partial \tilde{k}}{\partial \alpha} = 0 \tag{3.28b}$$

These results follow because additive technological shocks do not affect the marginal product of capital. Therefore, the immediate and only impact would be to increase consumption by the same amount as output has risen. An alternative interpretation of this result is in terms of environmental damage, $\partial\alpha < 0$, reducing output but leaving the marginal product of capital unaffected. Obviously, such a shock would only affect the economy by reducing the consumption.

Let us now continue with multiplicative technological shocks, which affect $c^*(t,\cdot)$ and $k^*(t,\cdot)$ through the parameter β. This question was touched upon by Weitzman (1976), who argued that previously unanticipated 'capital-augmented' technological progress would move the economy along the production possibility frontier by immediately causing consumption to fall and investments to rise. According to the results that we are about to derive, this is not necessarily true. Differentiating Equations (3.25) with respect to β we find that

$$\frac{\partial c^*}{\partial \beta} = \frac{\partial \tilde{c}}{\partial \beta} - \frac{\partial \tilde{k}}{\partial \beta} v_1^1 e^{\delta_1 t} \overset{\geq}{\underset{<}{}} 0 \tag{3.29a}$$

$$\frac{\partial k^*}{\partial \beta} = \left(1 - e^{\delta_1 t}\right)\frac{\partial \tilde{k}}{\partial \beta} \geq 0 \tag{3.29b}$$

To interpret these results, the reader should distinguish between long-run effects (i.e. steady state results) and impact effects (which occur immediately). In the long run (i.e. in the limit when $t \to \infty$), $\partial c^* / \partial \beta = \partial \tilde{c} / \partial \beta > 0$ and $\partial k^* / \partial \beta = \partial \tilde{k} / \partial \beta > 0$, which means that the long-run effect of multiplicative technological progress will be to increase both consumption and the capital stock. Put differently, in the long run the economy moves to a new steady state with higher consumption and a larger capital stock in comparison with the initial steady state. The impact effect at $t = 0$ on the capital stock is zero, which means that the economy is initially 'caught' with its existing capital stock. On the other hand,

a)   Consumption Rises Initially

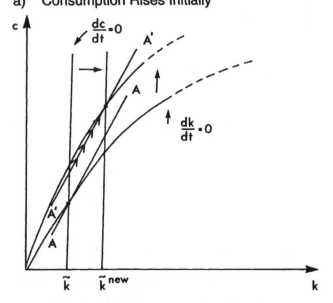

b)   Consumption falls Initially

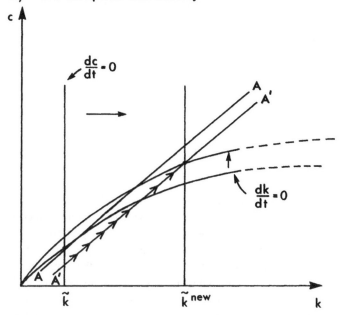

Figure 3.3   Comparative dynamic effects

the impact effect on consumption is ambiguous. However, from Equation (3.29a) we can at least draw the qualitative conclusion that the more the steady state consumption increases in relation to the steady state capital stock, the more likely it is that the impact effect on consumption is positive. This is illustrated in Figure 3.3.

In both parts of Figure 3.3, an increase in β rotates the $dk(t) / dt = 0$ locus upwards and shifts the $dc(t) / dt = 0$ line to the right. The initial saddle point path is denoted A – A and the new saddle point path is denoted A' – A'. In Figure 3.3(a), consumption rises initially as the new saddle point path is located above the old one, i.e. given the initial capital stock, consumption 'jumps up' to the new saddle point path and will then follow that path to the new steady state. In Figure 3.3(b), consumption falls initially, since the new saddle point path is located below the old one. This means that, given the capital stock in the initial steady state, consumption has to fall in order to reach the new saddle point path along which the economy should move to reach the new steady state. We can also in this case give the results an alternative interpretation in terms of previously unexpected environmental damage, which works to reduce the slope of the production function. In terms of Figure 3.3 this would rotate the $dk(t) / dt = 0$ locus downwards and shift the $dc(t) / dt = 0$ line to the left. Even if such a negative shock reduces the steady state values of both consumption and capital it may, nevertheless, cause consumption to rise initially.

Measuring Welfare Effects of Previously Unexpected Shocks

We shall now continue with measuring the welfare change following small increases or decreases in the technological parameters α and β. As mentioned previously, since technological change has intertemporal consequences, the correct evaluation of the welfare change requires knowledge of control variables, state variables and shadow prices along the optimal path. Put differently, since parametric changes in the production function affect future consumption possibilities, there is no observable static equivalent to the welfare change based on current prices. Deriving these welfare effects is, nevertheless, easier than may appear at first sight because of an envelope result in variational calculus. We start by presenting that result, which was derived by Caputo (1990a), and then continue with the welfare interpretation of previously unexpected technological or environmental change.

Along the optimal path, the relationship between consumption, output and net investments can be written $c^*(t;\alpha,\beta) = \alpha + \beta q(k^*(t;\alpha,\beta)) - dk^* (t;\alpha,\beta) / dt$, which is a restatement of Equation (3.2) and means that optimal consumption equals the difference between optimal output and optimal net investments. We can, therefore, write the maximum utility along the optimal path, or value function, as

$$V^*(t;\alpha,\beta) = \int_t^\infty u\Big(\alpha + \beta q\big(k^*(s;\alpha,\beta)\big) - \dot{k}^*(s;\alpha,\beta)\Big) e^{-\theta(s-t)} ds$$

$$= \int_t^\infty u\big(k^*(s;\gamma), \dot{k}^*(s;\gamma), \gamma\big) e^{-\theta(s-t)} ds \qquad (3.30)$$

where $\gamma = (\alpha, \beta)$. Our concern is to determine the effect on $V^*(\cdot)$ following a small change in γ, i.e. the derivative $\partial V^*(\cdot) / \partial \gamma$. The result derived by Caputo (1990a) is given in Proposition 3.2 below:

Proposition 3.2   *Given that the value function is differentiable, it holds that*

$$\frac{\partial V^*(t;\gamma)}{\partial \gamma} = \int_t^\infty u_\gamma\big(k^*(s;\gamma), \dot{k}^*(s;\gamma), \gamma\big) e^{-\theta(s-t)} ds$$

where $u_\gamma(\cdot) = \partial u(\cdot) / \partial \gamma$.

The proof of Proposition 3.2 is straightforward. Suppose that we were to choose γ such as to maximize

$$\Delta(t;\gamma) = \int_t^\infty u\big(k^*(s;\gamma_0), \dot{k}^*(s;\gamma_0), \gamma\big) e^{-\theta(s-t)} ds - V(t;\gamma) \qquad (3.31)$$

Since the parameter γ is time independent, static optimization techniques apply. Obviously, (3.31) reaches its maximum for $\gamma = \gamma_0$, which means that the first-order condition is

$$\frac{\partial \Delta(t;\gamma_0)}{\partial \gamma} = \int_t^\infty u_\gamma\big(k^*(s;\gamma_0), \dot{k}^*(s;\gamma_0), \gamma_0\big) e^{-\theta(s-t)} ds - V_\gamma(t;\gamma_0) = 0 \qquad (3.32)$$

where $V_\gamma(\cdot) = \partial V(\cdot) / \partial \gamma$. Since γ_0 was arbitrarily chosen, this establishes Proposition 3.2.

The interpretation of Proposition 3.2 is as follows. To derive the welfare effect of a parametric change in the model, we take the direct effect on the instantaneous utility, $u(\cdot)$, of the relevant parameter and then integrate over the time horizon along the optimal path. Indirect effects via the capital stock and investments (or consumption) – i.e. effects via the comparative dynamic derivatives given in the previous subsection – will vanish as a consequence of the fact that the economy follows the optimal path. This result, therefore, resembles the envelope theorem in static models.[10]

Let us now examine the welfare consequences of increases in the technological parameters α and β in more detail. By using the necessary condition (3.4a), $u_c(c^*)$ = λ^{c^*}, Proposition 3.2 implies that these welfare change measures are

$$\frac{\partial V^*(t;\alpha,\beta)}{\partial \alpha} = \int_t^\infty \lambda^{c^*}(s)e^{-\theta(s-t)}ds \qquad (3.33a)$$

$$\frac{\partial V^*(t;\alpha,\beta)}{\partial \beta} = \int_t^\infty \lambda^{c^*}(s)q\left(k^*(s)\right)e^{-\theta(s-t)}ds \qquad (3.33b)$$

where the arguments in the functions $\lambda^{c^*}(\cdot)$ and $k^*(\cdot)$ have been suppressed. As can be seen from Equations (3.33), to evaluate the welfare change following previously unexpected technological change (or a new project if we reinterpret α and β in terms of policy parameters), we would require equilibrium prices along the entire optimal path, which explains why a static measure based on current prices would not work in this case. Note also that these two measures differ in their informational requirements; given knowledge of the optimal path for consumption – which according to Equation (3.4a) means that we also know the optimal path for the costate variable – the welfare effect of a small change in α appears to be easier to evaluate than the corresponding welfare effect of β. The reason is that, to evaluate Equation (3.33a), we do not need information about the optimal path for the capital stock. However, the practical problem still remains as we do not know the future paths for equilibrium prices, which means that the welfare change measures are very difficult to evaluate in practice. On the other hand, discounting future utility implies – from a practical point of view – that we can obtain reasonable approximations of these welfare change measures, even if we neglect components far into the future.

3.4   CONCLUSIONS FROM THE BENCHMARK MODEL

What we have called 'the benchmark model' is the simplest form of a dynamic general equilibrium model, where agents have infinite horizons and act under perfect competition. These assumptions mean that the resource allocation in the decentralized economy is the same as would be chosen by a utilitarian social planner – i.e. the decentralized market economy solves society's optimization problem. The benchmark model enables us to derive a set of very convenient results, which are related to the welfare interpretation of the national product (or a national product related measure). First, welfare measured as the present value of future utility turns out to be proportional to the current value Hamiltonian along the optimal path, where the latter is essentially a measure of the net national product in utility terms. Second, because of a relationship between the present value of future utility and the utility value of accumulated investments, the same 'net national product measure' is also equal to interest on the utility value of accumulated investments (or the capital stock). As argued in Section 3.2, this implies a simple and straightforward connection between welfare, national product and the value of capital.

However, from the point of view of social accounting, the most important result is that welfare is adequately measured by market data available at time t, i.e. welfare measurement does not require explicit knowledge of what the optimal paths for consumption and the capital stock will look like in the future. Unfortunately, this convenient result turns out to be particularly sensitive to the assumptions on which the model is based. For example, in the presence of externalities, we know that the market economy does not solve society's optimization problem. Naturally, this will also have important implications for the possibility of measuring welfare using current market data. This and other problems are discussed in the next chapter, where we extend the benchmark model in various directions.

NOTES

1. Some of the classical papers on growth theory are collected in Harcourt and Laing (1971) and Sen (1970).
2. A utilitarian social planner maximizes a welfare function, which is defined as the sum of individual utility functions.
3. Population growth is introduced in Chapter 6.
4. Leisure is introduced in Chapter 5.
5. The reader should observe that this comparison between a finite horizon transversality condition and its counterpart under infinite horizons is made solely for the purpose of giving the transversality condition an economic interpretation. A more formal analysis would reveal that, for finite horizon transversality conditions to carry over to the infinite horizon case, a certain growth condition in terms of the state variable must be fulfilled. This growth condition serves the purpose of imposing restrictions regarding how the state variable affects the functions involved in the optimization problem. In the model discussed here, where the utility function does not contain the state variable, the transversality condition in (3.4c) only requires an upper bound on the derivative $\partial(dk(t)/dt)/\partial k$, which is equivalent to imposing restrictions on the production function. The reader is referred to Seierstad and Sydsæter (1987), theorem 16 in chapter 3, for further details.
6. Browning, Deaton and Irish (1985) refer to this type of demand as 'a Frisch demand' after the Norwegian economist and Nobel Prize winner Ragnar Frisch. See also Frisch (1932).

7. See e.g. Samuelson (1961) for a useful discussion of this subject.
8. It is not entirely clear that this definition of income originates from Hicks. The American economist Irving Fisher and the Swedish economist Erik Lindahl used similar definitions of income; see Fisher (1906) and Lindahl (1933).
9. See also Section 2.3 in Chapter 2.
10. See e.g. Varian (1992).

4. Welfare measures under technological change and externalities

It may seem surprising that a static welfare measure can tell us exactly the present value of future utility along an optimal path. One reason is, of course, that it is indeed an optimal growth path, but this, as we shall show, is not enough. Another reason is that the dynamic optimization problem is not fundamentally time dependent. In other words, neither the objective function nor the dynamic equations for the state variables contain any explicit time dependence, other than that which follows from the state and control variables, and the discount factor. The latter 'disappears' in the current value Hamiltonian.

In this chapter we shall generalize the simple Ramsey growth model introduced in Chapter 3. More precisely, we shall introduce technological progress and externalities. In this setting, we shall repeat the exercises carried out in Chapter 3, and show why and how the welfare measures change. In particular, we shall show that available market data are, except under special circumstances, no longer sufficient to estimate future welfare.

We shall also introduce the value function and show how cost–benefit rules can be derived in a dynamic setting. These cost–benefit rules are contrasted with the linearized NNP–welfare measures of Hartwick (1990) and Mäler (1991) introduced in Chapter 3. The latter type of measure looks very similar to what one would expect cost–benefit rules for the entire economy to look like, especially with respect to how unpriced environmental services enter the measure. We show, however, that they cannot, in general, be used in a social cost–benefit analysis of a parametric change in some environmental or natural resource parameter. The correct evaluation rules for such projects are reminiscent of those used for dealing with the welfare consequences in non-autonomous systems generated by externalities.

In this chapter, we employ new envelope results on the properties of the value function in dynamic optimization.[1] As suggested in Chapter 2, the dynamic envelope theorem says that the total effect on the value function of a small change in a parameter is obtained by taking the partial derivative of the present value Hamiltonian (or more generally the Lagrangean) with respect to the parameter, and integrating the result along the optimal path over the planning horizon. This result greatly simplifies the derivation of welfare measures (cost–benefit rules) in an intertemporal setting. We start, however, by deriving a general result which follows directly from the necessary conditions for an optimal path, and which is fundamental for most of the following analyses.

4.1   A NON-AUTONOMOUS CONTROL PROBLEM

As in Chapter 3, we can think of an economy as evolving over time. The state of the economy at time t can be described by a vector of real numbers

$$x(t) = [x_1(t), \ldots, x_n(t)] \quad \text{(state variables)} \tag{4.1}$$

The capital stocks in the different sectors of the economy are typical examples of state variables. The processes in the economy can be controlled to some extent in the sense that a vector of control functions

$$c(t) = [c_1(t), \ldots, c_m(t)] \tag{4.2}$$

influences the processes. The control functions are typically the decision variables of firms and households, such as consumption and the supply of production factors. The processes, or more precisely, the state variables, are governed by a system of differential equations of the form

$$\frac{dx_1}{dt} = f_1\big(x_1(t), \ldots, x_n(t), c_1(t), \ldots, c_m(t), t\big)$$
$$\vdots$$
$$\frac{dx_n}{dt} f_n\big(x_1(t), \ldots, x_n(t), c_1(t), \ldots, c_m(t), t\big) \tag{4.3}$$

or in vector notation

$$\frac{dx}{dt} = f\big[x(t), c(t), t\big] \tag{4.3a}$$

Hence, as in the previous chapter, it is assumed that the rate of change of all the state variables in general depends on all state variables and all control variables, but, in contrast to the previous chapter, they also depend explicitly on time. This explicit time dependence is necessary if we want to allow for exogenous factors such as technological progress, population growth, and also, as we shall see below, externalities.

To begin with, we shall assume that the integrand depends on all state and control variables and that in addition, it is an explicit function of time:

$$V = \int_0^\infty f_0\big(x_1(t),\ldots,x_n(t),c_1(t),\ldots,c_m(t),t\big)dt = \int_0^\infty f_0\big(x(t),c(t),t\big)dt \qquad (4.4)$$

where the explicit time dependence can represent a time dependent discount factor as well as an externality in consumption, or both.

In applications of optimal control theory one usually assumes that the control function $c(t)$ has, at most, a finite number of discontinuity points on each finite interval with finite jumps at each point of discontinuity, and that it takes values in a fixed set C in R^m. These properties are referred to as $c(t)$, being a piecewise continuous function.

On the functions $f_0, f_1, \ldots, f_n$ one usually imposes the assumptions that

$$f_i(x,c,t) \quad \text{and} \quad \frac{\partial f_i}{\partial x_j}(x,c,t) \qquad (4.5)$$

are continuous with respect to x, c and t.

The maximization problem can now be formulated as

$$\underset{c(t)}{\text{Max}} \int_0^\infty f_0\big(x(t),c(t),t\big)dt$$

subject to

$$\dot{x} = f\big(x(t),c(t),t\big)$$

$$x(0) = x_0 \qquad (4.6)$$

$$x(t) \text{ free when } t \to \infty$$

To derive the main result of this section, consider first the necessary conditions for an optimal path. From the maximum principle, we know that if a piecewise continuous control $c^*(t)$ solves the optimization problem (4.6) and $x^*(t)$ is the associated optimal path, then there exists a continuous and piecewise continuously differentiable vector function, $\lambda^*(t) = [\lambda_1^*(t),\ldots,\lambda_n^*(t)]$, such that for all $t \in [t_0, t_1]$

(i) $c^*(t)$ maximizes $H(x^*(t), c(t), \lambda^*(t), t)$ for $c \in C$ i.e.,

$H^*(x^*(t), c^*(t), \lambda^*(t), t) \geq H(x^*(t), c(t), \lambda^*(t), t)$ for all $c \in C$

(ii) Except at the points of discontinuities of $c^*(t)$, for $i = 1, \ldots n$:

$$\dot{\lambda}_i^* = -\frac{\partial H^*(\cdot)}{\partial x_i}$$

(iii) if C is convex and H is strictly concave in c, then $c^*(t)$ is continuous.

The reader is referred to Seierstad and Sydsæter (1987), chs 2–3 for more details. As was mentioned in Chapter 3, the transversality conditions presuppose the fulfilment of certain growth conditions in terms of the state variables, which means that the transversality conditions under an infinite horizon are more complicated than their counterparts under a finite horizon.

We are now ready to introduce our main result, which is of great importance for the following analysis.

Proposition 4.1 *If $\partial f_i/\partial t$, $i = 0,1, \ldots , n$ exist and are continuous, then*

$$\frac{dH\left(x^*(t),c^*(t),\lambda^*(t),t\right)}{dt} = \frac{\partial H\left(x^*(t),c^*(t),\lambda^*(t),t\right)}{\partial t}$$

at all points of continuity of $c^*(t)$.

If $c^*(t)$ is, in addition, differentiable the proposition follows directly from the necessary conditions for an optimal path. To see this, we differentiate the Hamiltonian along the optimal path totally with respect to t to obtain:

$$\frac{dH^*}{dt} = \frac{\partial H^*}{\partial x}\dot{x}^* + \frac{\partial H^*}{\partial c}\dot{c}^* + \frac{\partial H^*}{\partial \lambda}\dot{\lambda}^* + \frac{\partial H^*}{\partial t} \qquad (4.7)$$

Since

$$\frac{\partial H^*}{\partial x} = -\dot{\lambda}^*, \quad \frac{\partial H^*}{\partial \lambda} = f^* = \dot{x}^*, \text{ and } \frac{\partial H^*}{\partial c} = 0,$$

it follows that

$$\frac{dH^*}{dt} = \frac{\partial H^*}{\partial t}.$$

At a point of discontinuity of $c^*(t)$, for example, a switch point along a bang-bang control solution, the problem is that $\dot{x}(t)$ does not necessarily exist, and the solution curve of the state variable has a kink at the switch point.

In intertemporal economics there is, as soon as we discount the future, a fundamental explicit time dependence through the discount factor. In the Ramsey problem of the previous chapter, the *present value* Hamiltonian along the optimal path has the form

$$H^*(t) = u(c^*(t))e^{-\theta t} + \lambda^*(t)[f(k^*(t)) - c^*(t)] \tag{4.8}$$

where we interpret $\lambda^*(t)$ as the optimal value at time zero of an additional unit of capital at time t, i.e. $\lambda^*(t) = \lambda^{c^*}(t)e^{-\theta t}$. If we use Proposition 4.1 we obtain

$$\frac{\partial H^*}{\partial t} = -\theta u\big(c^*(t)\big)e^{-\theta t} \tag{4.9}$$

Solving this equation forwards yields

$$H^*(t) = \theta \int_t^\infty u\big(c^*(s)\big)e^{-\theta s}\,ds \tag{4.10}$$

If we multiply both sides of Equation (4.10) by $e^{\theta t}$, we have reproduced the main result of Chapter 3: the current value Hamiltonian at time t equals interest on the present value of future utility.

As mentioned in Chapter 3, the seminal paper by Weitzman (1976) is based on a linear utility function, $u(c(t)) = c(t)$. In that case, the above control problem has to be modified by imposing the additional constraint that $0 \leq c(t) \leq c_{\max}$, where $c_{\max}$ is an upper bound on the short-run consumption level. The current value Hamiltonian can now be written

$$H^c(t) = S(t)c(t) + \lambda^c(t)f(k(t)) \tag{4.11}$$

where $S(t) = [1 - \lambda^c(t)]$ is a switching function and $\lambda^c(t)$ is the current value costate variable. The economy will end up in a steady state in finite time, where $f_k(\tilde{k}(t)) = \theta$: the marginal product of capital equals the rate of time preference. The solution is then to choose

$$\begin{aligned} c^* &= 0 \text{ if } k_0 < \tilde{k} \\ c^* &= c_{\max} \text{ if } k_0 > \tilde{k} \end{aligned} \tag{4.12a}$$

and switch to

$$\tilde{c} = f((\tilde{k}(t)) \tag{4.12b}$$

when the steady state is reached at say time t^1. This means that the control function will have, at most, one point of discontinuity, and we can only use Proposition 4.1 sequentially on the intervals $[0, t^1)$, and $[t^1, \infty)$. Hence for a t in the interval $[0, t^1)$ we would for $k_0 > \tilde{k}$ have

$$H^{c^*}(t) = -\theta \int_0^t c_{max} e^{-\theta(s-t)} ds + H^c(0) \tag{4.13}$$

In the steady state, $t \in [t^1, \infty)$ we obtain

$$H^{c^*}(t) = \tilde{c} = f(\tilde{k}) = \theta \int_t^\infty \tilde{c} e^{-\theta(s-t)} ds \tag{4.14}$$

which is a trivial special case of 'Hartwick's rule'. The above discontinuity problem is not completely handled by Weitzman in his influential 1976 paper, which shows that it is sometimes more important to have the right idea, than to obtain exactly the right answer.[2]

Finally, it may be worthwhile to point out the analogy with physics. In a conservative system (represented, for example, by the principle of least action in analytical mechanics), the value of the Hamiltonian represents energy. Since there is no time preference in physics, and since the theory is independent of calendar time, we have $(\partial H^*)/(\partial t) = 0$, and $H^* = $ constant: energy is preserved.[3]

4.2   A MORE GENERAL RAMSEY MODEL

In this section we shall introduce a Ramsey growth model which contains externalities in terms of pollution, and technological progress. The model is, apart from the technological progress, identical to a growth model introduced by Brock (1977). There is a single homogeneous good used for consumption and investment. In order to introduce an externality, production is assumed to cause pollution, which negatively affects society's welfare. We suppress any natural resources, since they do not add to our principal findings. The instantaneous utility function at time t is written as follows

$$u = u(c(t), x(t)) \tag{4.15}$$

where $u(\cdot)$ is the twice continuously differentiable cardinal utility function, which is strictly concave and increasing in its first argument and decreasing in its second argument, $c(t)$ is consumption per unit of labour (per capita) and $x(t)$ stands for the stock of pollution per capita at time t.

Goods are produced by capital, labour, and emissions (through the use of energy inputs). As in Chapter 3, the labour endowment is assumed to be fixed, and is normalized to unity. Assuming that the production function is homogenous of degree one, the production per capita can be written as follows:

$$y(t) = f(k(t), e_i(t), t) \qquad (4.16)$$

where y denotes *net output*, so that depreciation has been accounted for, $f(\cdot)$ is the production function, $k = K/L$ is the capital–labour ratio, K is capital, $L\,(= 1)$ is labour, and e_i is energy used per unit of labour. The production function is assumed to be strictly concave, twice continuously differentiable and increasing in energy. All inputs are necessary, i.e. $f(0, e_i) = f(k, 0) = 0$, the signs of the cross-derivatives, i.e. $f_{ke}(\cdot) = \partial^2 f(\cdot)/\partial k \partial e_i$ etc., are strictly positive, and production cannot be increased without bounds by increasing the use of a single input. These are basically the assumptions employed by Tahvonen and Kuuluvainen (1993). The time argument t catches technological progress, and the production function is assumed to be non-decreasing and continuously differentiable in t.

The accumulation of capital follows the accumulation equation

$$\dot{k}(t) = f(k(t), e_i(t), t) - c(t) - I(\alpha) \qquad (4.17)$$

where $I(\cdot)$ is a strictly convex differentiable cost function which is increasing in the policy parameter α; it says how many inputs are needed in order to improve the environment's assimilative capacity from its 'natural' level γ (see below).

Finally, we assume that emissions are accumulated in nature, though the environment has an assimilative capacity. The stock of pollution develops according to the following equation:

$$\dot{x}(t) = e_f(t) - (\gamma + \alpha)x(t) \qquad (4.18)$$

where $e_f(t)$ is the flow of emissions from the production of ordinary goods, γ is a parameter reflecting the environment's assimilative capacity ($0 \le \gamma \le 1$), and α is a parameter reflecting man-made additions (e.g. wetlands) to the environment's assimilative capacity. Our treatment of emissions means that we have exploited an assumed relationship between a production factor, energy, and the production of emissions. In order to simplify the notation without any loss of generality, we shall assume in the remainder of the chapter that $e_f(t) = e_i(t)$ for all t, and suppress the production of energy.

Command Optimum

The command optimum problem to be solved can now be written

$$\underset{c,e_f}{\text{Max}} \int_0^\infty u\big(c(t), x(t)\big)e^{-\theta t} dt \tag{4.19}$$

(i) $\dot{k}(t) = f(k(t), e_f(t), t) - c(t) - I(\alpha)$

(ii) $\dot{x}(t) = e_f(t) - (\gamma + \alpha)x(t)$

(iii) $k(0) = k_0 > 0$
$\qquad\;\; x(0) = x_0 \geq 0$ (4.20)

(iv) $\lim_{t \to \infty} k(t) \geq 0$

$\qquad \lim_{t \to \infty} x(t) \geq 0$

If we neglect the time indicator, the present value Hamiltonian of this two-state-variable problem is

$$H = u(c,x)e^{-\theta t} + \lambda \dot{k} + \mu \dot{x} \tag{4.21}$$

In addition to (4.20), the necessary conditions for optimality are:[4]

(i) $\partial H/\partial c = u_c(c,x)e^{-\theta t} - \lambda = 0$

(ii) $\partial H/\partial e_f = \lambda f_e(k,e_f,t) + \mu = 0$

(iii) $\dot{\lambda} = -\lambda f_k(k,e_f,t)$ (4.22)

(iv) $\dot{\mu} = -u_x(c,x)e^{-\theta t} + \mu(\gamma + \alpha)$

The present value Hamiltonian along an optimal path can be written

$$H^*(t) = u[c^*(t), x^*(t)]e^{-\theta t} + \lambda^*(t)[f[k^*(t), e^*_f(t), t] - c^*(t) - I(\alpha)]$$
$$+ \mu^*(t)[e^*_f(t) - (\gamma + \alpha)x^*(t)] \tag{4.23}$$

We can now use Proposition 4.1 to write[5]

$$\frac{dH^*}{dt} = \frac{\partial H^*}{\partial t} = -\theta u\big[c^*(t), x^*(t)\big]e^{-\theta t} + \lambda^*(t)f_t\big[k^*(t), e^*_f(t), t\big] \tag{4.24}$$

Integrating (4.24) forwards yields

$$H^*(t) = \theta \int\limits_t^\infty u\Big[c^*(s), x^*(s)\Big]e^{-\theta t}ds - \int\limits_t^\infty \lambda^*(s)f_s\Big[k^*(s), e_f^*(s), s\Big]ds \quad (4.25)$$

Equation (4.25) can, after multiplication by $e^{\theta t}$, be rewritten in terms of the current value Hamiltonian:

$$H^{c^*}(t) + \int\limits_t^\infty \lambda^{c^*}(s)f_s\Big[k^*(s), e_f^*(s), s\Big]e^{-\theta(s-t)}ds = \theta \int\limits_t^\infty u\Big[c^*(s), x^*(s)\Big]e^{-\theta(s-t)}ds \quad (4.26)$$

where $\lambda^c(s) = \lambda(s)e^{\theta t}$. The interpretation is:

Proposition 4.2   *For the model (4.19)–(4.20), interest on the present value of future utility along the optimal path is measured by the current value Hamiltonian at time* t *plus the integral (sum) of the present value of the marginal technological progress (regress) along the optimal path.*

Hence, if there is non-attributable technological progress, the current value Hamiltonian along an optimal trajectory will not represent a static equivalent of welfare. Proposition 4.2 has a very intuitive interpretation. The correct measure of welfare at time t is the current welfare measured by $u^*(\cdot)$, and the present value of the future welfare caused by present measures. Today we consume c^* and x^*, which give rise to utility $u(c^*, x^*)$; we invest $\dot{k}^*$ in capital and $\dot{x}^*$ in emissions, which give rise to $\lambda^c \dot{k}^* > 0$ and $\mu^c \dot{x}^* < 0$, respectively, in current value. We also utilize one unit of time which gives additional welfare because of technological progress equal to Ω^c, where $\dot{\Omega}^c = \theta\Omega^c - \lambda^{c^*}f_t(\cdot)$.

Note that we can, in the original problem, define an additional state variable by putting

$$t = s$$
$$\frac{ds}{dt} = 1 \quad (4.27)$$

The costate variable corresponding to this state variable would then equal $\Omega^c(t)e^{-\theta t}$. This trick helps to make the welfare measure look like the one we produced in Chapter 3, but it is not possible to elicit the value of $\Omega^c(t)$ from current market data. In other words, practical welfare measurement is considerably more complicated than in a world without technological change.

Externalities in the Decentralized Economy

There is an additional problem. Even if technological change is zero, i.e., $f_t \equiv 0$ all t, the command optimum cannot automatically be supported by a market solution. Profit maximizing firms would not automatically be induced to produce the socially optimal level of emissions. A firm would typically take the shadow price of emissions, μ, equal to zero and overproduce emission, since emissions here have a positive marginal product to firms, but represent a negative externality to households. The first-order conditions corresponding to the uncontrolled market solution would coincide with Equations (4.22), with $\mu = \dot{\mu} = 0$. The consumer's utility maximization problem is written

$$\underset{c(t)}{\text{Max}} \int_0^{\infty} u\big(c(t), x(t)\big)e^{-\theta t}\, dt \qquad (4.28)$$

subject to

$$\dot{k}(t) = \pi(t) + r(t)k(t) + w(t) - c(t) - I(\alpha) \qquad (4.28a)$$

$$\lim_{t \to \infty} k(t)\exp\left(-\int_0^t r(s)\,ds\right) = 0 \qquad (4.28b)$$

Equation (4.28a) is the 'dynamic budget constraint' and follows from the fact that in a decentralized market economy, the consumer sells a fixed labour input $\ell = 1$ at a given wage $w(t)$, and rents capital at the market interest rate $r(t)$ to a representative firm, which maximizes profits under perfect competition. The term $\pi(t) \geq 0$ represents a possible 'pure profit', i.e. a profit which cannot be attributed to either capital or labour. Equation (4.28b) is the No Ponzi Game (NPG) condition, which we discussed in Chapter 3. Since emissions are a production factor for the firm, pure profit would, in general, be positive. In addition to (4.28b) and the transversality condition, the control problem (4.28) results in the following necessary conditions for an optimal path (again neglecting time arguments):

$$(i) \quad u_c(c,x)e^{-\theta t} - \lambda = 0$$

$$(ii) \quad \dot{\lambda} = -\lambda r \qquad (4.29)$$

$$(iii) \quad \dot{k} = \pi + rk + w - c - I(\alpha)$$

Firms would choose k and e_f such as to maximize

$$\pi = f(k,e_f) - rk - w \qquad (4.30)$$

and the following first-order conditions emerge:

(i) $f_k(k,e_f) - r = 0$ (4.31)

(ii) $f_e(k,e_f) = 0$

The condition (4.31ii) means that emissions are used up to a point when the marginal productivity of emissions is zero. If we plug the pure profit expression for the market solution into the dynamic budget constraint (4.29iii), we obtain

$$\dot{k}^0 = f(k^0, e^0_f) - c^0 - I(\alpha) \qquad (4.32)$$

where k^0, e^0_f, c^0 denote entities along the decentralized market solution. If we differentiate the Hamiltonian corresponding to the decentralized economy,

$$H^0 = u(c^0, x^0)e^{-\theta t} + \lambda^0(f(k^0, e^0_f) - c^0 - I(\alpha)) \qquad (4.33)$$

with respect to t, and use Proposition 4.1, we obtain

$$\frac{dH^0}{dt} = -\theta u\left(c^0(t), x^0(t)\right)e^{-\theta t} + u_x\left(c^0(t), x^0(t)\right)\dot{x}^0 e^{-\theta t} \qquad (4.34)$$

By integrating (4.34) and transforming the results to current value terms we find

$$H^{c^0}(t) + \int_t^\infty u_x\left[c^0(s), x^0(s)\right]\dot{x}^0(s)e^{-\theta(s-t)}ds = \theta\int_t^\infty u\left[c^0(s), x^0(s)\right]e^{-\theta(s-t)}ds \quad (4.35)$$

The interpretation is summed up in Proposition 4.3:

Proposition 4.3   *The correct estimate of 'interest' on the present value of future utility in a decentralized market solution under externalities is the current value Hamiltonian, plus the present value of the marginal externality along a competitive path.*

This should come as no surprise to the reader, since the externality, although produced within the economic system, is exogenous to the consumer. In other words, it is very reminiscent of the way in which technological progress enters the firm's production function[6] in the previous subsection.

With respect to 'green NNP' measurements the problem is that the additional things we want to measure would not be available in terms of market data. This is, of course, not unexpected, and the theory tells us what to look for: the present value of the marginal damage along the competitive path measured in utility units. To transfer this into a monetary measure we can, since the marginal utility of consumption equals the shadow price of capital, $u_c^0 (\cdot) = \lambda^{c0} (t)$, divide by $\lambda^{c0} (t)$.

In a steady state $\dot{x}^*(t) = 0$ and the standard NNP related measure, the current value Hamiltonian, applies. This is after all a very unlikely situation in a market economy. It means among other things that consumption, the capital stock, and the stock of externalities remain unchanged. No wonder that welfare is proportional to the current value Hamiltonian in the steady state.

One would venture to guess that market data would improve in usefulness for welfare measurement if environmental taxes and emission permits were introduced. Since taxes and permit markets in general are equivalent as policy means, we choose to investigate the Pigouvian tax case.

Since the firm is causing the negative externality, we introduce a unit tax on emissions, $\tau(t)$. The firm's maximization problem at time t can now be written

$$\underset{k(t),e_f(t)}{\text{Max } \pi(t) = \text{Max } f\left(k(t), e_f(t), t\right) - r(t)k(t) - \tau(t)e_f(t).} \quad \forall t \quad (4.36)$$

The first-order conditions for an interior optimum are

$$\frac{\partial \pi}{\partial k} = f_k\left(k, e_f\right) - r = 0$$

$$\frac{\partial \pi}{\partial e_f} = f_e\left(k, e_f\right) - \tau = 0 \quad (4.37)$$

The problem of the consumer reads

$$\underset{c(t)}{\text{Max}} \int_0^\infty u\left[c(t), x(t)\right]e^{-\theta t} dt \quad (4.38)$$

subject to

(i) $\dot{k}(t) = \pi(t) + r(t)k(t) + w(t) + T(t) - c(t) - I(\alpha)$

(ii) $\displaystyle\lim_{t \to \infty} k(t)\exp\left(-\int_0^t r(s)ds\right) = 0$

(iii) $k(0) = k_0$ (4.39)

where $T(t) = \tau(t)e_f(t)$ is the externality tax revenue, which is redistributed to the consumer in terms of a lump-sum subsidy. Except for the transversality condition and the NPG condition, the necessary conditions are written

(i) $u_c(c, x)e^{-\theta t} - \psi = 0$

(ii) $\dot{\psi} = -\psi r$ (4.40)

(iii) $\dot{k} = \pi + rk + w + T - c - I(\alpha)$

(iv) $k(0) = k_0$

Here $\psi(t)$ is the shadow price (costate variable) of capital. The policy problem is now to choose $\tau(t)$ so that the decentralized solution coincides with the social optimum. The answer to the policy problem is provided by the following proposition:

Proposition 4.4 *If $\tau(t) = -\mu^*(t)/\lambda^*(t)$ where $\lambda^*(t)$ is the shadow price of capital, and $\mu^*(t)$ is the shadow price of the stock of pollution in the social planner's optimal solution, the decentralized solution will coincide with the social optimum.*

To see this, we combine (4.36), (4.37) and (4.40) to obtain

(i) $u_c(c, x)e^{-\theta t} - \psi = 0$

(ii) $\dot{\psi} = -\psi f_k(k, e_f)$ (4.41)

(iii) $\dot{k} = f(k, e_f) - c - I(\alpha)$

(iv) $k(0) = k_0$

The development of the stock of emissions is given by

$$\dot{x} = e_f - (\gamma + \alpha)x$$ (4.42)

and $\tau(t) = -\mu^*(t)/\lambda^*(t)$ in (4.36) gives

$$\lambda^* f_e(k, e_f) + \mu^* = 0 \tag{4.43}$$

Finally, from (4.22iv) we know that

$$\dot{\mu}^* = -u^*_x e^{-\theta t} + \mu^*(\gamma + \alpha) \tag{4.44}$$

Comparing (4.40)–(4.43) with (4.22) and (4.20i, ii) we find that they coincide and, hence, the command optimum and the decentralized problem (top index d) have the same solution, i.e., $c^d(t) = c^*(t)$, $k^d(t) = k^*(t)$, $\psi^d(t) = \lambda^*(t)$, $e^d_f(t) = e^*_f(t)$, and hence $x^d(t) = x^*(t)$ for all t.

The dynamic tax, which contains information about the present value of the marginal externality along the optimal path, is, of course, the dynamic analogue to the atemporal Pigouvian tax. It has in this context the obvious advantage that welfare in the dynamic case can now be measured appropriately by a variation of Equation (4.26) with the technology term excluded. The reason why current market data are enough is that we are on an optimal path, since the externality has been optimally adjusted for by the dynamic Pigouvian tax.

What happens if the tax is suboptimal, i.e. if $\tau \neq -\mu^*/\lambda^*$? Would the Hamiltonian along the resulting suboptimal path measure welfare in the appropriate manner, and what about the market solution? Say that we choose $\tau(t) = \bar{\tau}$, which is a constant and arbitrarily chosen number. This would imply that firms release emissions such that $f_e(k, e_f) = \bar{\tau}$, meaning that we can define a 'reaction function' $\bar{e}_f = e_f(k, \bar{\tau})$ describing the firm's optimal choice of emissions as a function of k and $\bar{\tau}$. Substituting this function into the social planner's optimization problem, we obtain

$$\underset{c(t)}{\text{Max}} \int_0^\infty u[c(t), x(t)] e^{-\theta t} dt \tag{4.45}$$

subject to

(i) $\dot{k}(t) = f(k(t), e_f(k(t), \bar{\tau})) - c - I(\alpha)$

(ii) $\dot{x}(t) = e_f(k(t), \bar{\tau}) - (\alpha + \gamma)x(t)$ (4.46)

(iii) $k(0) = k_0$

(iv) $x(0) = x_0$

Suppose that maximization of (4.45) subject to (4.46) results in the trajectory $\bar{c}(t)$, $\bar{x}(t)$, $\bar{k}(t)$, $\bar{\lambda}(t)$, and $\bar{\mu}(t)$, which thus represents a second-best solution. This second-best command optimum is clearly different from the first-best command optimum. Nevertheless, from the Hamiltonian corresponding to the second-best optimal path one obtains

$$\theta \int_{t}^{\infty} u(\bar{c}(s), \bar{x}(s)) e^{-\theta(s-t)} = H^{c}\left(\bar{c}(t), \bar{k}(t), \bar{x}(t), \bar{\lambda}(t), \bar{\mu}(t)\right) \qquad (4.47)$$

which, if the second-best command optimum is supported by the decentralized market solution involving an emission tax $\tau(t) = \bar{\tau}$, would be possible to recover from current market data. Unfortunately, the decentralized solution would, in general, be different from $(\bar{c}, \bar{k}, \bar{x}, \bar{\lambda}, \bar{\mu})$. To see this we substitute the reaction function into the consumer's problem (4.38)–(4.39). The necessary condition for an optimal path involves

(i) $\quad u_c(c, x) e^{-\theta t} - \psi = 0$

(ii) $\quad \dot{\psi} = -\psi\left(r + \bar{\tau}\dfrac{\partial e_f}{\partial k}\right) = -\psi\left(f_k + f_g \dfrac{\partial e_f}{\partial k}\right) \qquad (4.48)$

Equation (4.48ii) is clearly different from the development over time of $\bar{\lambda}$, which is given by:

$$\dot{\bar{\lambda}} = -\bar{\lambda}\left[f_k + f_g \frac{\partial e_f}{\partial k}\right] - \bar{\mu}\frac{\partial e_f}{\partial k}$$

The reason for this is that the consumer in the decentralized economy still behaves as if the path of $x(t)$ is exogenous. The second-best command optimum would even be different from the decentralized market solution for $\bar{\tau} = 0$, since the differential equation for $\bar{\mu}$ in the second-best problem reads

$$\dot{\bar{\mu}} = -u_x e^{-\theta t} - \bar{\mu}\gamma \qquad (4.49)$$

which is different from the uncontrolled market solution, where $\dot{\mu}(t) \equiv 0$.

There is, however, an interesting situation in which the NNP related measure, in terms of the Hamiltonian along the competitive path, would be an appropriate welfare measure. If environmental policy, in the form of a tax or some alternative policy means, is conducted so that the stock of emissions is kept constant, the extra integral on the left-hand side of Equation (4.35) would vanish, since $\dot{x}^0(t) \equiv 0$. This means that the current value Hamiltonian along the competitive path at time t would measure the present value of future utility. The intuitive reason behind this is, of course, that for $\dot{x}^0(t) \equiv 0$, emissions are 'modelled' as a parameter.

4.3   LINEAR WELFARE MEASURES VERSUS COST–BENEFIT RULES

In practice it is impossible to estimate welfare in terms of a utility function for a whole nation. Weitzman (1976) 'solved' this problem by maximizing the present value of total consumption, but, as we have indicated above, discontinuities in the optimal control (the consumption path) make the welfare measure valid on an infinite interval only in a steady state. Moreover, a bang-bang control solution, which is optimal in this case, is not what we observe in real life, not to mention the fact that it is impossible to support the path by a market solution.

This has, as we saw in Chapter 3, stimulated researchers to approximate utility by a linear function, see e.g. Dasgupta and Mäler (1990), Hartwick (1990, 1992) and Mäler (1991). The resulting measures look very similar to what one would expect a cost–benefit rule for the entire economy to look like, especially with respect to how unpriced environmental services enter the measure. However, we shall show that they cannot, in general, be used in a social cost–benefit analysis of a project represented by parametric change in some environmental or natural resource parameter which is not optimally chosen. In particular, we show that the correct evaluation rules for such projects are reminiscent of those used for dealing with the welfare consequences of externalities. In doing so, we employ fairly new results on the properties of the value function (the optimized objective function) in dynamic optimization.[7] Roughly speaking the dynamic envelope theorem says that the total effect on the objective function of an infinitesimally small change in a parameter is obtained by taking the partial derivative of the present value Hamiltonian (or more generally the Lagrangean) with respect to the parameter, and integrating along the optimal path over the planning horizon. A complication in the present context is that the planning horizon is infinite, and the existing theorems on the differentiability of the value function concern finite horizon problems. We introduce a new theorem, supplied to us by Atle Seierstad, which gives sufficient conditions for the differentiability of the value function in the infinite horizon case.

We start by defining the value function for the first-best command optimum problem, which can be interpreted as if we are studying welfare measurement and cost–benefit rules in an economy where externalities have been optimally adjusted. The value function or optimal performance function for the optimal control problem (4.19)–(4.20) is

$$V^*(\beta) = \int_t^\infty u\big(c^*(s), x^*(s)\big)e^{-\theta(s-t)}ds =$$

$$\int_t^\infty v\big(c^*(\beta,s), x^*(\beta,s), \beta, s\big)ds \qquad (4.50)$$

where $\beta = (\alpha, \gamma, \theta)$ is a vector of 'policy parameters'; and the asterisk refers, as usual, to an optimal level, i.e. to the outcome of the maximization of (4.19) subject to (4.20). Given a set of assumptions involving growth conditions on the objective function and on the differential equations for the state variables (see Appendix for details), $V^*(\beta)$ is continuously differentiable in β and; the derivative with respect to β is

$$\frac{\partial V^*}{\partial \beta}(\beta) = \int_t^\infty \left[\frac{\partial u^*}{\partial c}\frac{\partial c^*}{\partial \beta} + \frac{\partial u^*}{\partial x}\frac{\partial x^*}{\partial \beta} + \frac{\partial u^*}{\partial \beta}\right]e^{-\theta(s-t)}ds =$$

$$= \int_t^\infty \left[\frac{\partial u^*}{\partial \beta} + \lambda^{c^*}\frac{\partial \dot{k}^*}{\partial \beta} + \mu^{c^*}\frac{\partial \dot{x}^*}{\partial \beta}\right]e^{-\theta(s-t)}ds = \int_t^\infty \frac{\partial H}{\partial \beta}\big(c^*, x^*, \beta, s-t\big)ds \qquad (4.51)$$

Thus the total effect on the objective function of an infinitesimally small change in a parameter is obtained by taking the partial derivative of the present value Hamiltonian with respect to the parameter, and integrating along the optimal path over the planning horizon, which here is taken to be infinite. Note that the above formula recalls very much the corresponding discrete time envelope result in Chapter 2, Equation (2.19), where the change in the value function is obtained by summing the partial derivatives of the Hamiltonian at all discrete points of time.

Let us start by re-examining the linear welfare measure. The linear net welfare measure was introduced in Chapter 3. Using the model set out here, we would like to approximate a measure such as

$$\theta V^*(\beta) = u(c^*, x^*) + \lambda^c \dot{k}^* + \mu^c \dot{x}^* \qquad (4.52)$$

where the right-hand side is the current value Hamiltonian along the optimal path. To linearize the utility function we measure the difference $u(c^*, x^*) - u(0, 0)$ by a linear approximation to obtain

$$u(c^*, x^*) \approx u_c^* c^* + u_x^* x^* = \lambda^{c^*} c^* + u_x^* x^* \qquad (4.53)$$

where the second equality follows after having made use of the first-order conditions. Inserting (4.53) into (4.52) and dividing by λ^{c^*} we obtain the approximation of (4.52) in real terms which reads

$$\frac{NWM}{\lambda^{c^*}} = c^* + \dot{k}^* + \lambda^{c^{*-1}} u_x x^* - \tau^* \dot{x}^* \qquad (4.54)$$

where we take the optimal environmental tax as equal to $\tau^*(t) = -\mu^{c^*}(t)/\lambda^{c^*}(t)$.

The first two terms on the right-hand side of (4.54) correspond to the conventional net national product measure (consumption + investment). However, to get a correct estimate of welfare in terms of discounted future utility, we have to add the negative marginal disutility of pollution times the stock of pollution, and also deduct the net accumulation of pollution times the Pigouvian tax at time t. The treatment of unpriced renewable and non-renewable resources in a net welfare measure is analogous to the treatment of pollution[8] in (4.54). In the case of technological progress, another term, representing (an approximation of) the present value of marginal technological progress along the optimal path, has to be added. Similar complications would arise, as we have seen, whenever the externalities are not handled in the optimal way.

The linear welfare measure in (4.54) closely resembles what one would expect a cost–benefit rule for the entire economy to look like. This would have been even clearer if variable leisure time, as in Mäler (1991), had been included in the utility function. Total payments to labour would then have had to be deducted in order to end up with a linear approximation of net welfare. The analogy with cost–benefit rules is, as we are about to show, a little misleading. In fact, the differentiation we performed in Equation (4.51) contains the clue to the shape of the cost–benefit rule. Say that we want to know the evaluation rule for a project which improves the environment's assimilative capacity. According to Equation (4.51), we simply differentiate the Hamiltonian partially with respect to α, and integrate the resulting partial derivative over the planning horizon. We obtain

$$\frac{\partial V^*(\beta)}{\partial \alpha} = \int_t^\infty \left[-\mu^{c^*}(s) x^*(s) - \lambda^{c^*}(s) I_\alpha(\alpha) \right] e^{-\theta(s-t)} ds \qquad (4.55)$$

where $\mu^{c\cdot}(s)$ is the optimal (and non-positive) current value shadow price of the stock of pollution, $\lambda^{c\cdot}(s)$ is the optimal current value shadow price of capital, and $I_\alpha(\cdot)$ is the marginal cost of the project. The integral expresses the difference between the present value of the marginal benefits and the present value of the marginal costs of the project. By dividing the integrand by $\lambda^{c\cdot}(s)$ the project evaluation rule can be expressed in real terms:

$$\frac{\partial V^R(\beta)}{\partial \alpha} = \int_t^\infty \left[\tau^*(s)x^*(s) - I_\alpha(\alpha) \right] e^{-\theta(s-t)} ds \qquad (4.55a)$$

where $\tau^*(t)$ is the optimal Pigouvian tax.

In other words, compared with the linear welfare measures of green NNP which only require entities available at the current date, the cost–benefit rule requires data along the optimal path. The reason, loosely speaking, is that the project is represented by a parameter, which is not optimally chosen. The reader may also observe the close connection between a cost–benefit rule such as Equation (4.55) and the measures of the welfare effects of previously unanticipated technological change in Chapter 3. If we think of the technological shock as 'the project' – the welfare effect of which we would like to evaluate – the 'cost–benefit rule' would correspond exactly to the measure of the welfare effect derived in Chapter 3.

There is a trick which will supply us with a static equivalent of the project evaluation rule. We can treat α as a state variable $\alpha(t)$ with $\dot{\alpha}(t) \equiv 0$. The costate variable, $\Omega^{c\cdot}(t)$, connected with α, would then be the cost–benefit rule; i.e.

$$\Omega^{c\cdot}(t) = \frac{\partial V^*(\beta)}{\partial \alpha} = \int_t^\infty \left[-\mu^{c\cdot}(s)x^*(s) - \lambda^{c\cdot}(s)I_\alpha(\alpha) \right] e^{-\theta(s-t)} ds \qquad (4.56)$$

Unfortunately, this static equivalent is not available in the market.

To sum up, a comparison between the augmented NNP measure (4.54) and the cost–benefit rule (4.55a) highlights the fact that we cannot meaningfully interpret (4.54) in terms of a cost–benefit analysis of the entire economy. Basically, it provides a static equivalent of welfare, which can be interpreted as an approximation of the interest on the present value of future utility. For example, a project with a persistent impact, such as a shift from more to less aggressive pollutants, as illustrated by $d\alpha$ in Equation (4.55), cannot be completely evaluated by looking at a static welfare measure; the future consequences must also be accounted for.

Hence, even if there is a static equivalent of expected future utility, such as the value of the Hamiltonian in Equation (4.52) or an approximation such as (4.54), this information is not sufficient to evaluate the welfare consequences of, say, changes in environmental policy which, almost by definition, is conducted to correct for inoptimal conditions. Since policy changes have intertemporal consequences the evaluation requires, in general, knowledge of the shadow prices, state variables, and control variables along the entire future optimal path of the economy. This means that we cannot base evaluations of potentially welfare improving projects solely on the shadow prices, which would be the case with the current estimate of green NNP. New projects should be evaluated in a way similar to externalities, not internalized in the process of optimization (or by the price system). We have to evaluate marginal projects using the shadow prices generated along the future optimal path. This is analogous to a correct treatment of the welfare consequences of an externality along the (sub)optimal path, which is to estimate the present value of the marginal externality using the shadow prices of the (sub)optimal programme.

However, as Equation (4.56) illustrates, the value of a potential project is indeed inherent in the problem. In command optimum, a static equivalent of this value can be elicited by means of a technical trick, which treats parameters as state variables with time derivatives equal to zero. This information is, unfortunately, never available in real markets. However, as long as the optimization problem is not fundamentally time dependent, there is 'a catcher in the rye' if one wants to base an evaluation of an intertemporal project on today's shadow prices. Using the fact that $H^{c^*}(t) / \theta = V^*(\beta)$, one obtains a kind of *static cost–benefit equivalent*, which is written

$$[dH^{c^*}(t) / d\alpha] / \theta = \partial V^* (\alpha) / \partial \alpha \qquad (4.57)$$

Thus, at least in principle, it should be possible to base the evaluation on currently available information. However, the left-hand side expression in Equation (4.57) does not reduce to the net welfare change measure in Equation (4.54) since

$$[dH^{c^*}(t) / d\alpha] / \theta = [\lambda^{c^*}(t)c_\alpha^*(t) + \lambda^c_\alpha{}^*(t)c^*(t) + u_x^*(\cdot)x_\alpha^*(t) + \lambda^c_\alpha{}^*(t)\dot{k}^*(t) +$$
$$\lambda^{c^*}(t)\dot{k}_\alpha^*(t) + \mu^c_\alpha{}^*(t)\dot{x}^*(t) + \mu^{c^*}(t)\dot{x}_\alpha^*(t)]/\theta \qquad (4.58)$$

where a subscript α refers to a partial derivative with respect to α. If the shadow prices $\lambda^{c^*}(t)$ and $\mu^{c^*}(t)$ remain approximately constant as α changes, Equation (4.58) indeed looks like a variation of the net welfare change measure (4.54). Unfortunately, it is not possible to say, in general, whether changes in the shadow prices are important factors in signing Equation (4.58). The answer depends on the kind of project one is assessing, i.e., it is ultimately an empirical question whether shadow price changes are important or not.

4.4   COST–BENEFIT RULES IN THE UNCONTROLLED MARKET SOLUTION

We shall end this chapter by deriving cost–benefit rules for the case where the Pigouvian tax equals zero, which corresponds to an undisturbed market solution under externalities. This means that the consumer maximizes (4.28) subject to (4.28a) and (4.28b) and that firms behave according to (4.31). The Hamiltonian of this problem along the market solution can be written

$$H^0(t) = u(c^0(t), x^0(t))e^{-\theta t} + \lambda^0[f(k^0(t), e_f^0(t)) - c^0(t) - I(\alpha)]   (4.59)$$

and the value function is

$$V^0(\beta) = \underset{c(t)}{\text{Max}} \int_0^\infty u[c(t), x(t)]e^{-\theta t} dt   (4.60)$$

subject to (4.28a), (4.28b) and (4.31). As the Hamiltonian is written here, the project parameter seems to enter only through the cost function. In our notation we have, in general, suppressed the fact that control and state variables depend on the parameter vector β. One reason for this is that, as Equation (4.51) (Claim 1 and Theorem 1 in the Appendix) shows, this indirect effect on the value function vanishes. There is, however, an important difference between the Hamiltonian (4.59), and the Hamiltonian corresponding to the command optimum: in the former the pollution stock is no longer a state variable, but an exogenous variable affecting the utility of the consumer. Its development over time is governed by the differential equation

$$\dot{x} = e_f^0 - (\alpha + \gamma)x   \qquad x(0) = x_0   (4.61)$$

where $e_f^0(t)$ is determined in the firm's optimization problem from the first-order condition that the marginal productivity of emissions equals zero. If we solve Equation (4.61) we obtain

$$x^0(t, \alpha) = x_0 e^{-(\alpha+\gamma)t} + \int_0^t e_f^0(s, \alpha)e^{-(\alpha+\gamma)(t-s)} ds   (4.62)$$

In other words, the stock of pollution is a function of the parameter α, both directly through its impact on the depreciation rate, and indirectly through the emission function. The latter relationship follows since $e^0_f(t)$ is a function of the capital stock at time t, and the differential equation for the capital stock contains the cost function $I(\alpha)$. The partial derivative with respect to α, $x^0_\alpha(t,\alpha)$, is presumably negative. The depreciation effect is obviously negative, and an increase in α leads to less capital being accumulated, $I_\alpha(\alpha) > 0$. If capital and energy emissions are technical complements in production, the output of emissions will decrease for all t.

Given that $x^0(t,\alpha)$ is exogenous to the consumer, the derivative of the value function with respect to α has the following slope:[9]

$$\frac{\partial V^0(\beta)}{\partial \alpha} = \int_0^\infty \frac{\partial H^0(s)}{\partial \alpha} ds = \int_0^\infty \left[u_x\left(c^0(s), x^0(s)\right) x^0_\alpha(s) e^{-\theta s} - \lambda^0(s) I_\alpha(\alpha) \right] ds \quad (4.63)$$

The first term in the last component is the benefits of the project, $u^0_x < 0$, $x^0_\alpha < 0$, and $u^0_x x^0_\alpha > 0$. The second component represents the cost of the marginal project in utility units.

Again we have to know the development over time of state, control, and exogenous variables to evaluate the project correctly. These information requirements are of course demanding, but in principle they are not less demanding in the first-best optimum case. To determine the magnitude of the optimal Pigouvian tax, one has to solve the command optimum problem. Here we have – without market data on the marginal disutility of the stock of emissions – to determine the net willingness to pay for the project.

In both cases we can 'ask for' the once and for all maximum decrease in real consumption, $dc < 0$, the consumer is willing to forego to carry out the project. This sum, the 'equivalent variation', equals the value of 'the project' $d\alpha$, i.e.

$$\int_0^\infty \left\{ \left[u^0_x(s) x^0_\alpha(s) \right] \lambda^0(s)^{-1} - I_\alpha(\alpha) \right\} ds = -\int_0^\infty dc e^{-\theta s} ds = -\frac{dc}{\theta} > 0 \quad (4.64)$$

The aggregation problem induced by more than one consumer will, however, remain unsolved, even if consumers are able to give an unbiased answer to the indicated contingent valuation question.

NOTES

1. See Seierstad (1981), Caputo (1990a) and La France and Barney (1991).
2. The problem is that $\lim_{T \to \infty} H^*(T) \neq 0$. To see this, define

$$H^*(T) = H^*(0) - \theta \int\limits_0^{t^1} c_{\max} e^{-\theta s} ds - \theta \int\limits_{t^1}^T \bar{c} e^{-\theta s} ds$$

Clearly, $\lim_{T \to \infty} H^*(T) = (c_{\max} - \bar{c})e^{-\theta t^1} + \lambda^*(0)\dot{k}^*(0) \neq 0$, and the Hamiltonian at time zero is a biased measure of future welfare.

3. Note that for $k_0 < \bar{k}$ we put $c = 0$ at time zero, and $(dH^c) / (dt) = 0$ on the interval up to the switching point.
4. See Seierstad and Sydsæter (1987), theorem 3.12. The natural transversality condition $\lim_{t \to \infty} \lambda(t) \geq 0 \leq \lim_{t \to \infty} \mu(t)$ is only necessary if certain growth conditions on the utility and production function are satisfied. This is formally stated in Seierstad and Sydsæter (1987), theorem 3.16.
5. Since the control region is convex $c^* \geq 0$, $e_f^* \geq 0$, the optimal control $c^*(t)$, $e_f^*(t)$ is continuous if the Hamiltonian is strictly concave in the control variables.
6. Obviously, if $f_t \neq 0$, Equation (4.35) would be augmented with a term representing the present value of the marginal technological progress.
7. See Seierstad (1981), Caputo (1990a) and La France and Barney (1991) for examples.
8. See Hartwick (1990) and Mäler (1991).
9. This can be understood from the calculations behind Claim 1 in the Appendix.

APPENDIX   AN INFINITE PLANNING HORIZON ENVELOPE RESULT

The optimal performance function:

$$J^*(\alpha) = \int\limits_0^\infty f\Big(x^*(\alpha,t), c^*(\alpha,t), \alpha, t\Big) dt$$

is the solution to the problem:

$$\operatorname*{Max}_c J = \int\limits_0^\infty f\big(x(t), c(t), \alpha, t\big) dt$$

subject to: (P1)

$$\dot{x}(t) = g[x(t), c(t), \alpha, t] \qquad \forall t \in [0, \infty)$$

$$x(0) = x_0 \text{ fixed}$$

$$\lim_{t \to \infty} x(t) \text{ free}$$

We shall assume that:

A1 $f(\cdot)$, and $g(\cdot)$ are twice continuously differentiable

A2 H is strictly quasi-concave in $c \in R^m$

A3 The optimal path, $\{x^*(\alpha, t), \lambda^*(\alpha, t), c^*(\alpha, t)\}$ is unique $\forall \alpha \in A$ where A is the set of admissible parameter values.

A4 $\lim\limits_{t \to \infty} \lambda^*(\alpha, t) \dfrac{\partial x^*}{\partial \alpha} = 0$ for $\forall \alpha \in A$

The following claim can now – given that the 'relevant' improper integrals converge – be proved:

Claim 1 If P1 satisfies A1–A4, then $J^*(\alpha)$is twice continuously differentiable in α, and:

$$\frac{\partial J^*}{\partial \alpha} = \int\limits_0^\infty \left(\frac{\partial f^*}{\partial x} \frac{\partial x^*}{\partial \alpha} + \frac{\partial f^*}{\partial c} \frac{\partial c^*}{\partial \alpha} + \frac{\partial f^*}{\partial \alpha} \right) dt =$$

$$= \int\limits_0^\infty \left(\frac{\partial f^*}{\partial \alpha} + \frac{\partial g^*}{\partial \alpha} \lambda^* \right) dt = \int\limits_0^\infty \frac{\partial H}{\partial \alpha}\left(x^*, c^*, \alpha, t\right) dt$$

Proof (sketch) The first-order conditions for a maximum are

$$\frac{\partial H}{\partial c} = \frac{\partial f}{\partial c} + \frac{\partial g}{\partial c} \lambda = 0 \qquad (A.1)$$

From A1 and A2, the closed-loop solutions for the control variables, $\hat{c}(x, \lambda, \alpha, t)$, are unique and continuous in (x, λ, α, t), on $[0, \infty)$ by the maximum theorem and continuously differentiable on $(0, \infty)$ by the implicit function theorem. The conditions are, furthermore, necessary and sufficient. Along the optimal path λ and x must satisfy the following conjugate differential equations on $[0, \infty)$:

$$\dot{\lambda}^* = -\left(\frac{\partial f^*}{\partial x} + \frac{\partial g^*}{\partial x} \lambda^* \right) \qquad (A.2)$$

$$\dot{x}^* = g(x^*, c^*, \alpha, t) \qquad x(0) = x_0 \qquad \forall \alpha \in A \qquad (A.3)$$

It follows from A1, A3 and Oniki (1973) that $x^*(\alpha, t)$ and $\lambda^*(\alpha, t)$ are continuously differentiable on $(0, \infty)$. To obtain the open-loop controls, we substitute $x^*(\cdot)$, $\lambda^*(\cdot)$ into $c^*(\cdot)$ to obtain

$$c^*(\alpha, t) = c^*[x^*(\alpha, t), \lambda^*(\alpha, t), \alpha, t] \tag{A.4}$$

Along the optimal path the state equations can be written as

$$\frac{\partial x^*(\alpha, t)}{\partial t} = g\left[x^*(\alpha, t), \lambda^*(\alpha, t), \alpha, t\right] \tag{A.5}$$

Since g, x^* and c^* are continuously differentiable on $(0, \infty)$

$$\frac{\partial^2 x^*}{\partial t \partial \alpha} \equiv \frac{\partial g^*}{\partial x}\frac{\partial x^*}{\partial \alpha} + \frac{\partial g^*}{\partial c}\frac{\partial c^*}{\partial \alpha} + \frac{\partial g^*}{\partial \alpha} = \frac{\partial^2 x^*}{\partial \alpha \partial t} \tag{A.6}$$

by Young's theorem.

Applying the chain rule to the optimal performance function yields

$$\frac{\partial J^*}{\partial \alpha} = \int_0^\infty \left(\frac{\partial f^*}{\partial x}\frac{\partial x^*}{\partial \alpha} + \frac{\partial f^*}{\partial c}\frac{\partial c^*}{\partial \alpha} + \frac{\partial f^*}{\partial \alpha}\right) dt \tag{A.7}$$

We now substitute for $\partial f^*/\partial c$ from (A.1) to obtain

$$\frac{\partial J^*}{\partial \alpha} = \int_0^\infty \left(\frac{\partial f^*}{\partial x}\frac{\partial x^*}{\partial \alpha} - \frac{\partial g^*}{\partial c}\frac{\partial c^*}{\partial \alpha}\lambda^* + \frac{\partial f^*}{\partial \alpha}\right) dt \tag{A.8}$$

Solving (A.6) for $(\partial g^*/\partial c)(\partial c^*/\partial \alpha)$ we have

$$\frac{\partial g^*}{\partial c}\frac{\partial c^*}{\partial \alpha} = \frac{\partial^2 x^*}{\partial \alpha \partial t} - \frac{\partial g^*}{\partial \alpha} - \frac{\partial g^*}{\partial x}\frac{\partial x^*}{\partial \alpha} \tag{A.9}$$

and substituting the result into (A.8),

$$\frac{\partial J^*}{\partial \alpha} = \int_0^\infty \left[\frac{\partial f^*}{\partial x}\frac{\partial x^*}{\partial \alpha} + \frac{\partial g^*}{\partial \alpha}\lambda^* + \frac{\partial g^*}{\partial x}\frac{\partial x^*}{\partial \alpha}\lambda^* - \frac{\partial^2 x^*}{\partial \alpha \partial t}\lambda^* + \frac{\partial f^*}{\partial \alpha}\right] dt \tag{A.10}$$

Integrating the fourth term in (A.10) by parts yields

$$-\int_0^\infty \frac{\partial^2 x^*}{\partial\alpha\partial t}\lambda^* dt = -\frac{\partial x^*}{\partial\alpha}\lambda^*\Big|_0^\infty + \int_0^\infty \frac{\partial x^*}{\partial\alpha}\frac{\partial\lambda^*}{\partial t} dt = \int_0^\infty \frac{\partial x^*}{\partial\alpha}\frac{\partial\lambda^*}{\partial t} dt \quad (A.11)$$

since $\lim_{t\to\infty} \lambda^*(\partial x^*/\partial\alpha) = 0$, and $\partial x^*(\alpha, 0)/\partial\alpha = 0$, because $x(\alpha, 0) = x_0$ is fixed.

If we substitute the open-loop solution $(x^*(\alpha, t), c^*(\alpha, t))$ into (A.2) we obtain

$$\frac{\partial\lambda^*}{\partial t} = -\left(\frac{\partial f^*}{\partial x} + \frac{\partial g^*}{\partial x}\lambda^*\right) \quad (A.12)$$

Finally, combine (A.10)–(A.12) to get

$$\frac{\partial J^*}{\partial\alpha} = \int_0^\infty \left(\frac{\partial f^*}{\partial\alpha} + \frac{\partial g^*}{\partial\alpha}\lambda^*\right) dt = \int_0^\infty \frac{\partial H}{\partial\alpha}\left(x^*, c^*, \lambda^*, \alpha, t\right) dt \quad (A.13)$$

Moreover, since $x^*, c^*, \lambda^*, \partial f(\cdot)/\partial\alpha$, and $\partial g(\cdot)/\partial\alpha$ are continuously differentiable in α, the integrand on the right-hand side of (A.13) is continuously differentiable. Hence $J^*(\alpha)$ is twice continuously differentiable.

The assumptions A1–A4 are together quite restrictive, and there is a risk that the theorem is quite vacuous. For example, a transversality condition such as $\lim_{t\to\infty} \lambda^*(t) = 0$ requires that certain growth conditions on $f(\cdot)$ and $g(\cdot)$ are satisfied. The reader is referred to Seierstad and Sydsæter (1987), theorem 3.16, which gives the necessary transversality conditions for infinite horizon optimal control problems. See also Theorem 1 below. Sufficient conditions for infinite horizon problems are given in Seierstad and Sydsæter (1987), theorem 3.17. These require among other things that $f(\cdot)$ and $g(\cdot)$ are non-decreasing in x for each (c, t), and concave in (x, c) for each t.

The strict mathematical problem with the above proof is that we have assumed that certain improper integrals converge. To assure this, certain growth conditions have to be satisfied. Moreover, to prove differentiability, a convex set important in the Fillippov–Cesari theorem on the existence of an optimal solution appears among the assumptions. Atle Seierstad has provided us with the following precise theorem (personal communication):

Theorem 1   Let $J^*(\alpha)$ be the value function of P1, and let f and g be continuously differentiable with respect to (x, c, α). For a given $\alpha^* \in A$, assume that there exists a unique optimal solution $\{x^*(\alpha^*, t), c^*(\alpha^*, t)\}$ where $c^*(\alpha^*, t) \in C$ is the control corresponding to $x^*(\alpha, t)$. The control region C is compact.

Let $B, b, Q, q, q > k$ be positive constants and assume that the following holds:

$$\left| f\big(x(\alpha, t), c, \alpha, t\big) \right| \le Be^{-bt} \qquad \text{for all } c \in C$$

$$\left| \frac{\partial f}{\partial x}(x, c, \alpha, t) \right| \le Qe^{-qt} \qquad \text{for all } x, u, t$$

$$\left| \frac{\partial g}{\partial x}(x, c, \alpha, t) \right| \le k \qquad \text{for all } x, u, t$$

Finally, assume that the set

$$N(t, x, C) = \{f(x, c, \alpha, t) + \gamma, g(x, c, \alpha, t) : c \in C, \gamma \le 0\}$$

is convex for all t, x.

Then $\left.\dfrac{\partial J}{\partial \alpha}\right|_{\alpha=\alpha^*}$ exists and equals $\displaystyle\int_0^\infty \frac{\partial H}{\partial \alpha}\big(x^*(\cdot), c^*(\cdot), \alpha, t\big)dt.$

Note: Under the above growth conditions $\lambda(\infty) = 0$ belongs to the set of necessary conditions.

The finite horizon version of the theorem can be obtained from Clarke (1983), 5.5.2, by treating α as a state variable ($\alpha(0) = \alpha, \dot\alpha(t) \equiv 0$). The growth conditions in the theorem make the extension to an infinite horizon possible.

5. Human capital – a recent issue in 'practical' national accounting

This chapter concerns social accounting and welfare analysis in an economy where investments in human capital are important determinants of economic growth. An application focusing on human capital is interesting for several reasons. First, several studies have emphasized the role of human capital in the process of economic growth; see e.g. Uzawa (1965), Lucas (1988), Romer (1986a, 1986b, 1990) and Chamley (1993).[1] Second, there is now an empirical literature originating from a series of papers by Dale Jorgenson and Barbara Fraumeni (see below), which concerns the role of investments in human capital in the national accounts. This literature focuses on, among other things, how one *should* measure the contribution of the education sector to economic growth and, consequently, how one should augment the national product measure to take appropriate account of the output from the education sector.

Human capital is also a challenging topic from the point of view of welfare analysis. The decision to invest in human capital, which is essentially a choice to spend time in education, is part of the individual's intertemporal utility maximization problem. In addition to the potential direct effects of human capital on utility, the incentive to invest has to do with the influence of the human capital stock on earnings. However, investments in human capital may also create positive external effects – endogenous growth theory is built on this notion – which means that the individuals in the decentralized economy do not necessarily make the correct investment decision from society's point of view.

We start by reviewing some recent empirical research related to the measurement of the value of investments in human capital, and how that information can be used to establish a more correct basis for national accounting. This should, we hope, give the reader a feeling for the practical importance of investments in human capital and an intuitive understanding of how to measure the value of these investments. We shall then continue with a formal analysis using a growth model which includes investments in human capital. Following the studies of Lucas (1988), Razin (1972), Stokey (1991), Chamley (1993) and others we assume that the accumulation of human capital depends on the time consumers spend in education. However, contrary to these studies, we also include leisure in the utility function, which means that labour supply is endogenous here.[2] Moreover, although the stock of human capital is controlled by the consumers, through their decision to spend time in education, it is also a separate argument in the production function facing firms, which means that human capital accumulation gives rise to an external effect.

Having developed a model along these lines, we derive the augmented national product measure representing welfare in a social optimum. We also discuss the tax and transfer system required to internalize the externality in a decentralized economy. An interesting result here is that, since the externality is caused by the stock (and not the flow) of human capital, educational subsidies are not sufficient to make consumers choose the correct investment policy. What we require could, instead, be characterized as 'a stock subsidy', since it relates to the stock of human capital. Naturally, to internalize this externality, the 'policy maker' needs an enormous amount of information. The case when the (stock) subsidy is not optimally chosen – meaning that the externality has not become fully internalized – is, therefore, important to consider. Given that the initial subsidy is not necessarily optimal, the final concern will be to derive the cost–benefit rule required to determine whether a change in the subsidy rate increases welfare.

5.1   HUMAN CAPITAL IN PRACTICAL NATIONAL ACCOUNTING

It is not easy to give a formal definition of the concept of human capital. According to the *New Palgrave Dictionary of Economics*, human capital is the 'stock of skills and productive knowledge embodied in people'. Following the contributions by Becker (1964), Mincer (1974) and Schultz (1961), economists have often found it useful to characterize *education* as an investment in human capital. If an individual chooses to pursue an educational programme, he/she will face the cost of foregone earnings during the period of education. At the same time, as a consequence of the rise in the individual's productivity following education, earnings are likely to increase in the future. This gives a clue to how to measure the value of investments in human capital from the individual's point of view.

On the other hand, in actual national accounting education is included as part of public consumption, which means that the contribution of education to the net national product is measured as the sum of the direct costs of providing the education (costs of teachers, equipment, buildings, etc.). This way of measuring the value of education suffers from a number of weaknesses. First, it contains no information about the value of education from society's point of view; it only measures the value of (part of) the resources consumed in the education sector. Second, as indicated before, the investment character of education is completely neglected, which means that the picture of capital formation provided by the national accounts may not be correct.

In a series of papers, Dale Jorgenson and Barbara Fraumeni suggest and apply a method to measure the value of education that serves to eliminate these weaknesses.[3] The idea behind their approach is, as it should be, to view education as an investment: by acquiring education, the individual's productivity will increase, which in turn increases future earnings. Suppose that an individual, at the beginning of period t, has to decide whether or not to spend an additional year in education. Formally, we can write the change in the present value of lifetime income following the investment as

$$\Delta W(t) = -y(t) + \sum_{s=t+1}^{T} \Delta y(s)(1+\theta)^{-(s-t)}$$

The first term on the right-hand side is the foregone income during the period of education, while the second term on the right-hand side is the increase in the present value of income thereafter because education increases the individual's productivity. If we disregard the possibility that investments in human capital create external effects, and by subtracting the costs of resources used in the educational process, R, we obtain the measure $\Delta WN = \Delta W - R$, which is essentially the basis for Jorgenson and Fraumeni's analysis. Regarding the way to measure 'income', Jorgenson and Fraumeni (1992a) argue that the increase in the present value of lifetime income following additional human capital should not only involve the change in the present value of labour income. It should also be important to consider the change in the present value of 'leisure income', since additional human capital makes leisure more valuable. We shall return to this income concept below.

Wage and employment profiles over the lifecycle for different educational groups can be recovered by econometric methods. By assuming that an individual of a certain age and a given education will follow the (estimated) paths corresponding to his/her years of schooling, it is possible to compute the expected change in the present value of lifetime income from additional education. As a final step, aggregation is accomplished by using knowledge of enrolment rates in different age groups and population statistics. The result is an aggregate measure of the increase in the present value of lifetime income generated by the education sector during a year, i.e. a measure of the output of the education sector.

Jorgenson and Fraumeni (1992a, 1992b) examine how different factors have contributed to the US economic growth during the postwar period. When human capital is present in the analysis, it is meaningful to talk about 'the quality of labour input', which has to do with the fact that, given the hours of work, individuals differ in ability or skills because of their different endowment of human capital. By allocating the US economic growth during the period 1948–86 to its sources, Jorgenson and Fraumeni (1992b) find that 61 per cent is attributable to labour input, while the corresponding numbers for capital input and productivity growth are 22 per cent and 17 per cent, respectively. About 40 per cent of the contribution of labour input is attributable to labour quality, which, if these numbers are correct, indicates a considerable influence of human capital in the growth process.[4] A recent attempt to value education 'correctly' in the Swedish national accounts can be found in Ahlroth et al. (1994). Their study applies the method used by Jorgenson and Fraumeni but is less focused on economic growth. Instead, the authors present results from a series of calculations based on different assumptions in order to recover the value of additional human capital. Although their results are very sensitive to the assumptions of discount rate and how to measure income (for example, whether or not leisure income is included), the conclusion is, nevertheless, that neglecting investments in human capital is likely to result in substantially biased measures of the value of capital formation in the Swedish economy.

5.2   A GROWTH MODEL WITH HUMAN CAPITAL

The Model

The review presented above of recent attempts to measure the value of investments in human capital and to replace 'old' numbers in the national accounts with these 'new' numbers should serve as a motivation to look a little more closely at welfare measurement in the presence of human capital formation. Although the empirical measurement of the value of human capital investments is still in its infancy, meaning that the results are very uncertain (to say the least), we nevertheless argue that the studies referred to in the last subsection indicate such important effects of human capital that welfare measures neglecting these effects may be substantially biased. Despite this, the theoretical literature on social accounting and welfare measurement has almost exclusively focused on issues other than human capital; for example, environmental externalities and different kinds of technological change. Some of these issues were dealt with in Chapter 4.

The analysis in this section is based on a model developed by Aronsson and Löfgren (1995b). In order to focus on human capital, we disregard other types of complications studied in previous chapters. We shall also here, as in Chapters 3 and 4, disregard population growth and normalize the population to equal one. However, contrary to previous chapters, leisure is now assumed to be an argument in the utility function, which means that the present value of future utility is written

$$U(0) = \int_0^\infty u(c(t), L(t)) e^{-\theta t} dt \tag{5.1}$$

We define leisure, L, as $L = T - \ell - x$, i.e. as a time endowment, T, less time spent in market work, ℓ, and time spent in education, x. The instantaneous utility function is assumed to be strictly concave as well as increasing in c and L. To avoid corner solutions, we also require that $u_c(0, L) = u_L(c, 0) = \infty$, implying that $c > 0$ and $L > 0$ along the optimal path. Turning to the production side of the economy, the accumulation of physical capital net of depreciation (i.e. net investments) is determined by the equation

$$\frac{dk(t)}{dt} = f[a(h(t))\ell(t), k(t), h(t)] - c(t) \tag{5.2}$$

where $f(\cdot)$ is a production function and defines a relationship between *net output* and the factors of production. This formulation is convenient, since it enables us to suppress depreciation of physical capital and, therefore, avoid notations not essential for the main results to be derived.

In Equation (5.2), h is the stock of human capital, and $a(h)$ is a function such that $a(0) = 1$ and $a'(h) = \partial a(h)/\partial h > 0$. The term $a(h)\ell$ may be interpreted as a measure of 'effective labour supply'; given the time spent in market work, it reflects the quality of labour input. When convenient, we shall use the short-hand notation $\overline{\ell}$ for effective labour supply, $\overline{\ell} = a(h)\ell$. According to (5.2), the human capital stock enters the production function both directly as a separate argument and indirectly by increasing the marginal product of labour, i.e.

$$df(\cdot) / dh = a'(h) f_{\overline{\ell}}(\cdot)\ell + f_h(\cdot)$$

The last term, which is the direct effect, captures the possibility that human capital has a value for society beyond the compensation for investments facing the consumer. For example, rather than assuming that technological change is exogenous – which we did in Chapter 4 – we may think of it as driven by knowledge or investments in human capital. In this case, the specification of the production function in Equation (5.2) means that we do not restrict the technological progress to be 'labour augmenting'. We assume that $f(\cdot)$ is twice continuously differentiable in ℓ, k and h, increasing in ℓ and h, and strictly concave in ℓ and k.

The accumulation of human capital is determined by

$$\frac{dh(t)}{dt} = g(x(t)) - \gamma h(t) \tag{5.3}$$

where $g(x)$ is a function such that $g(0) = 0$ and $g'(x) = \partial g(x) / \partial x > 0$, while γ is the rate of depreciation of the human capital. Depreciation does not mean that knowledge is forgotten, i.e. $\gamma > 0$ is perfectly consistent with the assumption that once the knowledge is gained it will always be there. It simply means that knowledge becomes obsolete and, therefore, loses part of its value. This will be made clear below.

A Measure of Social Welfare

Let us assume, as we have done several times in previous chapters, that the resource allocation is determined by a utilitarian social planner, who in this case is choosing c, ℓ and x such as to maximize (5.1) subject to (5.2), (5.3), initial conditions, $k(0) = k_0$ and $h(0) = h_0$, and non-negativity constraints, $\ell \geq 0$ and $x \geq 0$. Suppose also that a finite valued solution to this optimization problem exists.[5] If we neglect the time indicator for notational convenience, the present value Hamiltonian corresponding to (5.1), (5.2) and (5.3) is written

$$H = u(c, T - \ell - x)e^{-\theta t} + \lambda(f(a(h)\ell, k, h) - c) + \mu(g(x) - \gamma h) \tag{5.4}$$

where $\lambda(t)$ and $\mu(t)$ are the costate variables and measure, respectively, the marginal value at time zero of an additional unit of physical capital at time t and the marginal value at time zero of an additional unit of human capital at time t.

In order to formulate the maximum principle for the problem discussed here, we also have to impose a constraint qualification corresponding to the non-negativity constraints. We show in the Appendix that the constraint qualification is always fulfilled in the present model. Therefore, in addition to Equations (5.2) and (5.3), and in addition to the non-negativity constraints and initial conditions, the necessary conditions are

$$H_c = u_c(\cdot)e^{-\theta t} - \lambda = 0 \tag{5.5a}$$

$$H_\ell = -u_L(\cdot)e^{-\theta t} + \lambda a(h)f_{\tilde{\ell}}(\cdot) \leq 0, \quad H_\ell \ell = 0 \tag{5.5b}$$

$$H_x = -u_L(\cdot)e^{-\theta t} + \mu g'(x) \leq 0, \quad H_x x = 0 \tag{5.5c}$$

$$\dot{\lambda} = -(\partial H/\partial k) = -\lambda f_k(\cdot) \tag{5.5d}$$

$$\dot{\mu} = -(\partial H/\partial h) = -\lambda(a'(h)f_{\tilde{\ell}}(\cdot)\ell + f_h(\cdot)) + \mu\gamma \tag{5.5e}$$

$$\lim_{t \to \infty} \lambda k = 0 \qquad (5.5f)$$

$$\lim_{t \to \infty} \mu h = 0 \qquad (5.5g)$$

where the transversality conditions in (5.5f) and (5.5g) are necessary provided that growth conditions of the type discussed in Chapters 3 and 4 are fulfilled. In addition to the efficiency condition for consumption, which is similar to that in previous chapters, this model also involves efficiency conditions for hours of work and time in education. If these conditions both imply interior solutions at a given point in time, we obtain by combining (5.5b) and (5.5c) the condition

$$\lambda a(h) f_{\ell}'(\cdot) = \mu g'(x)$$

which means that an additional hour spent in the labour market gives rise to the same utility value as an additional hour spent in education.

Let $(c^*(t), \ell^*(t), x^*(t), k^*(t), h^*(t), \lambda^*(t), \mu^*(t))$ represent the optimal solution implicit in (5.5). Substituting back into the present value Hamiltonian and applying Proposition 4.1 we obtain

$$\frac{dH^*(t)}{dt} = -\theta u\big(c^*(t), L^*(t)\big)e^{-\theta t}$$

Solving this equation forwards and transforming the result to current value, the equivalent of the measure of social welfare derived in previous chapters becomes

$$\theta \int_t^\infty u\big(c^*(s), L^*(s)\big)e^{-\theta(s-t)}ds = u\big(c^*(t), L^*(t)\big) + \lambda^{c^*}(t)\frac{dk^*(t)}{dt} + \mu^{c^*}(t)\frac{dh^*(t)}{dt} \qquad (5.6)$$

where $\lambda^{c^*}(t) = \lambda^*(t)e^{\theta t}$ and $\mu^{c^*}(t) = \mu^*(t)e^{\theta t}$. Equation (5.6) is clearly a national product related welfare measure; it is essentially the net national product measured in utility units augmented by the utility value of leisure time and the utility value of investments in human capital. This is perhaps most easily seen if we derive the analogue to 'the net welfare measure' discussed in previous chapters. By neglecting the time indicator for notational convenience, and dividing by the marginal utility of consumption, the local approximation of the welfare measure is written in real terms as

$$\frac{NWM}{\lambda^{c^*}} = c^* + \frac{dk^*}{dt} + w^* L^* + \frac{\mu^{c^*}}{\lambda^{c^*}} \frac{dh^*}{dt} \qquad (5.6a)$$

where $w^* = a(h^*)f_{\bar{\ell}}(a(h^*)\ell^*, k^*, h^*)$. The first two terms on the right-hand side of (5.6a) are, together, the conventional net national product. The third term is the value of leisure time and is measured as the wage rate (i.e. the marginal product of labour) times the optimal time spent on leisure. Finally, the fourth term is the value of investments in human capital. Hence, Equation (5.6a) illustrates what the social accounts corresponding to the model given by (5.1), (5.2) and (5.3) should include. Note in particular that, although the value of leisure time increases with the stock of human capital (via the marginal product of labour), its presence in the welfare measure does not depend on human capital *per se*; it depends on the assumption that leisure is an argument in the utility function and should, as a consequence, be included in Equation (5.6a) even if $h = 0$.

Society's Valuation of Additions to the Stock of Human Capital

For the national accounts to provide the correct information about welfare in this economy, it is of critical importance to know the utility value of additional human capital, $\mu^{c^*}(t)$. In the last subsection we discussed empirical attempts to find that information. An interesting question is, therefore, what insights this model provides. Using the fact that $\mu^{c^*}(t) = e^{\theta t}\mu^*(t)$, we can rewrite Equation (5.5e) to read

$$\dot{\mu}^{c^*}(t) - \theta\mu^{c^*}(t) = -\frac{\partial H^{c^*}(t)}{\partial h(t)}$$

which has a solution of the form

$$\mu^{c^*}(t) = \int_{t}^{\infty} \lambda^{c^*}(s)\left[a'\left(h^*(s)\right)f_{\bar{\ell}}(s)\ell^*(s) + f_h(s)\right]e^{-(\theta+\gamma)(s-t)}ds \qquad (5.7)$$

The first term within brackets of Equation (5.7) is the change in labour income following a small increase in the stock of human capital (it is the change in labour productivity times the hours of work), while the second term has to do with the direct effect of human capital in the production function. This means that in the absence of a direct effect of human capital – which would imply that the technological change driven by human capital accumulation is 'labour 'augmenting' – the current social value of an additional unit of human capital would be equal to the increase in the present value of labour income.[6] Note also that the appropriate discount factor in (5.7) is not given by the rate of time preference alone, but by the sum of the rate of time preference and the rate of depreciation of human capital. This raises two questions related to the empirical papers by Jorgenson and Fraumeni (1992a, 1992b) and Ahlroth et al. (1994). First, these studies neglect depreciation of human capital – also noted by Conrad (1992) in a comment to Jorgenson and Fraumeni (1992b) – which means that there is a tendency to overestimate the value of additional human capital. Second, the relevant measure of income change in Equation (5.7) is the change in the present value of labour income, not the change in the present value of the sum of labour income and leisure income, as argued in some of the empirical papers.

Externalities in the Decentralized Economy

It should come as no surprise to the reader that, if external effects are present, the decentralized economy will not, by itself, produce a socially optimal allocation of resources and, as a consequence, welfare cannot be represented by a national product related measure. In the present model, the externality has to do with the fact that human capital not only affects the present value of labour income, which is the concern of consumers when they choose their investments, but it is also a separate argument in the production function. As such the stock of human capital will contribute to output – in addition to its indirect effect via labour productivity – as long as $f_h(\cdot) > 0$.

To illustrate these basic points, and to see what policy is required to internalize the external effect mentioned above, we start by briefly presenting the optimization problem facing the agents in the decentralized economy. The firm is assumed to maximize the present value of profits, i.e.

$$\underset{\ell(t),k(t)}{\text{Max}} \int_0^\infty \left\{ f\left[a(h(t))\ell(t), k(t), h(t)\right] - w(t)\ell(t) - r(t)k(t) \right\} \exp\left(-\int_0^t r(s)ds \right) dt \qquad (5.8a)$$

where w is the wage rate and r the interest rate. At each instant of time, the firm behaves according to the necessary conditions for labour and capital, $a(h)f_{\bar{\ell}}(\cdot) = w$ and $f_k(\cdot) = r$.

The consumer in the decentralized economy is assumed to maximize the utility function in (5.1) subject to an intertemporal budget constraint, the accumulation equation for human capital given by (5.3), non-negativity constraints for time in market work and time in education, and initial conditions for the stocks of physical and human capital. As mentioned in Chapter 3, a dynamic budget constraint and a No Ponzi Game (NPG) condition are, together, equivalent to an intertemporal budget constraint. The dynamic budget constraint and the NPG condition are written

$$\frac{dk(t)}{dt} = \pi(t) + r(t)k(t) + a(h(t))w_0(t)\ell(t) - c(t) \qquad (5.8b)$$

$$\lim_{t \to \infty} k(t)\exp\left(-\int_0^t r(s)ds\right) \ge 0 \qquad (5.8c)$$

The terms on the right-hand side of (5.8b) are, respectively, profit income (since the consumer is assumed to own the firm), capital income, labour income and consumption. From the definition of labour income, we see that the consumer takes into account the relationship between the wage rate and past investments in human capital. The wage rate is, in this case, given by $w(t) = a(h(t))w_0(t)$, where the function $a(h)$ was introduced in the previous subsection. The term w_0 is the wage rate paid to effective labour, $a(h)\ell$.

We shall return to several details of the solution in the decentralized economy (including the necessary conditions for the consumer) in later parts of the chapter. For the time being, we simply define $(c^0(t), \ell^0(t), x^0(t), k^0(t), h^0(t), \lambda^0(t), \mu^0(t))$ to be *the general equilibrium solution* in the decentralized economy. Our concern here is the consumer's valuation of human capital. From (5.8b) we see that the stock of human capital only affects the dynamic budget constraint via the wage rate. Therefore, since the consumer does not take the direct effect of human capital on output into account in his/her optimization problem, it is easy to show that the current value of additional human capital from the consumer's point of view is given by

$$\mu^{c^0}(t) = \int_t^\infty \lambda^{c^0}(s)a'\left(h^0(s)\right)f_{\bar{\ell}}(s)\ell^0(s)e^{-(\theta+\gamma)(s-t)}ds \qquad (5.9)$$

Comparing Equations (5.7) and (5.9), we see that the consumer's valuation of additional human capital in the decentralized economy differs from the social value of additional human capital. As indicated above, the reason is that the consumer does not value the direct effect of human capital on output. The consumer in the decentralized economy is, therefore, likely to spend less time in education and, hence, accumulate less human capital than is socially optimal.

If the consumer's investment decision is based on a suboptimal shadow price (from society's point of view), a national product related measure based on current entities will not provide the correct information about welfare. To illustrate, let us define the present value Hamiltonian along the general equilibrium path (suppressing the time indicator)

$$H^0 = u(c^0, T - \ell^0 - x^0)e^{-\theta t} + \lambda^0(f(a(h^0)\ell^0, k^0, h^0) - c^0) + \mu^0(g(x^0) - \gamma h^0)$$

$$(5.10)$$

By applying Proposition 4.1 we obtain

$$\frac{dH^0(t)}{dt} = -\theta u\left(c^0(t), L^0(t)\right)e^{-\theta t} + \lambda^0(t)f_h(\cdot)\frac{dh^0(t)}{dt} \qquad (5.10a)$$

where the last term on the right-hand side of (5.10a) reflects the fact that output becomes an explicit function of time when h is not optimally chosen. Similar results (although in other contexts) were discussed in Chapter 4. Solving (5.10a) and transforming to current value gives

$$\theta \int_t^\infty u\left(c^0(s), L^0(s)\right)e^{-\theta(s-t)}ds = u\left(c^0(t), L^0(t)\right) + \lambda^{c0}(t)\frac{dk^0(t)}{dt} + \mu^{c0}(t)\frac{dh^0(t)}{dt}$$

$$+ \int_t^\infty \lambda^{c0}(s)f_h(s)\frac{dh^0(s)}{ds}e^{-\theta(s-t)}ds \qquad (5.11)$$

The right-hand side of (5.11) contains two parts: the first is the current value Hamiltonian; and the second is the present value of the marginal external effect along the general equilibrium path. We make two important observations from Equation (5.11). First, if human capital gives rise to a positive external effect, the augmented NNP measure (the current value Hamiltonian) will underestimate welfare. Second, (5.11) represents a lower welfare level than Equation (5.6), since the allocation implicit in (5.11) is not socially optimal.

A Numerical Cobb–Douglas Example

In this subsection, we present a simple numerical version of the model. The numerical example has primarily two purposes. The first is to illustrate what the intertemporal labour supply and investment behaviour in the model may look like for a given set of parameters. Since it is analytically difficult to derive the behaviour implicit in the general model, such an example should give the reader a better feeling for how the model works. The second purpose is to shed some light on the importance of the externality for measuring welfare in the decentralized economy. To make the analysis as simple as possible, we assume that both the instantaneous utility function and the production function are of Cobb–Douglas type. Formally,

$$u(c, L) = c^{\omega} L^{(1-\omega)}, 0 < \omega < 1$$

$$f(a(h)\ell, k, h) = [a(h)\ell]^{\rho_1} k^{\rho_2} h^{(1-\rho_1-\rho_2)}, 0 < \rho_1, \rho_2 < 1 \text{ and } \rho_1 + \rho_2 \leq 1$$

For the functions $a(h)$ and $g(x)$ in Equations (5.2) and (5.3) we assume that

$$a(h) = 1 + v_0 h^{v_1}, v_0 > 0 \text{ and } 0 < v_1 < 1$$

$$g(x) = \varsigma_0 x^{\varsigma_1}, \varsigma_0 > 0 \text{ and } 0 < \varsigma_1 < 1$$

which fulfil the properties specified previously. By choosing values for the parameters in these four equations, initial values for k and h, as well as a time horizon (which has to be finite in this example) we are able to compute the paths for control, state and costate variables both when the resource allocation is decided upon by a social planner and in the decentralized economy. Naturally, in this kind of model, it is difficult to choose a set of 'realistic' parameter values. The basis for our choice is, first, the empirical observation that the labour share of output usually exceeds the (physical) capital share, and second the desire to obtain reasonable values for the labour supply.[7] To begin with, let $\omega = 0.45$, $\rho_1 = 0.45$, $\rho_2 = 0.30$, $v_0 = 0.1$, $v_1 = 0.3$, $\varsigma_0 = 10$ and $\varsigma_1 = 0.95$. We also assume that $\theta = 0.03$ and $\gamma = 0.01$, while the time horizon is set to 100.

Given the choice of functional forms for preferences and technology, as well as the assumptions about parameter values, Figure 5.1 presents the equilibrium paths for the variables. The results are obtained using the simulation program GAMS. The figure contains two paths for each relevant variable, one corresponding to the social optimum, and the other corresponding to resource allocation in the decentralized economy, where the externality is not internalized.

Figure 5.1 is organized as follows: (a) contains the time paths for consumption, (b) the paths for time in market work, (c) the paths for time in education, (d) the paths for the stock of physical capital and (e) the paths for the stock of human capital. To interpret these results, note first (from (a)) that the consumption path is single peaked, which is the result usually obtained when consumption is chosen so as to maximize the present value of future utility (see, for example, Dasgupta and Heal, 1979 and Pezzy and Withagen, 1995). Note also, from (b) and (c) that 'the individual' spends much time in education at the initial phase of the

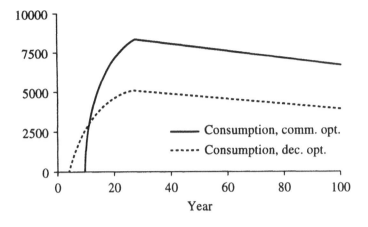

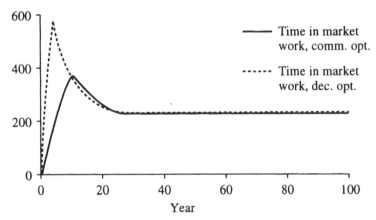

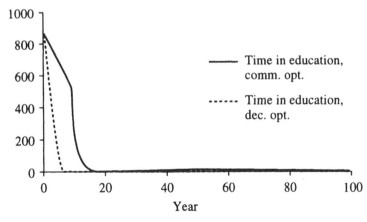

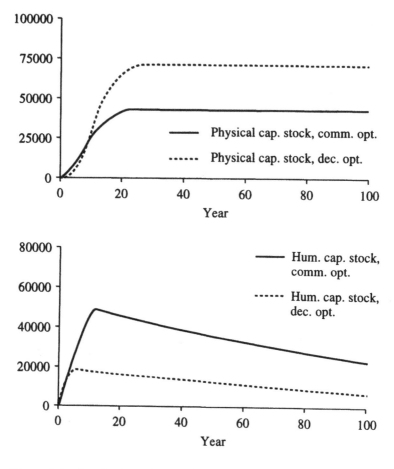

Figure 5.1   Results from the simulations

planning period (or lifecycle). This tendency is more pronounced in the command optimum – where the resources are allocated in an optimal way from society's point of view – in comparison with the decentralized solution. As a consequence, labour supply is greater in the decentralized economy than in the command optimum at the initial phase. Therefore, when the externality is not internalized, the economy will accumulate less human capital than is socially optimal, which is seen from (e).

Let us now turn to welfare measurement, which means that we compare the two allocation systems discussed above from the point of view of welfare. A particular concern here will be the importance of the externality for measuring welfare in the decentralized economy. As in the theoretical analysis, we shall measure welfare by the rate of time preference times the present value of future utility. The results are presented in Table 5.1.

Table 5.1   Welfare in the Cobb–Douglas example

ρ_1	ρ_2	Command optimum Welfare	Decentralized solution Welfare	NNP
0.45	0.30	1212.47	1104.53	729.74
0.55	0.30	962.86	929.16	709.08
0.35	0.30	1565.35	1315.56	721.27

The figures in the first two columns in Table 5.1 indicate the weights given to effective labour and physical capital in the production function. The first row corresponds to the parameter values used to simulate the paths in Figure 5.1 and may, therefore, be thought of as the reference case. When the resource allocation is determined by the decentralized economy, meaning that the external effect from human capital accumulation is not internalized, we also present a measure called 'NNP', which is the current value Hamiltonian evaluated at time zero (in the command optimum, the terms 'welfare' and 'NNP' coincide). In addition to the obvious conclusion that welfare is larger in the command optimum than in the decentralized economy, the results corresponding to the reference case imply that NNP clearly underestimates the welfare level in the decentralized economy. This means, in terms of Equation (5.11), that the present value of the marginal external effect is relatively large and, therefore, also an important contributor to the welfare level.

Naturally, the importance of the externality depends on the weight given to human capital, in comparison with the weights given to effective labour and physical capital, in the production function. It is, therefore, interesting to see what happens if human capital is given a greater or smaller weight than in the previous example. One way to accomplish this is to change the weight on effective labour, given the weight on physical capital. In the second row of Table 5.1 we have increased the weight given to effective labour to 0.55, and in the third row we have decreased the same weight to 0.35. The results in the second row indicate that the difference between the welfare level in the command optimum and that corresponding to the decentralized solution has decreased, and that NNP comes closer to measuring the welfare level in the decentralized economy than in the reference case. The reason is that the externality has become smaller. If we continue to increase the weight on effective labour, such that the weights given to effective labour and physical capital eventually sum to one, the externality will vanish, which means that the two systems for allocating the resources would become equivalent. On the other hand, in the example presented in the third row of Table 5.1, the external effect has increased. In this case, therefore, a comparison with the reference case yields the opposite conclusions.

5.3   INTERNALIZING THE EXTERNALITY

To internalize the externality in the decentralized economy, it is necessary to design a policy that makes the consumer value human capital in the same way as the social planner. A natural question is whether we can construct a tax and transfer system such that the command optimum is also attainable in the decentralized economy. This is indeed possible and the argument goes as follows. There is an extra gain corresponding to $\partial f(\cdot) / \partial h = f_h(\cdot) > 0$ of human capital, which is not internalized in the consumer's investment decision, i.e. $f_h(\cdot)$ does not affect the costate variable corresponding to h in the decentralized economy. By taxing the firm for its use of human capital, and then redistributing the tax revenues to the consumer as a subsidy per unit of human capital, where the subsidy rate is equal to $f_h(\cdot)$, additions to the stock of human capital will be valued correctly from society's point of view. Therefore, the best way to think about the tax transfer system is in terms of a subsidy from the firm to the consumer. The optimal tax transfer system is formally described in Proposition 5.1.

Proposition 5.1   *If the consumer receives a subsidy per unit of human capital of*

$$p_h^*(t) = f_h(a(h^*(t))\ell^*(t), k^*(t), h^*(t))$$

which is financed by a lump-sum tax on the firm equal to $p_h^*(t)h^*(t)$, the decentralized solution will support a command optimum.

To prove Proposition 5.1, we add the subsidy to the right-hand side of the consumer's dynamic budget constraint, which can now be written as

$$\frac{dk(t)}{dt} = \pi(t) + r(t)k(t) + a\big(h(t)\big)w_0(t)\ell(t) + p_h^*(t)h(t) - c(t) \quad (5.12)$$

where the consumer takes p_h^* as given. In addition to (5.3) and (5.12), as well as to the No Ponzi Game (NPG) condition, the initial conditions and the transversality conditions, the necessary conditions for utility maximization become (if we suppress the time indicator)

$$H_c = u_c(\cdot)e^{-\theta t} - \lambda = 0 \tag{5.13a}$$

$$H_\ell = -u_L(\cdot)e^{-\theta t} + \lambda a(h)w_0 \le 0, \quad H_\ell \ell = 0 \tag{5.13b}$$

$$H_x = -u_L(\cdot)e^{-\theta t} + \mu g'(x) \le 0, \quad H_x x = 0 \tag{5.13c}$$

$$\dot{\lambda} = -\lambda r \tag{5.13d}$$

$$\dot{\mu} = -\lambda(a'(h)w_0\ell + p_h^*) + \mu\gamma \tag{5.13e}$$

Using (5.13), together with the first-order conditions for firm behaviour and the definition of the subsidy rate, which are given by

$$f_k(\cdot) = r, \ f_{\tilde{\ell}}(\cdot) = w_0, \text{ and } p_h^* = f_h(\cdot)$$

we see that the necessary conditions in the decentralized economy exactly coincide with those of the command optimum, which proves Proposition 5.1.

Note that the subsidy to the consumer required to internalize the external effect is a stock subsidy: its size depends on the *stock* of human capital and is required to make the consumer value the human capital correctly from society's point of view. The reason is that the externality depends on the stock – and not the flow – of human capital. A subsidy directed explicitly to education would not bring the economy to a social optimum. If the consumer receives a transfer payment per unit of time spent in education, the problem caused by the external effect would still remain: the consumer would not value the direct effect of human capital on output when choosing his/her investment. In other words, the consumer's valuation of additional human capital would still be given by an expression such as Equation (5.9). Therefore, to internalize the externality, it is necessary to make the consumer – the investor – value human capital appropriately.[8]

5.4   WELFARE ANALYSIS WHEN THE SUBSIDY IS SUBOPTIMAL

The subsidy rate derived in the previous section varies over time according to the formula $p_h^* = f_h(a(h^*)\ell^*, k^*, h^*)$ which means that, to determine the optimal tax and transfer system, the government has to solve the command optimum problem. This can be interpreted to mean that, although there exists an optimal tax and transfer system such that the decentralized economy produces a socially optimal solution, the informational requirements are demanding. An implication of these informational requirements is that, even if the government wants to correct for the externality, it is less likely to be able to choose the optimal programme. It is, therefore, important to consider the case when the subsidy is suboptimal (meaning that the externality has not become fully internalized). More precisely, given that the initial subsidy rate is not optimal, is there a cost–benefit rule on the basis of which we can determine whether a (small) change in the subsidy rate will increase welfare? The derivation of such a cost–benefit rule is the subject of this section.

Suppose that the initial subsidy rate is equal to α, which is a constant and arbitrarily chosen number. The dynamic budget constraint facing the consumer may now be rewritten as

$$\frac{dk(t)}{dt} = r(t)k(t) + \pi(t) + a\big(h(t)\big)w_0(t)\ell(t) + \alpha h(t) - c(t) \qquad (5.14)$$

To derive the welfare effects following a change in α, it is necessary to characterize the general equilibrium solution that is determined *conditional* on α. In addition to (5.3), (5.14), the NPG condition, initial conditions for k and h, complementary slackness conditions and transversality conditions, and if we make use of the first-order conditions for the firm, the general equilibrium solution in the decentralized economy will involve

$$u_c(\cdot)e^{-\theta t} - \lambda = 0 \qquad (5.15\text{a})$$

$$-u_L(\cdot)e^{-\theta t} + \lambda a(h) f_{\tilde{\ell}}(\cdot) \leq 0 \qquad (5.15\text{b})$$

$$-u_L(\cdot)e^{-\theta t} + \mu g'(x) \leq 0 \qquad (5.15\text{c})$$

$$\dot{\lambda} = -\lambda f_k(\cdot) \qquad (5.15\text{d})$$

$$\dot{\mu} = -\lambda[a'(h)f_{\tilde{\ell}}(\cdot)\,\ell + \alpha] + \mu\gamma \qquad (5.15\text{e})$$

Let $(\hat{c}(t), \hat{\ell}(t), \hat{x}(t), \hat{k}(t), \hat{h}(t), \hat{\lambda}(t), \hat{\mu}(t))$ be the general equilibrium solution implicit in conditions (5.15) and define the value function

$$\hat{V}(\alpha, \gamma, \theta) = \int_0^\infty u\Big(\hat{c}(t;\alpha, \gamma, \theta), T - \hat{\ell}(t;\alpha, \gamma, \theta) - \hat{x}(t;\alpha, \gamma, \theta)\Big)e^{-\theta t}dt \qquad (5.16)$$

We see that α affects the value function via the equilibrium values of consumption and leisure. Now, suppose that the value function is continuously differentiable in its parameters, and consider the welfare effect of an increase in the subsidy rate α. After some tedious but straightforward calculations presented in the Appendix, the welfare change measure (or cost–benefit rule) is written

$$\frac{\partial \hat{V}}{\partial \alpha} = \int_0^\infty \hat{\lambda}(t) \left[f_h\left(a\left(\hat{h}(t)\right)\hat{\ell}(t), \hat{k}(t), \hat{h}(t)\right) - \alpha \right] \frac{\partial \hat{h}(t)}{\partial \alpha} dt \qquad (5.17)$$

The term within brackets on the right-hand side of (5.17) measures the difference between the marginal external effect and the initial subsidy rate, which indicates the magnitude of deviation (prior to the increase in the subsidy rate) from the optimal policy. The cost–benefit rule is easy to interpret: given that $\partial \hat{h}/\partial \alpha > 0$, and the higher the marginal external effect (or marginal product of human capital) in comparison with the initial subsidy rate, the more likely it is that the project is welfare improving. Note also that if $\partial \hat{h}/\partial \alpha > 0$ and $\alpha = 0$, then $\partial \hat{V}/\partial \alpha > 0$ (since $\hat{\lambda} f_h(\cdot) > 0$). By appealing to a continuity argument, this means that the introduction of a small stock subsidy in the uncontrolled market economy will improve the welfare level. Therefore, even if we cannot determine the sign of the welfare effect in general, the cost–benefit rule may, nevertheless, provide important insights into the consequences of policy reform in the uncontrolled market economy.

NOTES

1. See also Barro and Sala-I-Martin (1995).
2. Human capital accumulation in a model with endogenous labour supply has previously been studied by Blinder and Weiss (1976), where the primary focus is on consumer behaviour in the decentralized economy.
3. See for example Jorgenson and Fraumeni (1992a, 1992b).
4. This conclusion is strengthened by a recent paper on growth accounting based on data from Iceland; see Herbertsson (1994).
5. The reason for this concern is that the production function is not necessarily globally concave in the stock of human capital, which means that a finite valued solution may not exist unless further restrictions are imposed. Such restrictions have the character of bounds on the dependence of output on human capital and on the rate of growth of human capital. Just to give the reader some idea of this, suppose that (5.2) and (5.3) satisfy bounds such that

   $$f(\cdot) \leq \delta + h^\rho \text{ and } 0 \leq (dh / dt) / h \leq \beta.$$

   In this case, if $\beta \rho < \theta$, where δ, β and ρ are finite valued real numbers, the optimization problem will have a finite valued solution. This is perfectly consistent with a production function that is globally convex in h. To see this, note that if $\beta < \theta$, then $\beta \rho < \theta$ allows for $\rho > 1$. The reader is referred to Romer (1986a, 1986b) for further details.
6. The model assumes that no resources are explicitly used in the production of human capital. This assumption is made for convenience and does not affect the general conclusions of the chapter. In practice, when such costs are present, they should be deducted from Equation (5.7).
7. An individual working full time in Sweden usually reports about 2000 hours of work per year.
8. For a subsidy directed to education – a flow subsidy – to support a command optimum we would require that the externality be related to the flow (and not the stock) of human capital. Such a subsidy is described by Chamley (1993).

APPENDIX

The Constraint Qualification

In the model presented and analysed in this chapter, it is easy to show that the constraint qualification is always fulfilled, meaning that Equations (5.5) are necessary conditions. To see this, define the vectors $\Gamma(t) = (c(t), \ell(t), x(t))$ and $\Lambda(t) = (k(t), h(t))$. Following Seierstad and Sydsæter (1987), we say that $(\Gamma(t), \Lambda(t))$ is an admissible pair if $\Gamma(t)$ is piecewise continuous, $\Lambda(t)$ is continuous and piecewise continuously differentiable, while at the same time (5.2), (5.3), the initial conditions and the non-negativity constraints are fulfilled. In order to formulate the maximum principle for the optimization problem, a constraint qualification has to be imposed on the functions

$$q_1(t) = q_1(\Gamma(t), \Lambda(t)) = \ell(t) \geq 0 \tag{A1}$$

$$q_2(t) = q_2(\Gamma(t), \Lambda(t)) = x(t) \geq 0 \tag{A2}$$

Let $(\Gamma^*(t), \Lambda^*(t))$ be an optimal pair and define the sets

$$I_t^- = \{j \mid q_j(\Gamma^*(t^-), \Lambda^*(t)) = 0, j = 1,2\} \tag{A3}$$

$$I_t^+ = \{j \mid q_j(\Gamma^*(t^+), \Lambda^*(t)) = 0, j = 1,2\} \tag{A4}$$

At each point in time along the optimal path the constraint qualification requires that

(a) If $I_t^- \neq 0$, the matrix $\{\partial q_j (\Gamma^*(t^-), \Lambda^*(t)) / \partial \Gamma_i\}, j \in I_t^-$ and $i = 1, \ldots 3$, has a rank equal to the number of elements in I_t^-.

(b) If $I_t^+ \neq 0$, the matrix $\{\partial q_j (\Gamma^*(t^+), \Lambda^*(t)) / \partial \Gamma_i\}, j \in I_t^+$ and $i = 1, \ldots 3$ has a rank equal to the number of elements in I_t^+.

In this case, the matrix $\{\partial q_j (\Gamma(t), \Lambda(t)) / \partial \Gamma_i\}, j = 1,2$, and $i = 1, \ldots 3$ is given by

$$\begin{bmatrix} \partial q_1 / \partial c & \partial q_1 / \partial \ell & \partial q_1 / \partial x \\ \partial q_2 / \partial c & \partial q_2 / \partial \ell & \partial q_2 / \partial x \end{bmatrix} = \begin{bmatrix} 0 & 1 & 0 \\ 0 & 0 & 1 \end{bmatrix} \tag{A5}$$

where the time indicator has been dropped for notational convenience. We see from (A5) that the rank condition is always fulfilled.

The Cost-Benefit Rule

By differentiating Equation (5.16) with respect to α we obtain

$$\frac{\partial \hat{V}}{\partial \alpha} = \int_0^\infty \left[u_c(\cdot) \frac{\partial \hat{c}}{\partial \alpha} - u_L(\cdot) \frac{\partial \hat{\ell}}{\partial \alpha} - u_L(\cdot) \frac{\partial \hat{x}}{\partial \alpha} \right] e^{-\theta t} dt \qquad (A6)$$

where the time indicator has been suppressed for notational convenience. Using (5.15a), (5.15b) and (5.15c), Equation (A6) is rewritten

$$\frac{\partial \hat{V}}{\partial \alpha} = \int_0^\infty \left[\hat{\lambda} \frac{\partial \hat{c}}{\partial \alpha} - \hat{\lambda}a(\hat{h})f_{\tilde{\ell}}(\cdot) \frac{\partial \hat{\ell}}{\partial \alpha} - \hat{\mu}g'(\hat{x}) \frac{\partial \hat{x}}{\partial \alpha} \right] dt \qquad (A7)$$

Along the general equilibrium path, the equations of motion can be written

$$\frac{\partial \hat{k}}{\partial t} = f\left(a(\hat{h})\hat{\ell}, \hat{k}, \hat{h}\right) - \hat{c} \qquad (A8)$$

$$\frac{\partial \hat{h}}{\partial t} = g(\hat{x}) - \gamma\hat{h} \qquad (A9)$$

where the absence of direct effects of policy parameters in Equation (A8) has to do with the fact that taxes and transfers cancel out in general equilibrium. By applying Young's theorem on (A8) and (A9) we have

$$\frac{\partial^2 \hat{k}}{\partial t \partial \alpha} = a(\hat{h})f_{\tilde{\ell}}(\cdot) \frac{\partial \hat{\ell}}{\partial \alpha} + \left(a'(\hat{h})f_{\tilde{\ell}}(\cdot)\hat{\ell} + f_h(\cdot)\right) \frac{\partial \hat{h}}{\partial \alpha} + f_k(\cdot) \frac{\partial \hat{k}}{\partial \alpha} - \frac{\partial \hat{c}}{\partial \alpha} = \frac{\partial^2 \hat{k}}{\partial \alpha \partial t} \quad (A10)$$

$$\frac{\partial^2 \hat{h}}{\partial t \partial \alpha} = g'(\hat{x}) \frac{\partial \hat{x}}{\partial \alpha} - \gamma \frac{\partial \hat{h}}{\partial \alpha} = \frac{\partial^2 \hat{h}}{\partial \alpha \partial t} \qquad (A11)$$

Solve (A10) and (A11) for, respectively, $\partial \hat{c}/\partial \alpha$ and $g'(\hat{x})\partial \hat{x}/\partial \alpha$ and substitute into (A7):

$$\frac{\partial \hat{V}}{\partial \alpha} = \int\limits_{0}^{\infty}\left[\hat{\lambda}\left\{ -\frac{\partial^2 \hat{k}}{\partial \alpha \partial t} + a(\hat{h})f_{\hat{\ell}}(\cdot)\frac{\partial \hat{\ell}}{\partial \alpha} + (a'(\hat{h})f_{\hat{\ell}}(\cdot)\hat{\ell} + f_h(\cdot))\frac{\partial \hat{h}}{\partial \alpha} + f_k(\cdot)\frac{\partial \hat{k}}{\partial \alpha} \right\} \right.$$

$$\left. -\hat{\lambda}a(\hat{h})f_{\hat{\ell}}(\cdot)\frac{\partial \hat{\ell}}{\partial \alpha} - \hat{\mu}(\frac{\partial^2 \hat{h}}{\partial \alpha \partial t} + \gamma\frac{\partial \hat{h}}{\partial \alpha}) \right]dt \qquad (A12)$$

From the fact that $k(0)$ and $h(0)$ are fixed, and if we use the transversality conditions, it follows that

$$\int\limits_{0}^{\infty} \hat{\lambda}\frac{\partial^2 \hat{k}}{\partial \alpha \partial t}\,dt = \hat{\lambda}\frac{\partial \hat{k}}{\partial \alpha}\bigg|_{0}^{\infty} - \int\limits_{0}^{\infty}\frac{\partial \hat{\lambda}}{\partial t}\frac{\partial \hat{k}}{\partial \alpha}\,dt = -\int\limits_{0}^{\infty}\frac{\partial \hat{\lambda}}{\partial t}\frac{\partial \hat{k}}{\partial \alpha}dt \qquad (A13)$$

$$\int\limits_{0}^{\infty} \hat{\mu}\frac{\partial^2 \hat{h}}{\partial \alpha dt}\,dt = \hat{\mu}\frac{\partial \hat{h}}{\partial \alpha}\bigg|_{0}^{\infty} - \int\limits_{0}^{\infty}\frac{\partial \hat{\mu}}{\partial t}\frac{\partial \hat{h}}{\partial \alpha}\,dt = -\int\limits_{0}^{\infty}\frac{\partial \hat{\mu}}{\partial t}\frac{\partial \hat{h}}{\partial \alpha}dt \qquad (A14)$$

By substituting (A13) and (A14) into (A12) and using the differential equations for $\hat{\lambda}$ and $\hat{\mu}$, which are given by (5.15d) and (5.15e), we obtain Equation (5.17). These calculations presuppose that certain improper integrals converge, which require that certain growth conditions are fulfilled. For details, the reader is referred to the Appendix of Chapter 4 or Johansson and Löfgren (1994).

6. Sustainable development and its relation to welfare measures

The previous chapters have focused on different kinds of net national product related welfare measures. The typical result is that NNP, according to the conventional national accounts, must not only be augmented by the utility value of accumulated and decumulated stocks of natural and human capital in order to reflect human welfare, but must also be corrected for technological progress and externalities. There is also a conventional wisdom[1] that a correct welfare indicator should, in some way, be connected with the concept of 'sustainable development', which was first popularized by the report of the Brundtland Commission, chaired by Gro Harlem Brundtland, the Prime Minister of Norway. The report, issued by the World Commission on Environment and Development, argues for sustainable development, defined as 'development that meets the needs of the present without compromising the ability of future generations to meet their own needs'.[2]

The underlying concern of the Commission was, of course, that humanity is using up its natural endowments too rapidly. These endowments include appropriated non-renewable resources such as different kinds of energy resources, non-fuel minerals and soils; appropriated renewable resources such as forests, and key non-appropriated resources such as clean air and water, the stock of genetic material, and the present climate. The dangers which are anticipated include future economic decline and/or climatic apocalypse.

Ideas about sustainability in terms of sustainable income are, however, much older than the Brundtland Commission. They belong to the intellectual heritage of three great economists: Irving Fisher, Erik Lindahl and John Hicks. As Nordhaus (1995) points out, Irving Fisher was the first to make a clear distinction between income and wealth.[3] His basic argument was that income is the yield on society's capital, or as he puts it: 'The income from any instrument is thus the flow of services rendered by that instrument. The income of a community is the total flow of services from *all of* its instruments'. We have added the emphasis, since Fisher realized that all kinds of social capital should be included in the appropriate capital concept. The more modern discussion dates back to Lindahl (1933) and Hicks (1939). Both defined income as the maximum amount you can consume and still keep the capital intact (interest on the capital). Intuitively, it equals current consumption plus net capital accumulation since, as long as net investment is kept non-negative, the capital is held intact. As we are about to see below, in the case of heterogeneous capital it is not clear-cut which 'capital stock' should be kept constant.

More fundamentally, however, Hicks realized that there is an intertemporal dimension involved. He writes: 'Income must be defined as the maximum amount of money which the individual can spend this week, and still be able to spend the same amount in real terms in each ensuing week'.[4] In other words, Hicks's view (definition) comes very close to a theoretically reasonable definition of income as the sustainable level of consumption.

An even more demanding measure of sustainable welfare was suggested by Nordhaus and Tobin (1972), which acknowledged the existence of technological progress. Under special conditions, the path along which society consumes without short changing the future is one with per capita consumption growing steadily at the rate of technological progress.

It has been hinted at[5] that Weitzman (1976) reconciled the Fisher–Lindahl–Hicks view with optimal growth theory in the sense that the Hamiltonian along an optimal path measures the maximum sustainable utility (consumption) level. This idea is, as we shall see below, near at hand. It is obviously correct if capital is homogeneous, but unfortunately wrong when there is heterogeneous capital.

We start the formal analysis from a slightly different angle by noting that sustainable consumption, according to Hicks, implies a constant utility level over time.

6.1   RAWLSIAN CONSTANT CONSUMPTION PATHS

Maximum social welfare according to the Rawlsian criterion is defined by maximizing the utility for the generation with the lowest utility level. Although Rawls himself considered his principle 'the veil of ignorance' to be inappropriate for handling intergenerational equity problems,[6] it is instructive to apply it to an optimal growth problem. The maximization of the utility of the generation with the lowest utility level means that each generation obtains the same utility level. One can otherwise always improve the situation for the generation with the lowest utility level by reallocating consumption from generations with higher utility levels. We shall, following Solow (1974), conduct the analysis with and without population growth, as well as for a situation with both population growth and labour augmenting technological progress. To accomplish this, let the production function in the economy be

$$Y(t) = F(K(t), e^{at}L(t)) \tag{6.1}$$

here e^{at} measures labour augmenting technological progress which proceeds at a rate a. The production function is assumed to be homogeneous of degree one in capital, $K(t)$, and efficiency units of labour, $e^{at}L(t)$.[7] This means that we can define production per capita $y = Y/L$ as

$$y = e^{at}f(z) \tag{6.2}$$

where $z = K/e^{at}L$ is capital per efficiency unit of labour, and y is production per capita. Differentiating z with respect to time yields

$$\dot{z} = \frac{d}{dt}\left(\frac{K}{e^{at}L}\right) = \frac{\dot{K}e^{at}L - \left[ae^{at}L + \dot{L}e^{at}\right]K}{\left(e^{at}L\right)^2} = \frac{\dot{K}}{e^{at}L} - (a+n)z \tag{6.3}$$

where $n = \dot{L}/L$ is population growth, which is treated parametrically. Moreover

$$\frac{\dot{K}}{e^{at}L} = f(z) - ce^{-at} \tag{6.4}$$

where $c = C/L$ is consumption per capita. Substitution of (6.4) into (6.3) gives

$$\dot{z} = f(z) - (a+n)z - ce^{-at} \tag{6.5}$$

which is the accumulation equation for capital per efficiency unit of labour. We are now ready to go briefly through three cases: 'no growth' ($a = n = 0$), population growth ($a = 0$, $n > 0$), and population growth and technological progress.

Case 1   Neither Technological Progress nor Population Growth

If $a = n = 0$, Equation (6.5) reduces to our standard Ramsey accumulation equation

$$\dot{k} = f(k) - c \tag{6.5a}$$

With a Rawlsian utility function, and an inherited capital stock $k(0) = k_0$, there is not much scope for choice. The optimal rule is to choose

$$\bar{c} = f(k_0) \tag{6.6}$$

where $\bar{c}$ denotes the constant consumption level.

Capital is kept intact since $\dot{k} = 0$ for all t and consumption can be sustained for ever.

Case 2   Population Growth Equal to n > 0:

If $n > 0$ and $a = 0$, the accumulative equation reads

$$\dot{k} = f(k) - c - nk \qquad (6.5b)$$

Given the initial capital stock, k_0, the maximum constant consumption path is given by

$$\bar{c} = f(k_0) - nk_0 \qquad (6.7)$$

Obviously $\dot{k} = 0$ and capital per capita is kept intact, as shown in Figure 6.1.

If we choose a constant consumption path $\bar{\bar{c}} > \bar{c}$, capital per capita would decline to zero in finite time, and sustainability would be violated. If $\bar{\bar{c}} < \bar{c}$, capital could be built up to the maximum sustainable yield, but this would not be a constant consumption path.

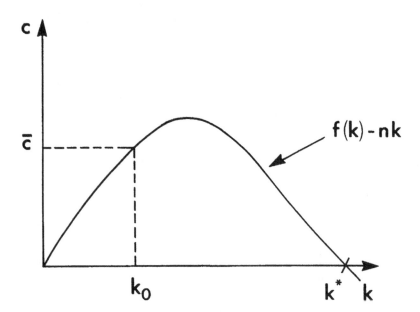

Figure 6.1   The maximum sustainable consumption per capita under population growth n > 0

Case 3 Population Growth and Labour Augmenting Technological Progress

In this case, the accumulation equation is given by Equation (6.5) above, which we repeat for the reader's convenience:

$$\dot{z} = f(z) - (a + n)z - ce^{-at} \qquad (6.5c)$$
$$z(0) = k_0 = z_0$$

Clearly, it would be too conservative to put $c = c_0 = f(z_0) - (n + a)z_0$ since, although $\dot{z}(0) = 0$, improved efficiency would mean $\dot{z} > 0$ for all $t > 0$. Hence it is optimal to have $\dot{z} \leq 0$ for all t.[8] Moreover, since $z < 0$ is not feasible, we have to choose a constant consumption path such that $\lim_{t \to \infty} z(t) = \lim_{t \to \infty} \dot{z}(t) = 0$ and

$$\bar{c} = (f(z) - (n + a)z - \dot{z})e^{at}, \text{ where } z(0) = z_0 \qquad (6.8)$$

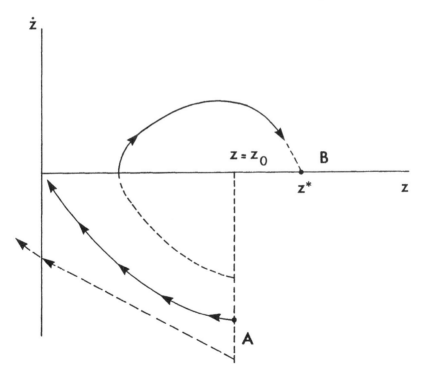

Figure 6.2 The optimal constant consumption path in capital/efficiency units of labour

The solution of this equation, which starts at $z = z_0$ with $\dot{z}(0) < 0$ and moves asymptotically towards $z(\infty) = 0$, is depicted as the path starting at A in Figure 6.2. If the path starts at $z = z_0$, but below A, it would reach the $\dot{z}$ axis in finite time with $\dot{z} < 0$ and z would become negative. If the path starts above point A, capital per efficiency unit of labour would first decline, and then increase towards a steady state level, independent of the chosen constant consumption level,[9] where $\dot{z} = 0$ and $z = z^* > 0$, say point B where $f(z^*) - (a + n)z^* = 0$. It can be shown that z^* (corresponding to k^* in Figure 6.1) is a stable node, which involves capital satiation in the sense that all capital accumulation is absorbed in order to keep the capital per efficiency unit of labour at a constant level.

6.2   INTRODUCING NATURAL RESOURCES

A natural next step would be to introduce heterogeneous capital in terms of one stock of man-made capital and a stock of a natural resource. The production function would then read

$$Y = F(K, L, R) \tag{6.9}$$

where R is the harvest of a non-renewable natural resource, which is available in limited supply, $\bar{R}$, implying that

$$\int_0^\infty R(t)dt \leq \bar{R} \tag{6.10}$$

The properties of the production function as a function of R are, of course, crucial. A fairly uninteresting case would be to assume that $F(K, L, 0) > 0$ for $K, L > 0$. This would mean that it is possible to produce positive output without any input of the natural resource, and we would essentially be back to a world with a homogeneous capital good. Instead, we should require $F(K, L, 0) = 0$, and possibly also that the average product of the natural resource goes to infinity as the input of it goes to zero. Clearly, if the average product is bounded, then we can only produce a finite amount of output from a fixed pool of resources. The two properties just introduced are, in combination, usually referred to as R, being an essential production factor.[10] A function which has these properties is

$$Y = F(K, L) R^h \tag{6.11}$$

where F is homogenous of degree $1 - h$. In the constant elasticity of substitution (C.E.S.) family only the Cobb–Douglas, with an elasticity of substitution equal to one, will do. If the elasticity of substitution between resources and other factors exceeds one, then resources are not indispensable to production, and, if it is less than one, the average product of the resource will be bounded (and consumption will therefore decline to zero). This important result was first proved by Dasgupta and Heal (1974), but Solow (1974) and Stiglitz (1974) also contain similar insights. For a recent and very general characterization of the conditions for indefinitely sustained consumption the reader is referred to Cass and Mitra (1991).

Given a Cobb–Douglas technology with Hicks's neutral technological progress, Solow (1974) reformulates and solves the constant consumption problem with an exhaustible resource, as well as man-made capital and labour as inputs. Although further complications are added, the main insights gained from the above analysis are preserved. The Rawlsian max–min criterion is a reasonable criterion for intertemporal planning decisions, except for three non-negligible difficulties. First, it requires an initial capital stock large enough to support a decent standard of living. Moreover, and perhaps less important, it is foolishly conservative under unlimited technological progress and no population growth. Finally, and certainly important, given a Cobb–Douglas production function, the constant consumption path exists if, and only if, the elasticity of output with respect to capital exceeds the corresponding elasticity with respect to the resource.[11] Under such conditions, a constant consumption path allows earlier generations to deplete the pool of exhaustible resources, as long as they add to the stock of man-made (reproducible) capital. The constant consumption path is, however, a knife-edge and the decumulation of the exhaustible resource and the accumulation of reproducible capital take place in an optimal manner. It should be remembered that we are maximizing an objective function, although it (trivially) leads to a constant consumption path.

Conversely, one could ask the following question: Given that we have a more general objective function, how do we know that the optimal consumption path is a constant consumption path? We answered this question in Chapter 3 by introducing Hartwick's rule, which tells us that $\lambda^*(t)\dot{k}^*(t) = 0$ for all t along an optimal path implies that utility (consumption) is constant for all t. Here $\dot{k}^*(t)$ (net investment) may be given a vector interpretation, and a neat interpretation of the rule is that when resource rents from exhaustible resources are invested in reproducible capital to keep the present (utility) value of net investment zero, this is sufficient to sustain a constant utility path.

It is, under these circumstances, a short step to guess that $\lambda^*(t)\dot{k}^*(t) \geqq 0$ all t implies that consumption (utility) is non-declining along the optimal path. As we shall show below, this is not necessarily true, but the reverse claim, that a non-declining consumption along the optimal path implies $\lambda^*(t)\dot{k}^*(t) \geqq 0$ all t, can be shown to be true. In particular, it is true that a constant utility for all t along an optimal path implies $\lambda^*(t)\dot{k}^*(t) = 0$. The latter result was first shown by Dixit, Hammond and Hoel (1980) and together with Hartwick's rule it means that $\lambda^*(t)\dot{k}^*(t) = 0$ all t is both necessary and sufficient for an optimal constant consumption path.

The single capital good case is suggestive in the sense that it might induce you to believe that $\lambda^*(t)\dot{k}^*(t) \geqq 0$ is both necessary and sufficient for utility at t to be sustainable, although not necessarily sustained, along an optimal path. For a closed economy with a constant population and a stationary technology, it is true that future consumption possibilities are not reduced if, and only if, net investments are non-negative. This means that NNP defined as

$$y(t) = c(t) + \dot{k}(t) \tag{6.12}$$

measures the maximum sustainable consumption level at time t, since $c(t) \leq y(t)$ is equivalent to $\dot{k}(t) \geqq 0$, and the capital is kept intact. Hence, the Hamiltonian at time t along an optimal path would certainly measure the maximum sustainable utility level.

As Asheim (1994a) has shown[12] (by a counter-example) this is no longer true if there are multiple capital goods. He uses a Cobb–Douglas type model with instantaneous utility $u(c) = -c^{-(\eta-1)}$, where $\eta > 1$, and technology $c + \dot{k}_m \leq y = (k_m)^a (-\dot{k}_n)^b$, where $b < a < a + b < 1$, while the subscripts m and n, respectively, refer to 'man-made' and 'natural' capital, respectively. The particular analytical model was introduced and analysed by Dasgupta and Heal (1974, 1979).

More particularly, he showed that even if $\lambda(t)\dot{k}(t) \geq 0$ – where $\dot{k}(t)$ is a vector of net investments in different types of capital goods and $\lambda(t)$ is a vector of shadow prices – consumption, $c(t)$, may actually exceed the maximum sustainable level. This is illustrated in Figure 6.3, which we have borrowed from Asheim (1994a). The upper part of Figure 6.3 illustrates the consumption path, while the lower part contains the path for the value of the net investments. The symbol * is used to indicate an *optimal* path. We make three broad observations from the figure. First, for $t = 0$, $\lambda^*(0)\dot{k}^*(0) > 0$ and $c^*(0)$ equals the maximum sustainable level. Second, for $t \in (0, t')$, $\lambda^*(t)\dot{k}^*(t) > 0$ and $c^*(t)$ exceeds the maximum sustainable level. Finally, for $t = t'$, $\lambda^*(t')\dot{k}^*(t') = 0$ and $c^*(t')$ exceeds the maximum sustainable level. This means – as was also pointed out by Asheim – that $\lambda^*(t)\dot{k}^*(t) \geq 0$ at a given point in time, t, is no indicator of sustainability, i.e. it does not imply that $c^*(t)$ is sustainable.

What is then measured by $\lambda^*(t)\dot{k}^*(t)$? It turns out that the shadow value of the net investment at a given point in time reflects consumption preferences in the sense that it measures a weighted sum of future changes in consumption along the optimal path. Hence, it is possible to provide an exact relationship between the net investment at a given point in time and future consumption preferences.

To establish this result, we use a generalized version of the Ramsey growth model. Specifically, we introduce a general function to discount future utility, which means that our result neither requires a constant rate of time preference nor an exponential discount function. In the next section we derive the main result, which follows directly from the properties of the Hamiltonian along the optimal path. We shall then relate this result to the concept of sustainability and in particular to Hartwick's rule.

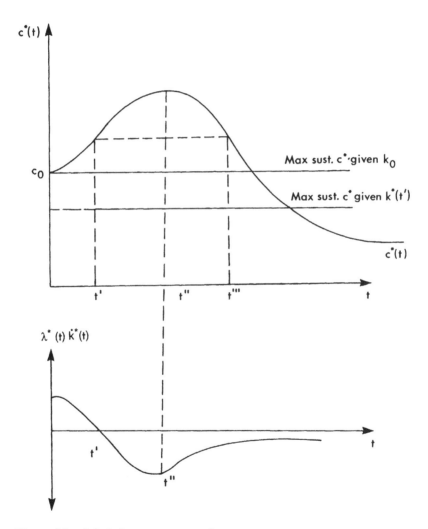

Figure 6.3   Asheim's counter-example

6.3   INVESTMENTS AND FUTURE CONSUMPTION PLANS

To make the analysis as simple as possible, let us assume, as in Chapter 3, that the resource allocation is decided upon by a social planner. If we neglect population growth (which is not essential here) and normalize the population to equal one, the social planner's optimization problem will be to maximize the individual's utility function subject to the economy's production possibilities and initial conditions. Using the notational convention of the previous section, let $k_m(t)$ be the stock of man-made capital, while $k_n^j(t)$, $j = 1, ...,J$, are the stocks of natural capital. We shall also define the vector of net investments, $\dot{k}(t)' = [\dot{k}_m(t),$ $\dot{k}_n^1(t), \dot{k}_n^2(t),...., \dot{k}_n^J(t)]$, and the vector of present value shadow prices of capital, $\lambda(t) = [\lambda_m(t), \lambda_n^1(t), \lambda_n^2(t),...., \lambda_n^J(t)]$. The social planner's problem is written

$$\text{(i)} \qquad \underset{c(t),R(t)}{\text{Max}} \int_0^\infty u(c(t))\Lambda(t)dt$$

$$\text{(ii)} \quad \text{s.t. } y(t) = f(k_m(t)R(t)) = c(t) + \dot{k}_m(t) \qquad\qquad (6.13)$$

$$\text{(iii)} \quad \dot{k}_n^j(t) = g^j(k_n^j(t)) - R^j(t), \qquad j = 1,....,J$$

and initial conditions $k_m(0) = k_{mo} > 0$ and $k_n^j(0) = k_{n0}^j > 0$, $j = 1,....,J$. The instantaneous utility function, $u(\cdot)$, is assumed to be twice continuously differentiable, increasing and strictly concave in its argument. Utility is discounted to present value by a general discount function, $\Lambda(t)$, which is continuously differentiable. We also assume that $\Lambda(0) = 1$, $\Lambda(\infty) = 0$ and $\dot{\Lambda}(t) < 0$ for $t \in (0, \infty)$. Turning to the production side, $R(t) = [R^1(t), R^2(t),....,R^J(t)]$ is a vector of harvests of natural capital involving both renewable resources ($g^j(\cdot) > 0$) and nonrenewable resources ($g^j(\cdot) = 0$). The production of net output, $y(t)$, depends on the stock of man-made capital and on the harvests of the natural capital stocks via the function $f(\cdot)$, We shall assume that $f(\cdot)$ is increasing in all arguments and strictly concave.

The present value Hamiltonian of the optimal growth problem can be written

$$H(t) = u(c(t))\Lambda(t) + \lambda(t)\dot{k}(t) \qquad\qquad (6.14)$$

where $\lambda(t)$ is a vector of costate variables, with elements representing the shadow prices of capital in terms of utility. Suppose that the economy follows the optimal path. In that case, by applying Proposition 4.1, we obtain

$$\frac{dH^*}{dt} = \dot{\Lambda}(t)u(c^*(t)) \qquad\qquad (6.15)$$

Equation (6.15) implicitly defines a relationship between the Hamiltonian along the optimal path and a weighted sum of maximized instantaneous utilities. To see this, we integrate forwards to obtain

$$H^*(t) = -\int_t^\infty \dot\Lambda(s) u\big(c^*(s)\big) ds \tag{6.16}$$

which – in terms of this more general model – is the analogy of the welfare result derived by Weitzman (1976), and discussed in some detail in Chapter 3. If we divide both sides of Equation (6.16) by $\Lambda(t)$, we find that the current value Hamiltonian along the optimal path (the net national product measured in utility units) equals a term involving the sum, from time t to infinity, of the products of the instantaneous utility function, $u(c^*)$, and the (negative of the) time derivative of the discount function, $-\dot\Lambda$. However, since the rate of time preference is not (necessarily) constant here, we cannot give NNP the usual Fisher–Hicks–Lindahl interpretation[13] in terms of 'interest on the value function'.

We are now in the position to derive the main result. Integrating the right-hand side of (6.16) by parts, and making use of the assumption that $\Lambda(\infty) = 0$, we obtain

$$H^*(t) = -\Big[\Lambda(s) u\big(c^*(s)\big)\Big]_t^\infty + \int_t^\infty \Lambda(s) u_c\big(c^*(s)\big) \dot c^*(s) ds$$

$$= u\big(c^*(t)\big)\Lambda(t) + \int_t^\infty \Lambda(s) u_c\big(c^*(s)\big) \dot c^*(s) ds \tag{6.17}$$

Since both $H^*(t)$ and the final expression in (6.17) contain $u(c^*(t))\Lambda(t)$, we can rewrite (6.17) to read

$$\lambda^*(t)\dot k^*(t) = \int_t^\infty \Lambda(s) u_c\big(c^*(s)\big) \dot c^*(s) ds \tag{6.18}$$

which relates the value of the net investments at time t to the future consumption path. In the special case where $\dot k(t)$ is a scalar, a division by $\lambda^*(t)$ converts Equation (6.18) to real terms (the division is, of course, not equally clear-cut if $\dot k(t)$ has a vector interpretation). The result can be summarized as follows:

Proposition 6.1 *The value of net investments along an optimal path is positive (negative) in the interval* (t, t + dt), *if, and only if, the discounted utility value of the sum of future changes in consumption along the optimal path is positive (negative).*

One interpretation of Proposition 6.1 is, of course, in terms of an exact relationship between net investments at a given point in time and future consumption plans. Future consumption preferences, therefore, contain all relevant information for determining $\lambda^*(t)\dot{k}^*(t)$; the value of the net investment at time t. Another, and equally appealing, interpretation is that the right-hand side of (6.18) is the (maximum) future willingness to pay – in utility units – for the net investment. Accordingly, the more the individual wants to consume in future periods, the higher his/her willingness to pay for net investments at time t.

Note also that Equation (6.18) is derived on the basis of a general discount function, $\Lambda(t)$. In the special – and frequently applied – case with a constant rate of time preference, θ, and an exponential discount function, $\Lambda(t) = e^{-\theta t}$, the analogue becomes

$$\lambda^*(t)\dot{k}^*(t) = \int_t^\infty e^{-\theta s} \frac{\left[u_c\left(c^*(s)\right)\right]^2}{u_{cc}\left(c^*(s)\right)} \left[\theta - f_k\left(k_m^*(s), R^*(s)\right)\right] d. \qquad (6.18a)$$

which means that the value of the net investment at time t is positive (negative) if, and only if, the weighted sum of differences between the rate of time preference and the marginal product of capital is negative (positive). Equation (6.18a) can, of course, be given the same 'willingness to pay' interpretation as Equation (6.18), which would imply that the smaller the rate of time preference, or the higher the future marginal product of capital, the higher the willingness to pay for net investments at time t.

Note finally that Equation (6.18) is easily extended to cover the influence of technological progress. Suppose the (vector) production function takes the form $f(k_m(t), R(t), t)$, where the separate time argument represents technological progress. By defining an artificial state variable, s, where $s \equiv t$, we can proceed in the same general way as above and derive an analogue to Equation (6.18):

$$\lambda^*(t)\dot{k}^*(t) + \Omega^*(t)\dot{s}(t) = \int_t^\infty \Lambda(t)u_c\left(c^*(s)\right)\dot{c}^*(s)ds \qquad (6.18b)$$

where $\Omega^*(t) = \int_t^\infty \lambda_m^*(s)f_s\left(k_m^*(s), R^*(s), s\right)ds$ and $\dot{s} = 1$.

The formulation of Equation (6.18b) is appealing in the sense that the present value of technological progress enters the formula in the same way as the value of net investments, which means that the concept of net investments can be redefined to include technological progress as an 'investment of time'. The interpretation is that the value of net investments – including the value of technological progress – at time t is positive (negative) if, and only if, the weighted sum of future changes in consumption is positive (negative).

6.4   SUSTAINABILITY AND THE RELATIONSHIP TO HARTWICK'S RULE

The result summarized in Proposition 6.1 – and extended by Equation (6.18b) – also relates, in a natural way, to Hartwick's rule. As we have seen in Chapter 3, Hartwick showed that in a closed economy with a constant population and a stationary technology which is steering along an optimal path with $\lambda^*(t)\dot{k}^*(t) = 0$ for all t, the utility level is constant and equal to the maximum sustainable level. If we use the extended definition of net investments suggested by (6.18b) and define $\Phi^*(t)\dot{K}^*(t) = \lambda^*(t)\dot{k}^*(t) + \Omega^*(t)\dot{s}(t)$, the analogue of Hartwick's rule becomes:

Let $(c^*(t), K^*(t), \dot{K}^*(t))$ be an optimal path for the above Ramsey problem, and suppose that, for each t, $\Phi^*(t)\dot{K}^*(t) = 0$. Then, $u(c^*(t))$ is constant for all t.

Note that since $u(c^*(t))$ is constant and $c^*(t)$ is optimal, $u(c^*(t))$ represents the maximum sustainable utility level. Dixit et al. (1980) showed that $\Phi^*(t)\dot{K}^*(t) = 0$ for all t is also necessary for the utility level to be constant along an optimal path. Formally:

If the utility is constant along an optimal path $(c^*(t), K^*(t), \dot{K}^*(t))$, then $\Phi^*(t)\dot{K}^*(t) = 0$ for all t.

These two results mean, together, that $\Phi^*(t)\dot{K}^*(t) = 0$ for all t is equivalent to $u(c^*(t))$ being equal to the maximum sustainable utility level. Equation (6.18) is a vehicle to prove both the necessity and sufficiency of $\Phi^*(t)\dot{K}^*(t) = 0$ for all t, for $u(c^*(t))$ to be the maximum sustainable utility level for all t. Loosely speaking, $\dot{c}^*(t) = 0$ for all t implies that $c^*(t)$ and $u(c^*(t))$ are constant and equal to their maximum sustainable levels for all t. It also means that $\Phi^*(t)\dot{K}^*(t) = 0$ for all t according to (6.18b). Conversely, $\Phi^*(t)\dot{K}^*(t) = 0$ for all t implies that $\dot{c}^*(t) = 0$ and $u(c^*(t))$ is constant for all t. To see this more clearly, note from Equation (6.18b) that $\Phi^*(t)\dot{K}^*(t) = 0$ for all t means that

$$\frac{d}{dt}\left[\Phi^*(t)\dot{K}^*(t)\right] \equiv \frac{d}{dt}\int_t^\infty u_c\left(c^*(s)\right)\Lambda(s)\dot{c}^*(s)ds \equiv -u_c\left(c^*(t)\right)\Lambda(t)\dot{c}^*(t) \equiv 0$$

and $u_c(c^*(t))\Lambda(t) > 0$. Hence, both necessity and sufficiency follow. However, the reader should note that $\Phi^*(t)\dot{K}^*(t) = 0$ at *some* t, in the context of a competitive economy, is no indication of sustainability. It only shows that the weighted sum of future changes in consumption, where the weights are defined as the discounted value of the future marginal utilities, is equal to zero.

Another intuitive implication of the model set out in the previous section is a relationship between consumption and the shadow price of reproducible capital along a sustainable path. To see this, let us define a sustainable path such that $c^*(t) > 0$ and $\dot{c}^*(t) \geq 0$ holds for all t. We denote the shadow price of man-made capital in current value terms by $\lambda_m^c(t) = \lambda_m^*(t)\Lambda(t)^{-1}$, where $\lambda_m(t)$ is an element of $\lambda(t)$. From the necessary conditions, we know that the marginal utility of consumption equals the shadow price of man-made capital, i.e.

$$u_c(c^*(t)) - \lambda_m^c(t) = 0 \qquad (6.19)$$

which defines a relationship between consumption and the current value shadow price of man-made capital along the optimal path. Differentiating with respect to time we obtain

$$u_{cc}(c^*(t))\dot{c}^*(t) = \dot{\lambda}_m^c(t) \qquad (6.20)$$

If $c^*(t) > 0$ and $\dot{c}^*(t) \geq 0$ for all t, Equation (6.20) means that the current value shadow price of man-made capital is non-increasing along the optimal path. In fact, given that the instantaneous utility function is strictly concave, a non-increasing shadow price of man-made capital is a both necessary and sufficient condition for a non-decreasing consumption path. We interpret (6.20) to mean that, in order to sustain a given consumption level, capital cannot become more scarce over time. This is a very intuitive result. The idea of sustaining a given consumption level may require that natural resource stocks are replaced by reproducible capital. Such a substitution means that increases in the stock of man-made capital counteract the increased scarcity of natural resources. Otherwise – if the net investments in man-made capital are not sufficient from that point of view – the current value shadow price of man-made capital will increase, implying that consumption falls.

6.5   THE DISTINCTION BETWEEN SUSTAINABLE AND SUSTAINED

One can ask about the generality of the shape of the optimal consumption path in the above example. Given an economy with no population growth, no technological progress, and a convex technology with labour, reproducible capital and a non-renewable resource as inputs, is the typical optimal consumption path first rising and then declining over time?

Clearly, if at time t^1 the optimal consumption path is declining from this time and onwards, $c^*(t)$ is obviously not sustainable for any $t \geq t^1$. This is because, if it were, the sustainable path would result in a higher present value than the optimal path, which contradicts the latter being optimal in the first place. In other words, given that the optimal consumption path is single peaked in the above sense, once on the declining part of the optimal consumption path, the sustainable consumption level is always below the optimal level.

For the particular utility function $u(c) = -c^{-(\eta-1)}$ and the Cobb–Douglas technology, one can show that the consumption path is indeed single peaked (strictly declining being a special case of single peakedness).[14] Moreover, consumption will in the limit go to zero. To see this, we introduce the Keynes–Ramsey equation for the model under consideration (see also Chapter 3, Equations (3.4b) and (3.4d)):

$$\frac{\dot{c}^*(t)}{c^*(t)} = \frac{a k_m^{*(a-1)}\left(-\dot{k}_n^*\right)^b - \theta}{\eta} \tag{6.21}$$

Clearly from feasibility $(-\dot{k}_n^*) = R(t) \to 0$ when $t \to \infty$, and if $\lim_{t \to \infty} k_m^* \to \bar{k}_m > 0$, then $\dot{c}^*(t) / c^*(t)$ is bound to become negative at some t and remain negative thereafter (i.e. $c^*(t) \to 0$). The only way for $\dot{c}^*(t) / c^*(t)$ to remain non-negative is that $k_m^*(t) \to 0$, and since both k_m^* and $R(t)$ go to zero, output and consumption also go to zero in the limit.

As Dasgupta and Heal (1979) point out, discounting is of course the culprit. The effect of the discount rate is that the utility of generations far away are discriminated, and, hence, are given a low capital stock, and consequently a low consumption level. Frank Ramsey, the inventor of optimal growth theory, viewed discounting as 'ethically indefensible' and solved his optimal growth problem using a zero discount rate. This was made possible by an assumption that the utility function is bounded from above by what he called the 'bliss level'. Since he worked in a framework in which the optimal policy leads to utility levels which approach the bliss level, he was able to solve his problem by minimizing the integral of the difference between the actual utility level and the bliss level.

His approach does not, however, work in general. This is unfortunately also true for the related overtaking criterion,[15] which was suggested by Von Weizsäcker (1965). The criterion will not yield a consumption path which is optimal in the usual sense of being comparable to, and at least as good as, any other feasible consumption path. Rather a set of non-comparable paths may be found, each of which is 'maximal', in the sense that no second feasible path can be found which is better. Hence, the criterion provides a partial pre-ordering of programmes. This was first pointed out by Koopmans (1960).

It is, however, clear that an asymptotically sustained consumption path is, as a rule, not the outcome of a standard present value exhaustible resource problem, where utilities are discounted. It helps if it is assumed that the stock of the resource is valued as such, but one might still feel that the resulting steady state is too discriminating against future generations. To elaborate on this, we introduce some recent ideas in Chichilnisky (1993) and Heal (1995), on discounting and sustainability.

Say that the growth problem is a pure depletion problem with an additively separable, increasing and strictly concave utility function

$$u[c(t), x(t)] = u_1[c(t)] + u_2[x(t)] \qquad (6.22)$$

where $x(t)$ is the stock of the resource at time t. This function is maximized subject to the depletion equation

$$\dot{x}(t) = -c(t) \qquad x(0) = x_0 > 0 \qquad (6.23)$$

The basic present value problem can now be written

$$\underset{c(t)}{\text{Max}} \int_0^\infty \left(u_1[c(t)] + u_2[x(t)]\right)e^{-\theta t}\,dt \qquad (6.24)$$

subject to Equation (6.23).

Since the resource is finite and is the only capital asset, a steady state requires that steady state consumption is zero. One can show that a steady state also requires that

$$u_1'(0) = u_2'(x^*)\theta^{-1} \qquad (6.25)$$

where $u_1'(0)$ is the marginal utility at zero consumption level and $u_2'(x^*)$ is the marginal utility of the resource at x^*. Clearly, for Equation (6.25) to hold $u_1'(0) < \infty$, and, hence, marginal utility of consumption must be bounded from above. Total consumption along the optimal steady state path will be $x_0 - x^*$ if $x_0 > x^*$ and zero otherwise.

In this way the utility level $u(0, x^*)$ will be sustained for ever, but it does not represent the maximum sustainable utility level. Following Phelps (1961) one can, like Heal (1995), ask for the path among feasible paths which gives the highest value of the long-run utility level or

$$\max_{\substack{\text{(feasible paths)}}} \lim_{t \to \infty} u[c(t), x(t)] \tag{6.26}$$

The solution of this problem is simple in the present example. Obviously, consuming nothing and conserving the entire initial stock maximizes the sustainable utility level. Heal calls this steady state path the green golden rule path, but it is also, in this particular case, the max–min path discussed in the introductory part of this chapter. The former steady state is what we can expect under a positive discount factor, and the latter arises when we neglect discounting entirely.

Is there a reasonable compromise? What discounting means is that there will always exist a future point in time such that whatever happens after this time, it cannot change the ranking between two utility paths. To see this, say that we are considering two paths yielding utility $u^0(\cdot)$ and $u^1(\cdot)$, and suppose that it holds that

$$\int_0^\infty u^0(\cdot) e^{-\theta t} dt = \int_0^\infty u^1(\cdot) e^{-\theta t} dt + A \tag{6.27}$$

where $A > 0$.

We want to show that if we worsen u^0 to a finite lower bound of utility, $\underline{u}$, and increase u^1 to a finite upper bound, $\bar{u}$, we can always find a T large enough such that

$$\int_T^\infty (\bar{u} - \underline{u}) e^{-\theta t} dt < A \tag{6.28}$$

This is true, since the integral on the left-hand side equals

$$\frac{(\bar{u} - \underline{u})}{\theta} e^{-\theta T} \tag{6.29}$$

which goes to zero as $T \to \infty$. The interpretation is that for T large enough, whatever is done to worsen the better path at T and onwards, it remains superior. Chichilnisky (1993) calls this property of discounted present value 'the dictatorship of the present'.

Conversely, a term like Equation (6.27) would represent the dictatorship of the future if there is a cut-off level, T^1, which makes what happens before T^1 irrelevant for the ranking of two utility paths with finite upper and lower bounds.

Chichilnisky (1993) shows that a welfare criterion which satisfies axioms that exclude both the dictatorships of the present and future, and which includes an intergenerational Pareto criterion (related to Brundtland's definition of sustainability), continuity of the utility sequence, and that total welfare is linear in the welfare of generations, can only be represented by the following objective function:[16]

$$\alpha \int_{0}^{\infty} u(t)\Lambda(t)dt + (1-\alpha) \lim_{t \to \infty} u(\cdot), \text{ where } 0 < \alpha < 1 \qquad (6.30)$$

where $\Lambda(t)$ is a measure such that

$$\int_{0}^{\infty} \Lambda(t)dt = 1,$$

i.e. it could be a conventional discount factor, $\Lambda(t) = e^{-\theta t}$. The first term represents the dictatorship of the present and the second is obviously the dictatorship of the future, since it depends only on what is left in the limit. Maximizing this utility functional subject to the depletion equation (6.23) consequently yields a depletion path somewhere in between the present value path and the green golden rule path. Figure 6.4, which is borrowed from Heal (1995), compares the present value and green golden rule paths with the path resulting from the Chichilnisky criterion. In other words, the latter criterion leads to a long-run stock, x^c, which is greater than under the present value path, x^*, but less than under the green golden rule path, (x_0).

When the resource is renewable, Heal (1995) shows that the resource management problem (6.24) has no solution under the Chichilnisky criterion, provided that the discount rate is a positive constant. The reason is, according to Li and Löfgren (1996), that the present and the future are treated as two disjoint sets by the criterion, and the objective function becomes discontinuous at any future 'transition date' T. It is a mere coincidence that the problem can be solved in the non-renewable resource case, since the discontinuity can be avoided when

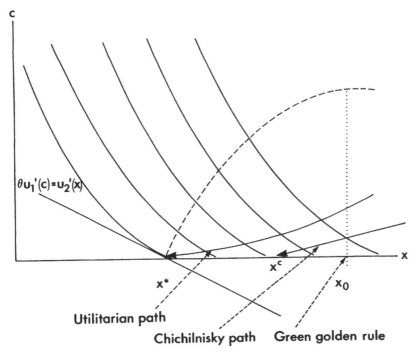

c

$\theta u_1'(c) = u_2'(x)$

x

x^*

x^c

x_0

Utilitarian path

Chichilnisky path   **Green golden rule**

Figure 6.4   Alternative solutions to a 'pure' depletion problem

long-run consumption goes to zero. The problem can be circumvented, as pointed out by Heal, by letting the discount factor vary over time and asymptotically approach zero. The interpretation and solution of such a problem is further discussed in Li and Löfgren (1996).

At the moment, and under more realistic assumptions, it is not clear how the implementation of the Chichilnisky criterion in a market economy can be achieved. Its value, so far, lies in its precise relationship to a set of axioms (iff), which seem reasonable as fundaments of the concretization of sustainable development. The present value criterion will, in general, not do in this respect, and the green golden rule and/or the max–min criterion are very likely to be too conservative.

As Heal (1995) points out, the optimal path under the Chichilnisky criterion fulfills all necessary conditions of the corresponding present value problem ($\alpha = 1$),[17] except the transversality conditions. This means that we can use optimal control theory and define

$$H^K = u(t)e^{-\theta t} + \lambda(t)\dot{x}(t) + \lim_{t \to \infty} u(t) \qquad (6.31)$$

and since $\lim_{t\to\infty} u(\cdot) = K = $ constant we have[18] (along an optimal path)

$$\frac{dH^K}{dt} = \frac{\partial H^K}{\partial t} = -\theta u(t)e^{-\theta t} \qquad (6.32)$$

and

$$H^K(t) = \theta \int_t^\infty u(s)e^{-\theta s} ds + K$$

with $\lim_{t\to\infty} H^K = K = \lim_{t\to\infty} u(t)$.

In other words the augmented Hamiltonian, H^K, will tell us about the value of the Chichilnisky criterion along the optimal path. Unlike the ordinary Hamiltonian, it does not go to zero in the limit, but approaches the sustainable utility level.

6.6   CONCLUDING COMMENTS

To conclude, it is worth mentioning that views on sustainable development are, to a large extent, ethical issues. The view taken in this chapter is very much neoclassical in the sense that sustainability requires that the overall stock of capital assets (man-made, natural, and human capital) is kept intact, although we have shown that it is generally impossible to find a static measure of this kind of capital. This view is often referred to as 'Solow sustainability'.

The environmental economists in London have argued for a modified version of Solow sustainability by introducing upper bounds of assimilative capacity, and lower bounds on the natural capital stocks necessary to support sustainable development.[19] They have, for example, introduced concepts such as critical natural capital, i.e., keystone species and keystone processes to mimic non-substitutability of certain types of natural capital.

Other critics – in particular ecologists[20] – have argued that the full contribution of component species and processes to the aggregate life support service provided by ecosystems cannot be captured in economic values. There are, therefore, risks that some of these processes will be eroded because of undervaluation, thereby reducing the stability and resilience of the ecosystem to future shocks and stress.[21]

Finally, there are economists and ecologists like Daly (1984, 1992) who emphasize the scale of human impact relative to global carrying capacity. The following quotation from Daly (1984) is illustrative of their argument:

> Suppose we want to maximize the load that the boat carries. If we place all the weight in one corner of the boat it will quickly sink or capsize. Therefore we spread the weight out evenly. To do this we invent a price system. The higher the waterline in any corner of the boat, the higher the price of putting another pound in that corner. The lower the waterline, the lower the price. We allocate the weight so that the price per pound is equal in all parts of the boat. This is the internal optimizing rule for allocating space (resources) among weights (alternative uses). This pricing rule is an allocative mechanism only, a useful but dumb computer that sees no reason not to keep on adding weight and distributing it equally until the optimally loaded boat sinks, optimally, to the bottom of the sea. (p. 29)

The approach reduces to a call for a steady state economic system based on thermodynamic constraints on the overall economy. The constant scale requires, e.g., zero economic growth and zero population growth.

Against the above background, we have only been able to cover very limited aspects of sustainable development. We hope, however, that what we have discussed shows that even our neoclassical weak form of sustainable development is neither irrelevant nor unproblematic.

NOTES

1. See e.g. Solow (1986, 1992), Mäler (1991), Hulten (1992) and Nordhaus (1995).
2. World Commission on Environment and Development, (1987), p. 43.
3. See Fisher (1906).
4. *Value and Capital*, p. 165.
5. See e.g. Solow (1986), Hulten (1992), Dasgupta and Mäler (1991), Mäler (1991) and Nordhaus (1995).
6. See Rawls (1971), pp. 284–93. The idea could be criticized, since even under a veil of ignorance an individual would not end up in the lowest end of the income distribution with probability one.
7. Compare with Chapter 5, where the notion of efficient labour comes from technological progress driven by investment in human capital.
8. Since $z > 0$ for some t would together with a constant path consumption mean that we could have sustained a higher constant consumption level.
9. Note that $\lim_{t \to \infty} c_0 e^{-at} = 0$, independent of the magnitude of c_0.
10. See e.g. Dasgupta and Heal (1974).
11. A more general case is treated in Dasgupta and Mitra (1983).
12. A similar result is proved by Pezzey (1995).
13. See Fisher (1906), Hicks (1939) and Lindahl (1933).
14. A formal proof can be found in Pezzey and Withagen (1995), but see also Dasgupta and Heal (1979), pp. 298–300.
15. See, for example, Seierstad and Sydsæter (1987), p. 232. The criterion states, roughly, that one consumption path is considered to be better than a second if a sufficiently large number of generations taken together poll a majority vote for the first path.

16. For the underlying mathematical principles, see also Radner (1967).
17. If this is not true for some interval, consumption can be reallocated over this interval to increase the value of the integral. Hence, a contradiction.
18. The proof is analogous to the proof in Chapter 3.
19. See Turner (1993).
20. See Ehrlich and Ehrlich (1992).
21. Yet another more ecumenical, interdisciplinary perspective is taken by economists like Richard Norgaard; see e.g. Howarth and Norgaard (1992), and the survey by Toman (1994).

7. A *smörgåsbord* of topics

This chapter contains a *smörgåsbord* of topics, such as open economies, non-constant utility discount rates (the consequences of which were not explored in Chapter 6), defensive expenditures and stochastic time horizons. The absence of these topics in Chapters 2–6 does not mean that we believe them to be less important than those already discussed. On the contrary, we believe them to be very important. However, given the focus of previous chapters, it was difficult to address these topics in a natural way, and this motivates a chapter briefly summarizing them. Section 7.1 extends the analysis to an open economy, and explores (among other things) the role of capital gains, while Section 7.2 concerns welfare measurement under a non-constant rate of time preference. Section 7.3 briefly treats the problem of defensive expenditures and their role in 'green' NNP measures. Finally, Section 7.4 relaxes the assumption that the economy will continue forever with perfect certainty. Instead, we assume that the time horizons are stochastic and finite, and we develop appropriate methods to analyse the consequences of that assumption from the points of view of resource allocation and welfare measurement.

7.1 CAPITAL GAINS AND CONSTANT CONSUMPTION PATHS IN THE OPEN ECONOMY

The bottom line of Chapter 6 is that there is no simple indicator of sustainability. However, if the economy follows a constant consumption (max–min) path, NNP, or more precisely the Hamiltonian, is indeed an exact indicator of sustainability. In a closed economy with no exogenous technological progress or externalities, and a constant population – the model in Chapter 3, Section 3.2 – we have along an optimal path that

$$H^{c^*}(t) = u\!\left(c^*(t)\right) + \lambda^{c^*}(t)\dot{k}^*(t) = \theta\!\int_t^\infty u\!\left(c^*(s)\right)e^{-\theta(s-t)}ds \qquad (7.1)$$

and we showed in Chapter 6 that $u(c^*(t)) = $ constant if and only if $\lambda^{c^*}(t)\dot{k}^*(t) = 0$ for all t.

Note, however, that if we use the same idea in an open economy, which lives solely by harvesting its non-renewable resource and trading it against consumption goods in the world market, the NNP measured as consumption plus net investment would be zero, since

$$NNP = c(t) + \bar{\lambda}_n(t)\dot{k}_n(t) = 0 \qquad \text{all } t \qquad (7.2)$$

where $-\dot{k}_n(t) = R(t)$ is the harvest at time t, $\lambda_n(t)$ is the current value price of natural resources in terms of goods, and k_n is the stock of natural capital.[1] As the resource has to be scarce to buy goods, such an 'oil economy' cannot have $\lambda_n(t)\dot{k}_n(t) = 0$ and $c(t) > 0$. Hence, Hartwick's rule implies that the maximum constant consumption level is zero in this case.

On the other hand, we can conceive of a case (the standard one, according to Hotelling's rule), where the resource price for the harvest of a natural resource in terms of consumption goods increases over time. This means exogenously improving terms of trade, or, which in principle amounts to the same thing, an exogenously improving technology. From Chapter 4, we know how to handle such a complication in welfare measurement, but this kind of capital gain will also have consequences for the sustainable consumption path. An 'oil economy' may, for this reason, be able to sustain a positive stationary consumption level, and an indicator of sustainability should acknowledge this possibility. In other words, the exogenous capital gains cannot be neglected.

At the opposite extreme, we can allow each country to fully include capital gains in the NNP measure. For the 'oil economy', this would result in the measure

$$NNP^g = c(t) + \bar{\lambda}_n(t)\dot{k}_n(t) + \dot{\bar{\lambda}}_n(t)k_n(t) = \dot{\bar{\lambda}}_n(t)k_n(t) \qquad (7.3)$$

where top-index g denotes that capital gains $\dot{\bar{\lambda}}_n(t)k_n(t)$ are included. The last equality in Equation (7.3) follows, since $c(t) = \bar{\lambda}_n(t)(-\dot{k}_n)$ by assumption. If the whole NNP^g is consumed we have

$$c(t) = c(t) + \bar{\lambda}_n(t)\dot{k}_n(t) + \dot{\bar{\lambda}}_n(t)k_n(t) \qquad \text{all } t \qquad (7.4)$$

implying that

$$\frac{d}{dt}\left[\bar{\lambda}_n(t)k_n(t)\right] = \bar{\lambda}_n(t)\dot{k}_n(t) + \dot{\bar{\lambda}}_n(t)k_n(t) = 0 \qquad \text{all } t \qquad (7.5)$$

In other words, the national wealth is kept intact over time. As Asheim (1994b) notes, this points to a more general result. If one wants to keep national wealth non-decreasing, an NNP concept which includes capital gains would measure the maximum allowable level of consumption.

We now have two seemingly conflicting results. If each country wants to keep its national wealth constant, consumption will equal a measure of NNP which includes capital gains. However, adding all countries together into a world economy, assuming that the objective is to keep the level of aggregate consumption constant, consumption will equal a measure of NNP which does not include capital gains.

To reconcile these results, we note that the maximum constant consumption is the interest on a properly defined measure of wealth, and constant wealth is not a sufficient condition for a constant consumption path. The interest rate (the marginal productivity of capital) can, however, change over time. Clearly, if positive capital gains (increasing wealth) come with a decreasing interest rate, a constant consumption path over time (interest on wealth = constant) implies increasing wealth. In other words, keeping wealth intact is no longer sufficient for ensuring a sustainable constant consumption path. This means, in particular, that if an 'oil economy' wants to sustain a constant consumption path, it can only consume part of its positive capital gains.[2] The rest must be used to augment wealth.

Hence, if we can show that there is, indeed, an inverse relationship between capital gains and the interest rate, we have reconciled the seemingly paradoxical results. Following an intuitive argument based on Asheim (1994b), let us reintroduce the technology from Section 6.3, with a constant returns to scale production function

$$y(t) = f(k_m(t), -\dot{k}_n(t)) \tag{7.6}$$

where k_m is man-made capital. If the consumption good serves as the numeraire, a competitive equilibrium entails the equality between the marginal productivity of the resource flow and the resource price, i.e.:

$$f_2(k_m(t), -\dot{k}_n(t)) = \bar{\lambda}_n(t) \tag{7.7}$$

where $f_2(\cdot)$ is the marginal productivity of the resource flow.

The marginal productivity of man-made capital measures the interest rate, and equals, since no arbitrage possibilities are left in a competitive economy, the growth rate of the resource price, or

$$f_1\left(k_m(t), -\dot{k}_n(t)\right) = r(t) = \frac{\dot{\bar{\lambda}}_n(t)}{\bar{\lambda}_n(t)} \tag{7.8}$$

With the consumption good as a numeraire, the capital gains of the resource equal $\dot{\overline{\lambda}}_n(t)k_n(t) = \overline{\lambda}_n(t)k_n(t)r(t)$, which means that the capital gains in the resource are positive. The last equality of Equation (7.8) is simply Hotelling's rule of resource extraction, i.e. the growth rate of the price of the resource equals the interest rate.

Now let $C(r,\overline{\lambda}_n)$ denote the minimum cost of producing one unit of output, i.e.

$$C\left(r,\overline{\lambda}_n\right) = \min_{k_m,k_n}\left\{rk_m + \overline{\lambda}_n\left(-\dot{k}_n\right)\middle| f(\cdot)=1\right\} \qquad (7.9)$$

The zero pure profit condition of the competitive economy under constant returns to scale gives

$$f(r,\overline{\lambda}_n) = C(r,\overline{\lambda}_n) = 1 \qquad (7.10)$$

The last equality defines a factor price contour or an isocost, which – by a standard result of duality theory – has a negative slope. To see this note that

$$\left.\frac{dr}{d\overline{\lambda}_n}\right|_{C=1} = \frac{-\partial C}{\partial \overline{\lambda}_n}\left[\frac{\partial C}{\partial r}\right]^{-1} = \frac{\left(\dot{k}_n\right)}{k_m} < 0$$

where the last equality follows from Shephard's lemma.[3] In other words, capital gains ($\dot{\overline{\lambda}}_n(t) > 0$) are equivalent to a falling interest rate ($\dot{r}(t) < 0$).

To conclude, since capital gains under constant returns to scale come with a falling interest rate, constant wealth cannot sustain a constant consumption (income path). A constant consumption path will require increasing wealth. Moreover, an 'oil economy' cannot sustainably consume the whole increase in its wealth, since part of it must be accumulated to compensate for the falling interest rate.

7.2   WELFARE MEASUREMENT UNDER NON-CONSTANT TIME PREFERENCES

By modifying the simple Ramsey model with a time dependent time preference, we ended up, in Chapter 6, with a relationship between the present value Hamiltonian and future consumption which has the following shape

$$H^*(t) = -\int_t^{\infty} \dot{\Lambda}(s)u\Big[c^*(s)\Big]ds \qquad (7.11)$$

where $\dot{\Lambda}(s)$ is the time derivative of the utility discount factor. Clearly, if $\Lambda(s) = e^{-\theta s}$ we can write

$$H^{c^*}(t) = \theta\int_t^{\infty} u\Big[c^*(s)\Big]e^{-\theta(s-t)}ds \qquad (7.12)$$

To find a 'static equivalent' to the present value of future utility under a general case with varying time preference, $-\dot{\Lambda}(t) / \Lambda(t) \neq$ constant, we can approach the problem in a more direct manner. Following Asheim (1995), we are looking for an entity $h(t)$ such that

$$\int_t^{\infty} \Lambda(s)h(t)ds = \int_t^{\infty} u\big(c^*(s)\big)\Lambda(s)ds \qquad (7.13)$$

i.e., such that the present value of $h(t)$, if sustained indefinitely, equals the present value of future utility. Solving for $h(t)$ yields

$$h(t) = \int_t^{\infty} \Big[c^*(s)\Big]\Lambda(s)ds\left[\int_t^{\infty} \Lambda(s)ds\right]^{-1} \qquad (7.14)$$

If $\Lambda(t) = \Lambda(0)e^{-\theta t}$, we have a constant time preference

$$\theta = \frac{-\dot{\Lambda}(t)}{\Lambda(t)} = \frac{\Lambda(t)}{\int_t^{\infty} \Lambda(s)ds} \qquad (7.15)$$

If not, we have a term structure of utility interest rates with the very short-term interest rate equal to

$$\theta_s(t) = -\dot{\Lambda}(t)[\Lambda(t)]^{-1}$$

and the very long-term interest rate equal to

$$\theta_\ell(t) = \Lambda(t)\left[\int_t^\infty \Lambda(s)ds\right]^{-1}$$

This means, among other things, that $1/\theta_\ell(t)$ is the price at time t in terms of utility of a utility annuity from time t onwards. We can now use the above definitions to write the 'static equivalent' as

$$h(t) = \theta_\ell(t)\int_t^\infty \frac{\Lambda(s)}{\Lambda(t)} u\big(c^*(s)\big)ds \qquad (7.16)$$

From a technical point of view, $h(t)$ bears a close resemblance to the national product related welfare measure in Equation (3.19). The interpretation is that $h(t)$ measures the infinitely long-term utility interest rate times current welfare. Like the Hamiltonian in the constant time preference case, the 'static equivalent' is a solution to a differential equation of the form

$$\dot{h}(t) = \theta_\ell(t)[h(t) - u(c^*(t))] \qquad (7.17)$$

The practical problem with the term $h(t)$ is that it cannot, in general, be measured by current entities such as prices and quantities at time t, since it contains forward looking components.

The Welfare Measure Expressed in Terms of Consumption

So far we have used a roundabout linear approximation of the utility function to come up with a market related approximation of the utility value of future consumption. A more straightforward approach is to use consumption and prices in the competitive economy directly. One can show, see Dixit et al. (1980), that under certain regularity conditions there exists a present value price path $\{p(s)\}_t^\infty$ such that maximization of the present value future utility also maximizes

$$\int_t^\infty p(s)c(s)ds \qquad (7.18)$$

over all feasible consumption paths. It also holds for all s that $c^*(s)$ maximizes

$$\Lambda(s)u[c(s)] - p(s)c(s)$$

with respect to $c(s)$, which means that along an interior solution

$$\Lambda(s)u_c[c^*(s)] = p(s) \tag{7.19}$$

As in the previous section, $p(s)$ determines a term structure of 'consumption' interest rates. The very short-term consumption interest rate is

$$r_s(t) = -\dot{p}(t) / p(t)$$

and the very long-term interest rate is

$$r_\ell(t) = p(t)\left(\int_t^\infty p(s)ds\right)^{-1}$$

We can now, in the same way as earlier, ask for an income $y(t)$ which, if sustained indefinitely, yields the same wealth as the wealth maximizing path, i.e.

$$y(t)\int_t^\infty p(s)ds = \int_t^\infty p(s)c^*(s)ds \tag{7.20}$$

or

$$y(t) = \int_t^\infty p(s)c^*(s)ds\left[\int_t^\infty p(s)ds\right]^{-1} = r_\ell(t)\int_t^\infty \frac{p(s)}{p(t)}c^*(s)ds \tag{7.21}$$

where the division by $p(t)$ in the last integral converts wealth into current value. Hence, the 'NNP measure' in terms of consumption equals the infinitely long-term consumption interest rate, times current wealth. As in the previous section, $y(t)$ obeys an equation

$$\dot{y}(t) = r_\ell(t)[y(t) - c^*(t)] \tag{7.22}$$

It is, of course, relevant to ask to what extent $y(t)$ is an exact indicator of utility, i.e. whether $h(t) = u(y(t))$. As Asheim (1995) shows, the static income $y(t)$ is a lower bound for an exact welfare indicator, i.e. $h(t) \geqq u(y(t))$.[4]
We are now in a position to combine (7.21) and (7.22) to yield

$$y(t) = c^*(t) + \dot{y}(t) / r_\ell(t) =$$

$$c^* + \frac{d}{dt}\left(\int\limits_t^\infty \frac{p(s)}{p(t)} c^*(s)ds\right) + \dot{r}_\ell(t) / r_\ell(t)\int\limits_t^\infty \frac{p(s)}{p(t)} c^*(s)ds \qquad (7.23)$$

This means that consumption NNP equals consumption plus the growth of current wealth plus the rate of change in the long-term interest rate times current wealth. For the special case, when the consumption interest rate is constant, i.e., when $p(s) = p(0)e^{-rs}$ we end up with the conventional NNP measure of consumption plus net investment. To see this note that the third term of (7.23) vanishes, since $\dot{r}_\ell = 0$. Moreover, direct calculation shows that the second term equals

$$B = \int\limits_t^\infty \frac{p(s)}{p(t)} c^*(s)ds = \int\limits_t^\infty p(0)e^{-r(s-t)}\dot{c}^*(s)ds \qquad (7.24)$$

From the fact that the price system supports an optimal path we have that $p(s) = \Lambda(s)u_c(c^*(s))$ for all s, and, hence, that

$$B = \frac{1}{\Lambda(t)u_c\left(c^*(t)\right)}\int\limits_t^\infty \Lambda(s)u_c\left(c^*(s)\right)\dot{c}^*(s)ds = \frac{1}{\lambda(t)}\int\limits_t^\infty \lambda(s)\dot{c}^*(s)ds \qquad (7.25)$$

where $\lambda(s)$ is the shadow price of capital along the optimal path. Proposition 6.1 now tells us that $B = \dot{k}(t)$, the real value of net investment at time t, so

$$y(t) = c^*(t) + \dot{k}^*(t) \qquad (7.26)$$

The price of capital in terms of consumption goods is one when goods can be used as capital in a one to one fashion. If there is more than one capital good, we write the second term $Q(t)\dot{k}^*(t)$ where $Q(t)$ are the competitive prices of capital in terms of consumption goods. The relationship (7.26) will also hold for $c^*(t)$ = constant, since along such a path the Dixit, Hammond and Hoel result reproduced in Chapter 6 tells us that the value of net investment is identical to zero along such a path.

A Fundamental Reason for no Capital Gains

One can like Asheim (1995) ask why there are no capital gains included in the consumption NNP measure derived for the closed economy with no exogenous technological progress, and a constant consumption interest rate. If a constant returns to scale economy such as that in Section 7.1 is imposed, one can show that[5]

$$Q(t)k(t) = \int_t^\infty \frac{p(s)}{p(t)} c^*(s)ds \qquad (7.27)$$

where $Q(t)$ are the competitive prices of the capital goods in terms of current consumption. Rewriting Equation (7.23) using (7.27) yields

$$y(t) = c^*(t) + Q(t)\dot{k}^*(t) + \dot{Q}(t)k^*(t) + \frac{\dot{r}_\ell(t)}{r_\ell(t)} Q(t)k(t) \qquad (7.28)$$

Since under these circumstances the last term is zero ($\dot{r}_\ell = 0$) and, as we have just shown that $y(t) = c^*(t) + Q(t)\dot{k}^*(t)$, it follows that $\dot{Q}(t)k(t) = 0$: there are no capital gains.

As Asheim suggests, Weitzman's original result that capital gains are not part of the NNP measure is based on a more restrictive model than the one set out here. Under a constant consumption interest rate, constant returns to scale and no non-attributable technological progress there are no capital gains. The same reasoning can, of course, be applied when one works directly through the utility function, as we have been doing in the main part of this volume, and assumes that the time preference is constant.

7.3 DEFENSIVE EXPENDITURES AND 'GREEN' NNP MEASURES

In many cases, individuals can affect the quality of the services they derive from the environment. This makes it fruitful to view individuals as producing services using the environment as one of several inputs. One example is provided by recreational services such as visiting a ski resort or a fishing site. In these cases, private goods and factors such as petrol and time are inputs.

There are also public good inputs related to the site such as size and quality attributes. The individual uses these private and public inputs to produce a recreational experience. Similarly, individuals can sometimes protect themselves against the effects of pollution, i.e. undertake defensive expenditures. A simple example is provided by the installation of a filter in one's water tap to improve the quality of the drinking water and reduce the health risks of consuming contaminated water. In this case, too, the individual can be viewed as producing environmental quality.

Empirical studies within the field usually concentrate on health risks. To study individuals' averting behaviour is intuitively appealing, since this is really a case where individuals buy themselves a risk reduction for money. For example, Åkerman et al. (1991) examined households living in houses with indoor radiation arising from radon decay products. Given information on radiation levels and the health risks, households decide whether or not they should take measures against the radiation. This decision obviously involves a consideration of how much they are willing to pay for a radiation reduction. Using data on measures undertaken, costs and radiation levels, Åkerman et al. estimated a willingness to pay (WTP) and the implied value of statistical life. Other examples of averting behaviour are purchases of smoke detectors; see Dardis (1980), and the use of seatbelts; see Blomquist (1979).

There has also been some discussion, see e.g. Dasgupta et al. (1995) and Mäler (1991) for reviews, of how to classify household defensive expenditures in 'green' national income measures: should such expenditures be deducted or not? It has been argued that an increase in household defensive expenditure will increase the gross national product. In order to prevent increases in pollution (via their impact on household defensive expenditures) increasing the level of welfare, it is claimed that household defensive expenditures should be *deducted* from 'the NNP' to obtain a properly defined welfare measure. In this section, we shall introduce a household production function approach so as to shed light on the question of how to treat household defensive expenditures in 'green' national product measures.

The Model and the Main Result

The analysis in this subsection is based on the model set out in Chapter 4, augmented by a household production function, so as to model defensive actions taken by the individual against the effects of pollution. It is also important to distinguish between the actions taken by the individual to protect himself/herself against a given level of pollution, and the actions taken by the government to affect the level of pollution. We shall, therefore, also include what we call 'a public pollution treatment sector' in the model.

Let us here write the instantaneous utility function as $u(c(t), x(t))$, where $x(t)$ is an indicator of environmental quality. We also require that the instantaneous utility function is increasing in both arguments and strictly concave. To capture the possibility that the individual undertakes actions to protect himself/herself against pollution, let

$$x(t) = h(c^P(t), z(t))$$

be a household production function, where $c^p(t)$ represents the private goods used as inputs in the production of environmental quality, and $z(t)$ the stock of pollution. We assume that $\partial h(\cdot) / \partial c^p(t) > 0$, while $\partial h(\cdot) / \partial z(t) < 0$ for all t. The equations of motion for physical capital and pollution, Equations (4.17) and (4.18), are modified to read

$$\dot{k}(t) = f(k(t), e_f(t)) - c(t) - c^p(t) - I[\alpha(t)] \qquad (7.29)$$

$$\dot{z}(t) = e(\alpha(t), e_f(t)) - \gamma z(t) \qquad (7.30)$$

In comparison with its counterpart in Chapter 4, Equation (7.29) also contains the expenditures chosen by the individual to protect himself/herself against pollution. Another difference between this version of the model and the one in Chapter 4 is that the variable α, which represents the scale of the operations undertaken by the government to affect the stock of pollution, enters the pollution production function instead of affecting the rate of decay of pollution. We assume that the pollution production function is such that $\partial e(\cdot) / \partial e_f > 0$ and $\partial e(\cdot)/\partial \alpha < 0$.

Apart from the household production function (and the neglect of exogenous technological progress), the model is identical to the one in Chapter 4. If we were to compare the command optimum solution with the resource allocation in the decentralized economy, we would, therefore, reach the same general conclusion as in Chapter 4 about the source of the external effect and the policy required to internalize this external effect. As a consequence, we concentrate the analysis to the command optimum solution and the treatment of defensive expenditures in the national product related welfare measure.

The social planner's decision problem is to choose the control variables $c(t)$, $c^p(t)$, $e_f(t)$ and $\alpha(t)$ such as to maximize

$$U(0) = \int_t^\infty u\Big(c(t), h\big(c^P(t), z(t)\big)\Big)e^{-\theta t} dt$$

subject to (7.29), (7.30) and initial conditions. Let

$$(c^*(t), c^{p^*}(t), e_f^*(t), \alpha^*(t), k^*(t), z^*(t))$$

be the solution to the social planner's optimization problem. Along the optimal path, the present value Hamiltonian is written

$$H^*(t) = u(c^*(t), h(c^{p^*}(t), z^*(t)))e^{-\theta t} + \lambda^*(t)\dot{k}^*(t) + \mu^*(t)\dot{z}^*(t) \quad (7.31)$$

Applying methods that should by now be familiar to the reader, the national product related welfare measure can be written

$$\theta\int_t^\infty u\Big(c^*(s), x^*(s)\Big)e^{-\theta(s-t)}ds = u\Big(c^*(t), x^*(t)\Big) + \lambda^{c^*}(t)\dot{k}^*(t) + \mu^{c^*}(t)\dot{z}^*(t) \quad (7.32)$$

where $x^*(t) = h(c^{p^*}(t), z^*(t))$. The right-hand side of Equation (7.32) is the current value Hamiltonian along the optimal path, which is defined by multiplying (7.31) by $e^{\theta t}$. As mentioned previously, it is often convenient to approximate the instantaneous utility by a linear function when relating the welfare measure to the national accounts. Using the approximation

$$u(c^*, h(c^{p^*}, z^*)) \approx \lambda^{c^*}c^* + \lambda^{c^*}c^{p^*} + u_x(\cdot)h_z(\cdot)z^*$$

which follows from the necessary conditions (which we leave for the reader to derive), the linear – or net – welfare measure is given by

$$NWM = \lambda^{c^*}c^* + \lambda^{c^*}c^{p^*} + u_x(\cdot)h_z(\cdot)z^* + \lambda^{c^*}\dot{k}^* + \mu^{c^*}\dot{z}^* \quad (7.32a)$$

where the time indicator has been neglected for notational convenience. Both the benefit and the cost associated with the defensive actions are captured by (7.32a): the benefit is the utility value of improved environmental quality, i.e. the second term on the right-hand side, while the cost in terms of foregone consumption is included in the fourth term. Note also that the costs and benefits associated with defensive actions cancel out in the linear welfare measure.

The costs and benefits associated with public pollution control are included in the fourth and fifth terms, respectively, of (7.32a). Note also that, even if the pollution treatment sector is optimally scaled (meaning that α is optimally chosen), households may still undertake defensive actions. The reason is that the government's pollution control affects the level of pollution, whereas private defensive actions do not, which means that these two activities are not perfect substitutes.[6]

7.4 GLOBAL WARMING, STOCHASTIC TIME HORIZONS AND THE PROBABILITY OF 'DOOMSDAY'

We have thus far assumed that mankind will survive forever. Unfortunately, this assumption does not hold; according to the natural laws governing the evolution over time of the universe, sooner or later mankind will become extinct. Meanwhile, however, we can affect the probability that civilization survives. This is illustrated by our concern for the greenhouse effect. Many people fear that this effect, in particular through an increased volatility in the climate, will have a devastating impact on the living conditions of future generations. At the same time, measures aimed at reducing/eliminating global warming are requested, i.e. it is believed that we can affect the probability that pollution causes a breakdown of future living conditions.

In this section, we incorporate the dynamic and stochastic features of global warming into the analysis. The problem of global warming is, in a fundamental way, related to uncertainty and depends on the impact of greenhouse gases on the climate. If the stock of greenhouse gases exceeds a certain, stochastic level, this may seriously affect the climate and, therefore, the living conditions of mankind. An economic analysis related to the problem of global warming must, therefore, take this uncertainty into account. The outline of this section is as follows. First, we introduce a dynamic growth model which is designed so as to capture the dynamics and stochastics related to the problem of global warming. This model involves, among other things, a stochastic finite time horizon for the individual. In the next two subsections, we show how to handle this complication in an optimal control problem, and discuss its implications for welfare measurement by applying methods that were originally introduced in the health economic literature.[7] In the final subsection, we present results from the simulation of a numerical version of the model, which enables us to examine how this type of uncertainty affects the paths of certain key variables such as consumption and investments in physical capital.

A Growth Model with a Stochastic Time Horizon

The deterministic part of the model
The analysis to be carried out is based on a model suggested by Backlund et al. (1995), which relates to the model of Chapter 4. To specify consumer preferences in a straightforward way, let us here simplify the utility function in Chapter 4 by neglecting the impact of pollution, and write the instantaneous utility as a function only of the consumption of goods

$$u = u(c(t))$$

which is strictly concave and increasing in its argument. The production side of the model is also slightly changed compared with Chapter 4, since it involves both final goods and a natural resource (forest). Final goods are produced by labour (normalized to one), capital, k, and a forest harvest, m. We also allow a stock of greenhouse gases (GHGs), denoted by z, to affect the output as 'an externality production factor'. The production function is written

$$y(t) = f(1, k(t), m(t), z(t))$$

where $\partial f(\cdot) / \partial m > 0$ and $\partial f(\cdot) / \partial z < 0$. Physical capital accumulates according to

$$\dot{k}(t) = f(1, k(t), m(t), z(t)) - c(t) \tag{7.33}$$

Since output is determined by a forest harvest, the next step will be to specify how the forest stock, $k_n(t)$, accumulates over time. In order to take the potential interaction between forest growth and GHGs into account, we assume that the forest stock accumulates according to the differential equation

$$\dot{k}_n(t) = \kappa(k_n(t), z(t)) - m(t) \tag{7.34}$$

where the forest growth function, $\kappa(\cdot)$, is strictly concave in the forest stock, k_n. The forest growth is also affected by the size of the stock of GHGs. Since one can conceive of cases in which the growth of a forest is either stimulated or harmed by GHGs, we shall not specify the qualitative effect of z on the growth function. To close the deterministic part of the model, we assume that the stock of GHGs accumulates according to

$$\dot{z}(t) = \varsigma(k_n(t), m(t)) - \gamma z(t) \tag{7.35}$$

where $\varsigma(\cdot)$ is the emission production function, and γ represents the absorption capacity of the environment. The properties of Equation (7.35) are important for analysing global warming, and a reasonable assumption may be that the emission growth is decreasing in the forest stock and increasing in the forest harvest.

The stochastic part of the model

The most important change in comparison with the model set out in Chapter 4 is that we here relax the assumption that the economy continues forever with perfect certainty. The reason is that uncertainty about biological and meteorological relationships is fundamental to the global warming problem. Although our understanding of these relationships is incomplete, it seems indisputable that a high concentration of GHGs in the atmosphere may lead to substantial changes in the environment that could severely damage human health and the living conditions for mankind. We incorporate this possibility into the analysis by what we call 'a probability for doomsday'. The term 'doomsday' should not be interpreted too literally. We can think of situations when the climate becomes wildly erratic, which makes the earth uninhabitable in certain places. More specifically, the implications of a 'doomsday' are that, if the catastrophe scenario discussed above becomes reality, then the instantaneous utility drops to zero and stays so ever after. This implies that the model's time horizon is stochastic and finite.[8] However, the reader should note that the assumption that the stock of GHGs may cause the extinction of mankind (i.e. that the utility level drops to zero) is not necessary for the analysis to hold. It is made only for analytical convenience; we could equally well assume that pollution may cause the utility to drop to a positive 'fallback level'.

To introduce the concept of stochastic time horizons, we begin with the assumption that society has survived until time T. Then, the present value utility of society at time zero can be written as

$$U(0,T) = \int_0^T u(c(t))e^{-\theta t}\,dt \qquad (7.36)$$

The probability that society faces a 'doomsday' in a short time interval $(T, T + dT)$, conditional on having survived until time T, is assumed to be given by the hazard function

$$[F_d(T) / (1 - F(T))]\,dT = \delta(z(T), T)\,dT \qquad (7.37)$$

where $F_d(T)$ is the probability density function and $F(T)$ is the cumulative distribution function. The hazard is assumed to be a function of both the stock of GHGs at time T, and the 'age' of society, and we specify the qualitative relationships to be such that $\partial\delta(z, T) / \partial z > 0$ and $\partial\delta(z, T) / \partial T > 0$, and we also require that $\delta(\cdot)$ is non-negative.

The model set out here means that 'mankind' can affect the probability of a 'doomsday' through its behaviour. This is so because the stock of GHGs, which increases the probability that mankind will become extinct, is determined endogenously in the model. If we solve Equation (7.37) for $1 - F(T)$, we obtain the probability that mankind has survived up to time T, i.e.

$$1 - F(T) = e^{-\int_0^T \delta(z(s), s)\,ds} = e^{-\Delta(T)} \qquad (7.38)$$

Equation (7.38) means that the stock of GHGs decreases the life expectancy of humanity. Equations (7.37) and (7.38) have important implications for the analysis to follow. In the Appendix we show that, given the assumptions implicit in these functions, the expected present value of future utility takes the form

$$E[u_0] = \int_0^\infty F_d(T) \int_0^T u(c(t)) e^{-\theta t} \, dt \, dT = \int_0^\infty u(c(t)) e^{-(\theta t + \Delta(t))} \, dt \qquad (7.39)$$

Equation (7.39) has two important implications. First, the utility maximization problem with a stochastic, finite time horizon is transformed to a problem with an infinite time horizon. Second, the uncertainty shows up as an addition to the utility discount rate: the relevant utility discount rate at time t now becomes the rate of time preference, θ, plus the conditional probability of a 'doomsday' at time t, $\delta(z(t), t)$.

The Social Planner's Optimization Problem

To derive the social optimum, we proceed in the same general way as in previous parts of the book by assuming that the resource allocation is decided upon by a social planner. Since the utility discount rate depends on a state variable, the social planner's utility maximization problem is not a standard control problem under an infinite time horizon. However, there is a trick which enables us to transform the optimization problem into such a control problem, meaning that we can apply the same analytic tools as in previous chapters. The trick is to introduce an additional, and artificial, state variable of the form

$$\Delta(t) = \int_0^t \delta(z(s), s) \, ds, \text{ where } \Delta(0) = 0$$

which gives a differential equation

$$\dot{\Delta}(t) = \delta(z(t), t) \qquad (7.40)$$

We can now write the social planner's optimization problem as a standard control problem under an infinite time horizon. Formally,

$$\underset{c,m}{\text{Max}} E[u_0] = \underset{c,m}{\text{Max}} \int_0^\infty u\big(c(t)\big)e^{-(\theta t+\Delta(t))}dt$$

subject to equations of motion for the state variables, i.e. (7.33), (7.34), (7.35) and (7.40), as well as initial conditions $k(0) = k_0$, $k_n(0) = k_{n0}$, $z(0) = z_0$ and $\Delta(0) = 0$. The present value Hamiltonian is written

$$H(t) = u(c(t))e^{-(\theta t + \Delta(t))} + \lambda(t)\dot{k}(t) + v(t)\dot{k}_n(t) + \mu(t)\dot{z}(t) + \psi(t)\dot{\Delta}(t) \quad (7.41)$$

where $\lambda(t)$, $v(t)$, $\mu(t)$ and $\psi(t)$ are present value costate variables. In addition to (7.33), (7.34), (7.35) and (7.40), as well as to initial conditions and transversality conditions, the necessary conditions are (if we neglect the time indicator)

$$u_c(c)e^{-(\theta t + \Delta(t))} - \lambda = 0 \quad (7.42a)$$

$$\lambda f_m(1, k, m, z) - v + \mu\varsigma_m(z, m) = 0 \quad (7.42b)$$

$$\dot{\lambda} = -\frac{\partial H}{\partial k} = -\lambda f_k(1, k, m, z) \quad (7.42c)$$

$$\dot{v} = -\frac{\partial H}{\partial k_n} = -v\kappa_{k_n}(k_n, z) - \mu\varsigma_{k_n}(k_n, m) \quad (7.42d)$$

$$\dot{\mu} = -\frac{\partial H}{\partial z} = -\lambda f_z(1, k, m, z) - v\kappa_z(k_n, z) + \mu\gamma \quad (7.42e)$$

$$\dot{\psi} = -\frac{\partial H}{\partial \Delta} = u(c)e^{-(\theta t + \Delta(t))} \quad (7.42f)$$

Now, suppose that

$$(c^*(t), m^*(t), k^*(t), k_n^*(t), z^*(t), \lambda^*(t), \mu^*(t), v^*(t), \psi^*(t))$$

is the solution to society's optimization problem (i.e. the path obeying the first-order conditions). Since $z^*(t)$ affects the utility discount rate, it will also have an impact on the consumption path. To see this, let us combine (7.42a) and (7.42c) to obtain

$$\dot{c}^*(t) = \frac{u_c\left(c^*(t)\right)}{u_{cc}\left(c^*(t)\right)}\left[\theta + \delta\left(z^*(t),t\right) - f_k\left(1, k^*(t), m^*(t), z^*(t)\right)\right] \qquad (7.42\text{g})$$

which clearly indicates that the probability of a 'doomsday' affects the differential equation for consumption. The higher the stock of GHGs, the higher the state dependent part of the utility discount rate. Moreover, the higher the state dependent part of the utility discount rate, *ceteris paribus*, the more likely it is that consumption is declining. This can be interpreted to mean that the risks associated with global warming provide an incentive to consume more now and less in the future, compared with the case when these risks are absent. In other words, the probability of a 'doomsday' gives rise to an 'impatience effect'. However, since $z^*(t)$ is endogenous, there are also incentives to increase the present value of future utility by reducing the stock of GHGs. This is accomplished by reducing the forest harvest and, as a consequence, producing fewer final goods. If fewer final goods are produced, the state dependent part of the utility discount rate decreases, which provides incentives to postpone consumption. This implies that the probability of a 'doomsday' scenario also gives rise to a 'patience effect'. It also means that the effect of the stock of GHGs (via the utility discount rate) on the consumption path depends both on the preferences and the technology and cannot be determined without additional assumptions. This is further discussed in the next subsection, where the results from simulating a numerical version of the model are presented.

Let us now turn to the measurement of welfare in the 'global warming model'. Note that, although the economy follows the command optimum path, it is not possible to design a welfare measure solely on the basis of currently observed entities. The reason is, as we indicated in Section 7.2, that when the utility discount rate is time dependent, there is no observable static equivalent to future utility. As we are about to show, the national product related current value Hamiltonian will, in this case, overestimate the welfare level both because of the non-constant utility discount factor and because time itself affects the conditional probability of a 'doomsday'. Substituting the optimal path into the present value Hamiltonian in Equation (7.41) and applying Proposition 4.1, we can derive the welfare measure

$$\theta\int_t^\infty u\left(c^*(s)\right)e^{-\left(\theta(s-t)+\bar{\Delta}(s-t)\right)}ds = H^{c^*}(t) - \int_t^\infty \delta\left(z^*(s),s\right)u\left(c^*(s)\right)e^{-\left(\theta(s-t)+\bar{\Delta}(s-t)\right)}ds$$

$$+ \int_t^\infty \psi^{c^*}(s)\delta_s\left(z^*(s),s\right)e^{-\left(\theta(s-t)+\bar{\Delta}(s-t)\right)}ds \qquad (7.43)$$

where $\bar{\Delta}(s - t) = \Delta(s) - \Delta(t)$. The first term on the right-hand side is the current value Hamiltonian, which would be the appropriate welfare measure under a constant utility discount rate. This means that the other two terms are related to the non-constant utility discount rate. The second term measures the discounted sum (over the planning horizon) of products of the instantaneous utility function and the 'doomsday' probability. It reflects the expected utility loss following a non-zero probability of a 'doomsday' (for example, the expected loss following the likelihood of climate erosion). The third term, finally, takes into account that time itself, through the aging of society, affects the probability of a 'doomsday'. Formally, the interpretation of Equation (7.43) is given in Proposition 7.1.

Proposition 7.1 *Interest on the expected future (lifetime) utility of society at time* t *is adequately measured by the current value Hamiltonian at time* t *minus the discounted sum of expected utility losses following from a non-zero probability of a 'doomsday', plus the (negative) present value of the future marginal utility lost through an age dependent conditional death risk for society.*

A Numerical Example

This section analyses a numerical version of the model and presents some of the simulation results from the Backlund et al. (1995) paper. The purpose here is to illustrate some implications of a state dependent utility discount rate, in particular, the implications for consumption and capital accumulation. This requires functional forms for the utility function, the production function and the two growth functions (for the forest stock and the stock of GHGs). These functions and their properties are given in the Appendix. To incorporate the probability of a 'doomsday' in the numerical version of the model, the utility discount rate is assumed to contain two parts: a constant rate of time preference and a term depending on the stock of GHGs. To facilitate the impact of the state dependent part of the utility discount rate, i.e. how the probability of a 'doomsday' is affected by the stock of GHGs, the utility discount rate at time t is written $\theta + \delta(z(t))$. This means that time will only have an indirect impact via the stock of GHGs. The function $\delta(\cdot)$ is linear in the stock of GHGs, and we assume that $\partial\delta(z) / \partial z = 0.000025$. We also assume, to begin with, that the rate of time preference, θ, is 2 per cent.

Introducing a state dependent utility discount rate has two implications in this case: it makes the discount rate higher as well as dependent on what may be thought of as a bad (i.e. the stock of GHGs). In the previous subsection we mentioned that, even if a higher utility discount rate itself provides incentives to consume more at present, introducing a state dependent utility discount rate will affect several parts of the economic system and may, as a consequence, not affect consumption in the same way as an increase in the rate of time preference, θ. Figure 7.1 presents time paths for consumption, investments in physical capital, the stock of GHGs, the physical capital stock and the forest harvest both under a constant utility discount rate and under a utility discount rate including the probability of a 'doomsday', which is defined in the way suggested above.

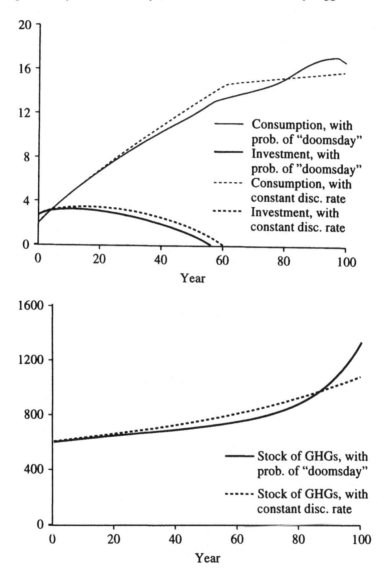

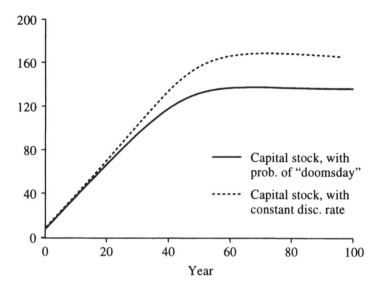

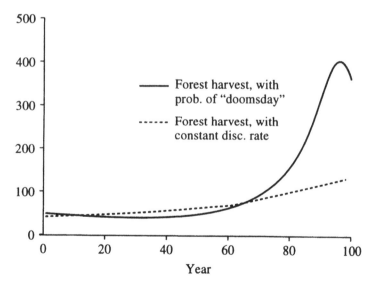

Figure 7.1   Results from the simulations

It is interesting to relate the results in Figure 7.1 to the distinction between 'patience and impatience effects' made in the previous subsection. In this example, it is clear that the 'patience effect' dominates the 'impatience effect'.

Figure 7.1(a) reveals that, in the constant utility discount rate case, more is consumed earlier than in the case when the utility discount rate depends on the stock of GHGs. The reason is that, by introducing the probability of a 'doomsday' into the analysis, the social planner becomes more cautious in his/her production behaviour during the first part of the planning period. This means harvesting less of the forest (Figure 7.1(d)) and producing fewer final goods, which also implies that the stock of GHGs is smaller in the case in which this stock determines the utility discount rate. The latter can be seen from Figure 7.1(b).

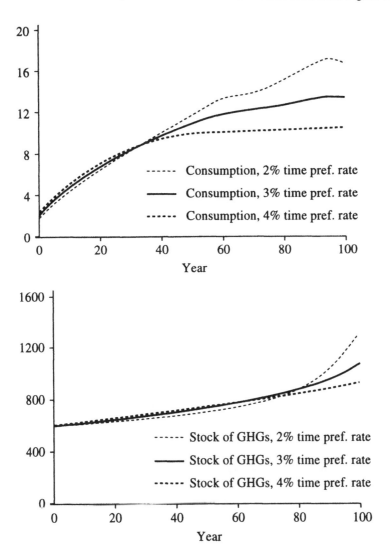

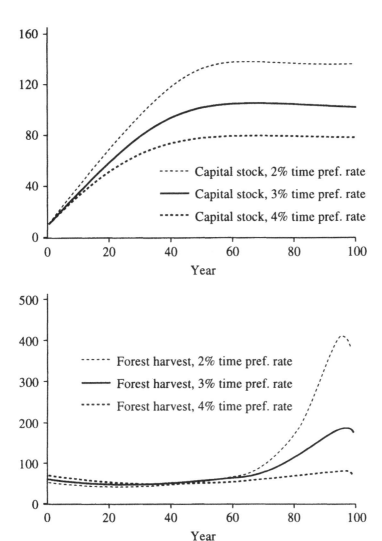

Figure 7.2 Sensitivity analysis

Another interesting observation concerns the configuration of the consumption paths in Figure 7.1(a). In the constant utility discount rate case, there is a tendency to smooth the consumption during the later part of the planning period. On the other hand, when the utility discount rate depends on the stock of GHGs, consumption increases rapidly from period 60 to period 95. The closer the economy comes to the time horizon, the less important will be the increases in the utility discount rate following an increase in the stock of GHGs. This means that both production and consumption increase in the later part of the planning period, when the utility discount rate depends on the stock of GHGs.

Naturally, the paths for the variables involved are sensitive to the assumption about the *level of the utility discount rate* (which we may interpret as the rate of time preference). Because of the long time period involved, the level of the utility discount rate has very powerful effects. This is shown in Figure 7.2, where all graphs relate to versions of the model with a state dependent utility discount rate.

Figure 7.2 compares the paths for consumption, the stock of GHGs, the physical capital stock and the forest harvest when the rate of time preference is 2, 3 and 4 per cent, respectively. The results in these graphs are easy to interpret. For example, Figure 7.2(a) implies that, in the model set out here, the lower the rate of time preference, the greater the consumption in the later phase of the planning period. Similarly, Figure 7.2(b) reveals that the lower the rate of time preference, the faster will be the rise in the stock of GHGs in the later phase of the planning period. The reason is, of course, that a low rate of time preference makes it worthwhile to postpone both production and consumption to future periods. Figures 7.2(c) and 7.2(d) may be interpreted in an analogous manner. Note finally, by comparing Figures 7.1 and 7.2, that a change in the level of the utility discount rate (i.e. increasing or decreasing θ) is fundamentally very different from introducing a state dependent part of the utility discount factor. This is so because, even if these two experiments may have similar effects on the consumption path in a partial equilibrium analysis, their impacts on production (and, therefore, their impacts on consumption in the general equilibrium model) are different.

NOTES

1. We drop the superindex ^{c} (current value) for notational convenience.
2. The exact relationship between the constant consumption path and current prices and stocks is found in Asheim (1994b), proposition 2.
3. See Varian (1992), pp. 74–5.
4. To see this we compute

$$A = \int_t^\infty \Lambda(s)\big[h(t) - u(y(t))\big]ds = \int_t^\infty \Lambda(s)\big[u(c^*(s)) - u(y(t))\big]ds$$

$$-\int_t^\infty \big[\Lambda(s)u_c(c^*(s))c^*(s) - y(t)\Lambda(s)u_c(c^*(s))\big]ds$$

where the last term is zero from (7.20) and since $\Lambda(s)u_c(c^*(s)) = p(s)$ for all s. Rewriting the expression in the following manner

$$A = \int_t^\infty \Lambda(s)\left[u^*\left(c^*(s)\right) + u_c\left(c^*(s)\right)\left(y(t) - c^*(s)\right) - u\left(y(t)\right)\right]ds$$

shows that $A \geqq 0$. $u(\cdot)$ is concave, implying that the expression within brackets is non-negative, and since $\Lambda(s) \geqq 0$, all s, the claim follows.
5. See Asheim (1994a).
6. The analysis of welfare measurement when α is not optimally chosen is left to the reader.
7. See Aronsson et al. (1994).
8. An analysis of nuclear power along these lines is found in a paper by Aronsson, Backlund and Löfgren (1996).

APPENDIX

The Expected Present Value of Future Utility

The objective function to be maximized can be written as follows:

$$E[u_0] = \int_0^\infty \delta[z(T), T]e^{-\int_0^T \delta[z(s), s]ds}\left[\int_0^T u(c(t))e^{-\theta t}dt\right]dT \qquad (A.1)$$

The following equivalence between areas of integration is true:

$$\begin{matrix} 0 \leq T \leq \infty \\ 0 \leq t \leq T \end{matrix} \Leftrightarrow \begin{matrix} t \leq T \leq \infty \\ 0 \leq t \leq \infty \end{matrix}$$

Changing the order of integration and integrating out T, we can, therefore, write (A.1) as in Equation (7.39).

The Numerical Model

The numerical model in the Backlund et al. (1995) paper assumes that the instantaneous utility is a logarithmic function

$$u(c(t) = \ln(c(t)) + \vartheta(t) \cdot trans(t) \qquad (A.2)$$

where $\vartheta(t)$ is a dummy variable taking the value one at the terminal point and zero otherwise, while *trans(t)* is a terminal condition that we use in order to avoid the effects of premature truncation. The role of the terminal condition is, essentially, to 'mimic' the case with an infinite time horizon; see Nordhaus (1993).

Output is given by a Cobb–Douglas production function, which exhibits constant returns to scale in capital, labour (normalized to one) and the forest harvest:

$$f(1, k(t), m(t), z(t)) = q(t)k(t)^{\rho_1} \cdot 1^{\rho_2} \cdot m(t)^{(1-\rho_1-\rho_2)} \tag{A.3}$$

where $q(t)$ is an efficiency variable, representing the effect of the residual production factor, i.e. it measures the impact on output of climate changes due to the emissions of GHGs. The variable relates to the stock of GHGs in the following way:

$$q(t) = \phi_0 + \phi_1 z(t) \tag{A.4}$$

The capital stock develops according to

$$\frac{dk}{dt} = q(t)k(t)^{\rho_1} \cdot 1^{\rho_2} \cdot m(t)^{(1-\rho_1-\rho_2)} - c(t) \tag{A.5}$$

The development over time of the forest stock is written

$$\frac{dk_n}{dt} = \Gamma(z(t)) \cdot \left(\omega_0 k_n(t) + \omega_1 k_n(t)^2\right) - m(t) \tag{A.6}$$

The parameters ω_0 and ω_1 are set so that forest growth is a concave function of the forest stock, while the function $\Gamma(z)$ implies a negative, linear relationship between forest growth and the stock of GHGs.

What remains now is the dynamics of the GHGs. We assume a simple relationship for the accumulation of GHGs, although we are aware of the complexity of this problem

$$\frac{dz(t)}{dt} = \beta_1 \cdot m(t) - \beta_2 \cdot k_n(t) - \gamma \cdot z(t) \tag{A.7}$$

where β_1 and β_2 are constants. The first part on the right-hand side is the flow of GHGs in the atmosphere, the second part 'a carbon sink' function of the forest stock, and the third part represents the absorption capacity (the oceans) of the ecological system.

The parameters used in the simulation referred to in the text are:

- for Equations (A3) and (A4), $\rho_1 = 0.40$, $\rho_2 = 0.45$, $\phi_0 = 1.015$ and $\phi_1 = -0.000025$;
- for Equation (A6), $\omega_0 = 0.06$, $\omega_1 = -0.000004$, while $\Gamma(z(t)) = 1.5 - 0.00083 \cdot z(t)$;
- for Equation (A7), $\beta_1 = 0.08$, $\beta_2 = 0.01$ and $\gamma = 0.001$.

The time horizon is set to 100. The results are obtained using the programme package GAMS.

8. Welfare measurement under uncertainty

From what we have seen so far, it holds within a deterministic autonomous Ramsey problem that there is a static equivalent of welfare. We have also seen that technological progress and second-best conditions will complicate welfare measurement, and add terms that contain forward looking components. In this chapter we shall show that the results derived under the assumption of perfect certainty are special cases of more general results which are part of the tool kit of stochastic dynamic programming. More precisely they follow as special cases of the first-order conditions of a stochastic Ramsey problem. We shall here, as in Chapter 6, introduce population growth explicitly into the analysis, and also discuss intuitively some of the technicalities which are created by the introduction of growth as a continuous-time stochastic process called Brownian motion (often named a Wiener process).

The chapter is organized as follows: Section 8.1 briefly reviews some of the mathematical tools of stochastic control theory. In Section 8.2, we use these tools to analyse a stochastic Ramsey problem originally introduced by Merton (1975). Finally, in Section 8.3 we derive stochastic versions of previous welfare measures.

8.1 CONTINUOUS-TIME STOCHASTIC PROCESSES

A stochastic process is a variable, $X(t)$, that evolves over time in a way that is, at least in part, random. In economic modelling, continuous-time stochastic processes are typically introduced in capital theory and financial markets. The most widely studied continuous-time process is a Brownian motion. The name originates from the English botanist Robert Brown who suggested a stochastic process to model seemingly random movements of particles. Einstein (1905 [1956]) is generally given the credit for the precise mathematical formulation of the Brownian motion process, but an even earlier equivalent formulation was given by Louis Bachelier (1900) in his theory of stock option pricing.

A stochastic process $X(t)$ is characterized by its distribution function $G(x, t)$:

$$\text{Prob } \{X(t) \le x\} = G(x,t) \tag{8.1}$$

Equation (8.1) tells us that the probability of finding the process not above some level x at time t is given by the value of the (possibly time dependent) distribution function evaluated at x. If the derivative $\partial G(x,t) / \partial x = g(x,t)$ exists, it can be used to characterize $x(t)$ as follows:

$$\text{Prob } \{x \leq X(t) \leq x + dx\} = G(x + dx,t) - G(x,t) = \tag{8.2}$$

$$= \left\{ G(x,t) + \frac{\partial G}{\partial x}(x,t)dx + O(dx) \right\} - G(x,t) = g(x,t)dx + O(dx)$$

The second equality of Equation (8.2) follows from a Taylor expansion of $G(\cdot)$ around the point x. Here $O(dx)$ denotes terms that are of higher order than dx and, therefore, can be ignored when dx is small. More specifically, a term is of order $O(dx)$ if $\lim_{dx \to 0} O(dx) / dx = 0$. The function $g(x, t) = \partial G(x, t)/\partial x$ is obviously the density function evaluated at $X = x$.

A Brownian motion, $B(t)$, or a Wiener process, is a stochastic process with the following properties:

(i) The sample paths of $B(t)$ are continuous
(ii) $B(0) = 0$
(iii) The increment $B(t + \tau) - B(\tau)$ is normally distributed with mean zero and variance $\sigma^2 \tau$
(iv) If (t, τ) and (t^1, τ^1) are disjoint intervals, then $B(\tau) - B(t)$, and $B(\tau^1) - B(t^1)$ are independent random variables.

Let $dB = B(t + dt) - B(t)$. Then, if we denote the standard normal density function by $\phi(\cdot)$, the normality of the increments means that

$$\text{Prob}[\beta \leq dB \leq \beta + d\beta] = \frac{1}{\sqrt{\sigma^2 dt}} \phi(\beta)d\beta = \left(\frac{1}{\sqrt{2\pi\sigma^2 dt}} \right) \exp\left(\frac{-\beta^2}{2\sigma^2 dt} \right) d\beta$$

$$\tag{8.3}$$

for a sufficiently small $d\beta$. Moreover, the first two moments of the distribution are

$$E\{dB\} = 0 \qquad E\{(dB)^2\} = \sigma^2 dt \tag{8.4}$$

The variance of the increment dB is of order dt (proportional to the small interval dt), and this creates many mathematical difficulties. Dividing both sides of the expression for the variance with $(dt)^2$ we obtain

$$E\left\{\left(\frac{dB}{dt}\right)^2\right\} = \frac{\sigma^2}{dt} \rightarrow \infty \quad \text{as } dt \rightarrow 0 \tag{8.5}$$

In other words $B(t)$ is not differentiable (see also below), but nevertheless everywhere continuous.

The fourth condition of the increments of a Brownian motion process is frequently referred to as the Markov property. This reflects a kind of lack of memory, since it means that the past history of the process does not influence its future position. To require independent increments is, however, more restrictive than to require that the 'future' state only depends on the present state, which is the true Markov property.

There are other special features of a Brownian process. For example, let the capital stock $K(t)$ follow a Brownian motion, i.e. $E[dK] = 0$ and $E(dK^2) = \sigma_K^2 dt$, where σ_K^2 is the variance of the increments in the capital stock. Let the production function be $Y = F[t, K(t)]$. Estimating dY at (t, K) for changes dt and dK by a second-order Taylor expansion yields

$$dY = \frac{\partial F}{\partial t} dt + \frac{\partial F}{\partial K} dK + \frac{1}{2}\left[\frac{\partial^2 F}{\partial t^2}(dt)^2 + 2\frac{\partial^2 F}{\partial t \partial K} dt dK + \frac{\partial^2 F}{\partial K^2}(dK)^2\right] \tag{8.6}$$

Since $K(t)$ is stochastic so is Y, and the differential dY therefore makes sense in terms of moments or distributions. Taking expectations of (8.6) conditional on $K(t) = k$ gives

$$E\{dY \mid K(t) = k\} = \frac{\partial F(t,k)}{\partial t} dt + \frac{1}{2}\frac{\partial^2 F(t,k)}{\partial K^2}\sigma_K^2 dt + O(dt) \tag{8.7}$$

The first second-order derivative within brackets in (8.6) is merged in the term $O(dt)$, while the second vanishes because $E(dK) = 0$. The third term within brackets, which contains the second derivative of the production function times the variance of dK, surfaces since $E[dK^2]$ is of order dt rather than $(dt)^2$. Therefore, the expected change in production over the short interval dt consists of two terms. The first can be interpreted as technological progress, and the second measures the effect from an additional unit of capital on the marginal product of capital, which is scaled by $E[dK^2] = \sigma_K^2 dt$. This term is presumably non-positive since production functions are usually assumed to be strictly concave. The interpretation is that the uncertainty of K is greater the longer the time horizon, so the expected value of a change in a strictly concave function is reduced by an amount that increases with time (a consequence of Jensen's inequality $E[f(x)] >(<) f(E(x))$ for a strictly concave (convex) function).

Clearly, Brownian motion induces a new calculus (the Ito calculus after the inventor, see Ito, 1944) in which it symbolically writes

$$E[dY] = \frac{\partial F}{\partial t} dt + \frac{\partial F}{\partial K} dK + \frac{1}{2} \frac{\partial^2 F}{\partial K^2} \sigma_K^2 dt + O(dt) \qquad (8.8)$$

where $\lim_{dt \to 0} O(dt) / dt = 0$.

Equation (8.8), as a measure of the first-order differential of a function which contains a stochastic variable following a Brownian motion process, is frequently referred to as Ito's lemma.

We can be more exact about the stochastic process by specifying the following general Brownian motion process:

$$dK = a(K, t)dt + b(K, t)dz \qquad (8.9)$$

Here $a(K, t)$ and $b(K, t)$ are known non-random functions, which are usually referred to as the drift and variance components of the process; dz is the increment of the process, and it holds that $E[dz] = 0$ and $E[dz^2] = dt$. This means that dz can be represented by $dz = \varepsilon \sqrt{dt}$ where $\varepsilon \sim N(0, 1)$. Substitution of (8.9) into (8.8) now gives

$$dY = \left[\frac{\partial F}{\partial t} + a(K,t) \frac{\partial F}{\partial K} + \frac{1}{2} b^2(K,t) \frac{\partial^2 F}{\partial K^2} \right] dt + b(K,t) \frac{\partial F}{\partial K} dz + O(dt) \quad (8.10)$$

Note that

$$dK^2 = a^2 dt^2 + 2ab\,dt\,dz + b^2 dz^2 = b^2 dz^2 + O(dt) = b^2 dt + O(dt) \qquad (8.11)$$

since $dt\,dz = \varepsilon\, dt^{3/2} \propto dt^{3/2}$, and $dz^2 = \varepsilon^2 dt \propto dt$ (the sign $\propto$ means 'proportional to').

To introduce a more specific example, let $Y = \log K$, and let dK follow a Brownian motion of the following shape:[1]

$$dK = \alpha K dt + \sigma K dz \qquad (8.12)$$

We now have

$$\frac{\partial F}{\partial t} = 0, \quad \frac{\partial F}{\partial K} = \frac{1}{K} \quad \text{and} \quad \frac{\partial^2 F}{\partial K^2} = -\frac{1}{K^2}$$

Moreover, $a(K, t) = \alpha K$ and $b(K, t) = \sigma K$, which substituted into (8.10) yields:[2]

$$dY = \left(\alpha - \frac{\sigma^2}{2}\right)dt + \sigma dz \qquad (8.13)$$

This means that over any finite interval ΔT, the change in log K is normally distributed with mean $(\alpha - \sigma^2/2)\,\Delta T$ and variance $\sigma^2 \Delta T$. Again, the reason why the expected value of the change in production grows slower than the drift in the capital accumulation equation is the strict concavity of the production function, and Jensen's inequality.

8.2   A CONTINUOUS-TIME STOCHASTIC RAMSEY MODEL

We are now ready to move towards a continuous-time optimal growth problem under uncertainty. The early contributions in this area confined themselves to linear technologies. Phelps (1962), and, later, Levhari and Srinivasan (1969), Hahn (1970), and Leland (1968), for example, examined the optimal consumption saving decision under uncertainty with a given linear production technology. In two seminal papers, Mirrlees (1965, 1971) treated the stochastic Ramsey problem in a continuous-time neoclassical one-sector model, subject to uncertainty about technological progress. Mirman (1973) and Brock and Mirman (1972) worked with the corresponding problem in a discrete-time context. They proved, among other things, the existence, uniqueness and stability of a steady state (asymptotic) distribution.

The analysis below relies heavily on a paper by Merton (1975), where he treats the asymptotic properties of both the neoclassical model of growth developed by Solow (1957), and the Ramsey optimal growth model (Ramsey, 1928), when the growth of the labour force follows a geometric Brownian motion process. We shall concentrate on welfare measurement and in particular examine the relationship between the welfare measures following from stochastic and deterministic optimal growth problems.

Let $F(K, L)$ be a linear homogeneous net production function (i.e. depreciation has been accounted for), where K denotes units of capital input and L denotes units of labour input. To simplify the analysis, we depart from the deterministic Ramsey models of previous chapters by assuming that a fraction, s, of net output is invested at each point in time. This means that the capital stock evolves according to

$$\dot{K} = s\, F(K,\, L) \qquad (8.14)$$

where $0 < s < 1$. Let $k = K/L$ and differentiate totally with respect to time. It follows that

$$\dot{k} = s\, f(k) - nk \qquad (8.15)$$

where $f(k)$ is net output per capita and n is population growth. It is assumed that $L(t) = L(0)e^{nt}$, $L(0) > 0$, $0 < n < 1$. Equation (8.15) is the Solow neoclassical differential equation of capital stock growth under certainty. Note that $dL\,/\,dt = nL$ or $dL = nLdt$.

In all previous chapters except Chapter 6 we neglected the possibility of population growth, since it was not essential to the analysis under perfect certainty. Now, suppose that the growth of the labour force is described by the stochastic differential equation

$$dL = nLdt + \sigma Ldz \qquad (8.16)$$

The stochastic part is dz, where $z = z(t)$ is a Brownian motion process defined on some probability space. This means that the increments of the process, dz, are independent random variables with mean zero and variance $\sigma^2(t - s)$, $t \geq s$. They are sometimes referred to as white noise. In particular we have seen that $z(t)$, $t \geq 0$ (the sample path) is nowhere differentiable, which induces a well known problem of the integration of the differential equation (8.16).[3,4] The drift of the process is governed by the expected rate of labour growth per unit of time, n. In other words, over a short interval of time, dt, the proportionate change of the labour force (dL/L) is normally distributed with mean ndt and variance σ^2dt.

We are now ready to transform the uncertainty about the growth of the labour force to uncertainty about the growth of the capital–labour ratio $k = K/L$. We shall make use of Ito's lemma or, more particularly, Equation (8.8) above. To this end define

$$k(t) = \frac{K(t)}{L} = G(L, t) \qquad (8.17)$$

From Equation (8.8) we know that

$$dk = \frac{\partial G}{\partial t}\, dt + \frac{\partial G}{\partial L}\, dL + \frac{1}{2}\frac{\partial^2 G}{\partial L^2}\, dL^2 \qquad (8.18)$$

By noting that

$$\frac{\partial G}{\partial t} = \dot{k} = sf(k) \quad dL = nLdt + \sigma Ldz$$

$$\frac{\partial G}{\partial L} = -\frac{K(t)}{L^2} = -\frac{k}{L} \quad (dL)^2 = \sigma^2 L^2 dt \qquad (8.19)$$

$$\frac{\partial^2 G}{\partial L^2} = 2\frac{K(t)}{L^3} = \frac{2k}{L^2}$$

we obtain after substitutions into (8.18)

$$dk = [sf(k) - (n - \sigma^2)k]dt - k\sigma dz \qquad (8.20)$$

In other words, we have translated uncertainty with respect to labour into uncertainty with respect to capital per unit of labour, and indirectly to uncertainty with respect to output per unit of labour.

We are now ready to formulate Merton's version of the stochastic Ramsey problem. Let $u(c)$ be a twice continuously differentiable and strictly concave utility function, where c denotes per capita consumption. The optimization problem is then to find an optimal saving policy function $s^0(k, t)$ such that we have

$$\max E_0\left\{\int_0^\infty u(c(t))e^{-\theta t}dt\right\} \qquad (8.21)$$

subject to

$$dk = [sf(k) - (n - \sigma^2)k]dt - \sigma kdz; \qquad k(0) = k_0 \qquad (8.22)$$

and $k(t) \geqq 0$ for each t with probability one. E_0 denotes that expectations are taken conditional on the information available at time zero. The only non-autonomous time dependence in the above problem is introduced through the discount factor. As we are about to see below, the absence of such time dependence will simplify the analysis. However, we have seen in previous chapters that a more fundamental time dependence, generated by, for example, technological progress or externalities, adds extra complications to welfare measurements. For this reason, we shall need a general formulation of the first-order conditions for maximum. Readers not interested in the mathematical technicalities below can move directly to Section 8.3, where we discuss welfare measurement, as well as compare the deterministic and the stochastic first-order conditions.

The optimization problem can be formulated in terms of an optimal saving policy $s^*(k, t)$. To this end we note that $c = (1 - s)f(k)$, and that the maximization of (8.21) subject to (8.22) can be analysed in the following manner: Define

$$J(k(t),t) = \underset{s}{\text{Max}}\, E_t \int_t^\infty u[(1-s)f(k)]e^{-\theta\tau}d\tau$$

$$= \underset{s}{\max}\, E_t \int_t^{t+\Delta t} u[k,s]e^{-\theta\tau}d\tau + \underset{s}{\max}\, E_{t+\Delta t} \int_{t+\Delta t}^\infty u(k,s)e^{-\theta\tau}d\tau$$

$$= \underset{s}{\max}\, E_t\left[\int_t^{t+\Delta t} u[k,s]e^{-\theta\tau}d\tau + J(k(t+\Delta t), t+\Delta t)\right]$$

$$= \underset{s}{\max}\, E_t[u(k(t), s(t))e^{-\theta t}\Delta t + J(k(t),t) +$$

$$J_k(k(t),t)\Delta k + J_t(k(t),t)\Delta t + \frac{1}{2}J_{kk}(k(t),t)(\Delta k)^2$$

$$+ J_{kt}(k(t),t)\Delta k\Delta t + \frac{1}{2}J_{tt}(k(t),t)\Delta t^2 + O(\Delta t)] \tag{8.23}$$

The first equality in (8.23) follows from Bellman's principle of optimality – 'every part of the optimal path must be optimal'. The second equality is a consequence of the definition of a value function, and, finally, the third equality follows from the Taylor expansion of the value function, which means that we have assumed that $J(\cdot)$ has continuous partial derivatives of all orders less than three. If Equation (8.22) is approximated by

$$\Delta k = [sf(k) - (n - \sigma^2)k]\Delta t - \sigma k\Delta z + O(\Delta t)$$
$$= h(k, s; \sigma, n)\Delta t - \sigma k\Delta z + O(\Delta t) \tag{8.22a}$$

we can substitute for Δk in (8.23), and use the multiplication rules for Ito calculus – in particular $(\Delta z)^2 = \Delta t$ – to obtain the first-order differential as

$$\text{Max } E_t \left[u(k,s)e^{-\theta t} + J_k h + J_t + \frac{1}{2} J_{kk} \sigma^2 k^2 \right] \Delta t$$

$$+ J_k \sigma \Delta z + O(\Delta t) = 0 \qquad (8.24)$$

Note that the value function at time t appears on both sides of Equation (8.23), so netting out creates the zero in the right-hand member of Equation (8.24). Taking expectations, dividing both sides by Δt, and taking the limit as $\Delta t \to 0$ one obtains

$$0 = \max_s \left[u(k(t),s(t))e^{-\theta t} + J_t + J_k h + \frac{1}{2} J_{kk} \sigma^2 k^2 \right] \qquad (8.25)$$

This equation is known as the Hamilton–Jacobi–Bellman equation of stochastic control theory, and it is usually written as[5]

$$-J_t = \max_s \left[u(k,s)e^{-\theta t} + J_k h + \frac{1}{2} J_{kk} \sigma^2 k^2 \right] \qquad (8.25a)$$

Equation (8.25a) is a partial differential equation. Given an optimal saving policy, $s^*(k, t)$, it is a function of both k and t. If certain growth conditions are satisfied it usually also has a boundary (transversality) condition

$$\lim_{t \to \infty} E_0 \{ J(k(t),t) \} = 0 \qquad (8.26)$$

8.3   WELFARE MEASUREMENT

After a great many preliminaries we are finally ready to perform the welfare analysis. The only non-autonomous time dependence in the above problem is introduced through the discount factor, which means that the model discussed here is a stochastic analogue to the model in Chapter 3, where welfare was appropriately measured by the utility value of the net national product. Following Aronsson and Löfgren (1995a) we shall show that similar results can be derived using the present model, which contains uncertainty from the point of view of the social planner. Our starting point will be the function

$$J(k(t),t) = \underset{s}{\text{Max}}\, E_t\left\{\int_t^\infty u[(1-s)f(k)]e^{-\theta\tau}d\tau\right\} \qquad (8.27)$$

subject to Equation (8.22), which is the Brownian motion equation for the capital stock, and $k(0) = k_0$. We now have

$$e^{\theta t}J(k(t),t) = \underset{s}{\text{Max}}\, E_t\left\{\int_t^\infty u[(1-s)f(k)]e^{-\theta(\tau-t)}d\tau\right\} \qquad (8.28)$$

$$= \underset{s}{\text{Max}}\, E_0 \int_0^\infty u(\cdot)e^{-\theta y}dy = W(k(0)) \qquad (8.29)$$

where $y = \tau - t$ and $W(k(0))$, which is the value function of time zero, is independent of t. This means that

$$J_t = \frac{d}{dt}\left[e^{-\theta t}W\right] = -\theta e^{-\theta t}W$$

and, in particular, that the Hamilton–Jacobi–Bellman equation can be written

$$\theta W = \underset{s}{\text{Max}}\left[u[(1-s)f(k)] + W_k h(k,s;\sigma,n) + \frac{1}{2}\sigma^2 k^2 W_{kk}\right] \qquad (8.30)$$

where $h(\cdot) = sf(k) - (n - \sigma^2)k$, $W_k = \partial W(\cdot)/\partial k$ and $W_{kk} = \partial^2 W(\cdot)/\partial k^2$. We can now define a costate variable $p(t)$ as

$$p(t) = W_k(k(t)) \qquad (8.31a)$$

and its derivative

$$\frac{\partial p(t)}{\partial k} = W_{kk}(k(t)) \qquad (8.31b)$$

Suppose that there exists a saving function $s^* = s^*(k, p, \partial p/\partial k)$, which solves the maximization problem. Given the optimal saving policy, (8.30) becomes

$$\theta W(k(t)) = u(k, s^*) + ph(k, s^*; n, \sigma) + \frac{1}{2} \frac{\partial p}{\partial k} \sigma^2 k^2 = \mathcal{H}^*\left(k, p, \frac{\partial p}{\partial k}\right) \quad (8.32)$$

The term $\mathcal{H}^*(\cdot)$ can be interpreted as a 'generalized' Hamiltonian in current value terms (see below). This generalized Hamiltonian will play a key role in the welfare measure we are about to derive. However, prior to the welfare analysis, and in order to relate the results in this chapter to those in Chapter 3, we shall derive the conditions describing how the variables k and p develop over time. Using (8.20) and the definition of $\mathcal{H}^*$, we obtain

$$dk = h(k, s^*; n, \sigma)dt + \sigma k dz = \left[\mathcal{H}^*_p\left(k, p, \frac{\partial p}{\partial k}\right)\right]dt + \sigma k dz = \mathcal{H}^*_p dt + \sigma k dz \quad (8.33)$$

where $\mathcal{H}^*_p = \partial \mathcal{H}^* / \partial p$. Equation (8.33) describes how k develops over time under the optimal saving policy. To find the corresponding condition for p, we use Ito's lemma and derive

$$d\bar{p} = \left[J_{kt} + J_{kk}h + \frac{1}{2}J_{kkk}\sigma^2 k^2\right]dt + J_{kk}\sigma k dz \quad (8.34)$$

where $\bar{p}(t) = p(t)e^{-\theta t}$. As in the case of perfect certainty, it is often convenient to relate $d\bar{p}$ to derivatives of 'the Hamiltonian'. Using the expression $-J_t = \mathcal{H}^* e^{-\theta t} = \theta W e^{-\theta t}$ to compute J_{kt}, we can rewrite (8.34) to read

$$d\bar{p} = -\mathcal{H}^*_k e^{-\theta t}dt + \sigma k e^{-\theta t}W_{kk}dz \quad (8.35)$$

where $\mathcal{H}^*_k = \partial \mathcal{H}^* / \partial k$. Finally, since $d\bar{p} = (dp - \theta p dt)e^{-\theta t}$, (8.35) is easily transformed to current value terms, i.e.

$$dp - \theta p dt = -\mathcal{H}^*_k dt + \sigma k W_{kk}dz \quad (8.36)$$

Let us now interpret Equations (8.32), (8.33) and (8.36) as well as relating them to their counterparts under certainty. First, Equation (8.32) clearly implies that the generalized Hamiltonian in current value terms equals interest on the expected future utility. This means that (8.32) is the welfare measure we are looking for. Using the definition of $W(\cdot)$ from (8.27)–(8.29) and substituting into (8.32), the analogue of the welfare measure in Chapter 3 becomes

$$\theta E_t\left\{\int_t^\infty u\!\left(k,s^*\right)e^{-\theta(\tau-t)}d\tau\right\} = \mathcal{H}^*\!\left(k,p,\frac{\partial p}{\partial k}\right) = u(\cdot) + ph + \frac{1}{2}\frac{\partial p}{\partial k}\sigma^2 k^2 \quad (8.32a)$$

The interpretation of the generalized Hamiltonian is that it is the sum of the instantaneous utility, the expected infinitesimal increment of capital valued at its marginal expected current value, plus the valuation of the risk associated with a given investment. If the individual is risk averse (loving), $\partial p/\partial k = W_{kk}$ is negative (positive). Loosely speaking, welfare is lower (higher) under uncertainty than under certainty. The stochastic differential equation (8.33) tells us how capital evolves over time along the optimal path, and Equation (8.36) is the corresponding stochastic differential equation for the development of the costate variable over time.

In the deterministic case $\sigma = 0$ and

$$\mathcal{H}^* = u\!\left(k,s^*\right) + ph\!\left(k,s^*;0,n\right) = \theta\int_t^\infty u(\cdot)e^{-\theta(s-t)}ds \quad (8.37)$$

which is the welfare measure corresponding to the deterministic Ramsey problem in Chapter 3. Moreover, since the white noise is eliminated from the equations for dk and dp, the time derivates dk/dt and dp/dt are well defined. Hence we have

$$\frac{dk}{dt} = h\!\left(k,s^*;0,n\right) = sf(k) - nk$$

$$\frac{dp}{dt} - \theta p = -\frac{\partial\mathcal{H}^*}{\partial k}$$

which are dynamic equations of the deterministic Ramsey problem corresponding to Equations (3.2) and (3.4b) in Chapter 3.

As a final part of the analysis, consider the case of non-attributable technological progress, such that time becomes a separate argument in the production function. Following the analysis in Chapter 4, this means that the per capita production function can be written $f(k, t)$, where $\partial f(\cdot)/\partial t$ measures the influence on output from non-attributable technological progress. Using this production function, the present value function is written

$$J(k(t),t) = \underset{s}{\text{Max}}\, E_t\left[\int_t^\infty u\big[(1-s)f(k,\tau)\big]e^{-\theta\tau}d\tau\right] \tag{8.38}$$

subject to

$$dk = [sf(k,t) - (n - \sigma^2)k]dt - \sigma kdz, \qquad k(0) = k_0 \tag{8.39}$$

and $k(t) \geq 0$. Now, define the current value function

$$W(k(t),\, t) = e^{\theta t}\, J(k(t),\, t) \tag{8.40}$$

Since $J_t = [-\theta W + W_t]\, e^{-\theta t}$, where $W_t = \partial W / \partial t$, we can write the Hamilton–Jacobi–Bellman equation as

$$\theta W - W_t = \underset{s}{\text{Max}}\left[u\big[(1-s)f(k,t)\big] + W_k h(k,s,t;\sigma,n) + \frac{1}{2}W_{kk}\sigma^2 k^2\right] \tag{8.41}$$

Let $s^*(k,t)$ be the optimal saving policy. Substituting it into (8.41) gives the welfare measure

$$\mathcal{H}^*\left(k, p, \frac{\partial p}{\partial k}, t\right) + W_t^* = \theta W^* \tag{8.42}$$

where

$$\mathcal{H}^* = u(\cdot) + ph + \frac{1}{2}\frac{\partial p}{\partial k}\sigma^2 k^2$$

evaluated along the optimal path and p has the same interpretation as previously. The interpretation of Equation (8.42) is that the expected future utility, W^*, is proportional to the sum of the generalized Hamiltonian, $\mathcal{H}^*$, and the expected present value of the marginal technological progress, W_t^*. The result derived in Chapter 4 follows as the special case when $\sigma \to 0$.

8.4   SUMMARY AND CONCLUDING COMMENTS

We have shown how the Hamilton–Jacobi–Bellman equation from stochastic control theory can be used to derive the appropriate welfare measure under uncertainty, which turns out to be analogous to its deterministic counterpart. A generalized Hamiltonian is directly proportional to the expected future utility along the optimal path. Not surprisingly, but neatly, the stochastic welfare measure collapses to the corresponding deterministic measure, when $\sigma \to 0$.[6]

The main part of the analysis is based on the assumption that a non-autonomous time dependence enters only through the discount factor. In the more general case with non-attributable technological progress or externalities, treated in Löfgren (1992), and Aronsson and Löfgren (1993, 1995a) for the deterministic case, the situation is only slightly more complex. The generalized Hamiltonian will be augmented with an extra component measuring the expected present value of marginal technological progress along the optimal path.

The welfare analysis can also be related to a competitive equilibrium under uncertainty. Here it is worth mentioning the pioneering work by Lucas and Prescott (1971), who considered the rational expectations equilibrium of investment in a competitive industry using a discrete-time Markov chain model. They established the optimality of the equilibrium. Moreover, as has been shown by Brock and Magill (1979), the idea of a *competitive path* introduced by Magill (1977) generalizes in a natural way to a *competitive process* in the case of uncertainty. They also show that a competitive process, under suitable regularity conditions, maximizes objective functions of the above type. Hence, there is a potentially exploitable theoretical connection between the stochastic welfare measure and data generated by a *market process*. To move from this to a practical application in national accounting is, of course, a big leap, and the fact that uncertainty introduces an extra cost under risk aversion is something we can say without introducing Ito-calculus. Nevertheless, stochastic tools are getting more and more common in economic analyses and it is worthwhile learning about these tools.

We have, of course, only given a narrow, but we hope self-contained, presentation of the modern stochastic methods in economics and finance. There are many interesting topics remaining to be covered. A statistician or even an economist would at times be interested in answering a question of the following type: If the capital stock $k(t)$ follows a particular stochastic process, say a Brownian motion, and its current value is k_0, what is the probability that the capital stock would be in a certain range at some later time t? To answer such a question we need a description of how the probability distribution of the capital stock evolves over time. In particular, one would be interested in deriving a steady state or equilibrium distribution of the capital stock, which would, through utility, production and saving functions enable us to calculate the moments of essentially all relevant entities of the growth problem. This turns out to be a rather difficult task. The existence problem of a stationary distribution for a stochastic differential equation has been solved in the mathematical literature for special cases. The particular model used in this chapter was analysed in this respect by Merton (1975). He showed that the stationary distribution for the capital stock is, in general, not unique, but for a Cobb–Douglas production function the existence problem can be solved by asking which constant saving function is optimal.

Today, there exist many textbook presentations of Ito calculus and stochastic control theory which are accessible to non-mathematicians. We would like to recommend the recent book by Dixit and Pindyck (1994) as a starter. Essentially the same material from a strict finance perspective is available at a more advanced level in Duffie (1992). Malliaris and Brock (1991) is a good survey of the whole field, starting with measure theory, and including Ito calculus, stochastic control, and ending with applications in economics and finance.

NOTES

1. Samuelson (1965) called this specific process geometric Brownian motion with drift.
2. Terms of magnitude $O(dt)$ are ignored in Equation (8.13).
3. Since $dz = \varepsilon\sqrt{(dt)}$ we have

$$\frac{dz}{dt} = \frac{\varepsilon}{2} dt^{-\frac{1}{2}} \text{ and } \lim_{dt \to 0} \frac{\varepsilon}{2} dt^{-\frac{1}{2}} = +\infty \text{ for } \varepsilon > 0,$$

    we cannot write (8.16) as a derivative.
4. For more details the reader is referred to Malliaris and Brock (1991) and/or Åström (1970).
5. Note that also J_t is not a function of s since we have assumed that J is a value function, and hence that s is maximized out from the expression.
6. For an analysis of sustainability in a stochastic environment, the reader is referred to Asheim and Brekke (1993).

9. Afterwords

In previous chapters we have introduced an intertemporal framework for welfare measurement, cost–benefit analysis, sustainable development and economic growth. The analysis is based on an ingenious idea put forward by Weitzman (1976), that, in an intertemporal perfect market economy, the present value of future utility can be accurately measured by current market data. We have dealt with more general conditions than those covered by Weitzman, although the consequences of some of them were hinted at in his seminal paper.

The key findings are that technological progress and externalities complicate welfare measurement to an extent that cannot be ignored, and in their presence it is generally no longer possible to measure future welfare solely by looking at current market data. We show, however, that if externalities are handled by means of dynamic Pigouvian taxes, they can be appropriately accounted for in welfare measurement based on current market data. Technological progress in the spirit of modern growth theory is endogenous.Thus, for example, the spillovers from human capital treated in Chapter 5 are positive externalities, and their welfare consequences can, in theory, also be accounted for through Pigouvian subsidies. Simulations in a recent paper – see Aronsson et al.(1996) – indicate that even second-best taxes can considerably improve welfare under externalities, and the second-best information they contain may prove useful in attempts to approximate future wealth.

Technological progress which is exogenous in the strict sense that it cannot be controlled by economic measures is the real problem. To account appropriately for its welfare consequences one has to measure the present value of the marginal technological progress along the future growth path of the economy. Formally, one can always find a static equivalent of future welfare in this context by computing an annuity equivalent – a hypothetical constant utility level which, if preserved for ever, would yield the same present value as the utility along the future growth path.

The problem is that we cannot estimate the future pace of progress from current market data. We can, however, forecast future growth parameters, and Weitzman (1996) derives a simple formula to calculate by how much the static equivalent of future welfare is augmented by technological progress. The answer is obtained by guessing the future average growth rate of the economy, as well as the average future Solow residual. It turns out that the impact on future welfare from technological progress can, under reasonable estimates of the parameters, be considerable. This is, to some extent, well known from standard growth theory. Barro and Sala-I-Martin (1995) introduce a straightforward calculation showing that if the US growth rate had been 1 per cent higher from 1870 until today, GDP would have been three times as high as it is today. The important questions – whether development is sustainable, whether there is a non-declining consumption path, and whether indeed the future growth path is sustained – are not answered by knowledge of the size of the static equivalent of future utility.

Weitzman's recent paper and the paper by Nordhaus (1995) are formally about sustainability; unfortunately the chosen definition of sustainability – as a static equivalent of the present value of future utility – is unable to tell us whether future consumption goes to zero or not. As shown by Asheim (1994), and further clarified in Chapter 6 in this book, the value of the Hamiltonian at time t – whether augmented by including technological progress or not – is not an exact indicator of sustainability. The information contained in the value of net investment at time t plus the present value of future technological progress refer to whether the discounted average future value of the change in consumption along the optimal path is positive or not. This can be seen from Proposition 6.1. The reader is also referred to a recent paper by Hartwick and Long (1995). This paper treats constant consumption paths in a very general setting which includes technological progress. The conclusion is that the appropriate measure of income at time t is, at best, a static equivalent of future welfare, but it is not an indicator of whether or not the present consumption level can be, or will be, sustained.

Some of the complications which are created by open economies and trade are dealt with in Chapter 7. However, we do not consider that this area is fully understood, despite the availability of several interesting results. The handling of uncertainties, which is the topic of Chapter 8, is still in its infancy.

The interesting question of whether and when the 'green NNP' concept, possibly augmented by an estimate of future technological progress, can be implemented in practice is largely unanswered. There have been some recent attempts to do so, of which the best known are Repetto et al. (1989) and Hultkrantz (1992). There are a number of ongoing projects aiming at 'green satellite' accounts in, for example, Sweden and the USA (see e.g. US Commerce Department, 1994).

One of the lessons from Weitzman's seminal paper is that all capital stocks – man-made, environmental, and human capital – should be treated in the same manner in welfare accounting. The future output from human capital is, today, standardly measured in the national accounts by the cost of the educational sector, and not by the net future income generated by the present investment in human capital. Jorgenson and Fraumeni (1992a) is a pioneering attempt to measure the output from the US educational sector. This study is replicated by Ahlroth et al. (1994) and Löfgren and Markland (1996) using Swedish data. The latter study presents an estimate of the net output from secondary and tertiary education in Sweden, which is about 2 per cent of GDP. This could lead one to infer, that, roughly speaking, the net output from the Swedish educational system is very low. A more reasonable conclusion is that the positive externalities, which are not measured in either of the studies, are of considerable importance, in the same way as technological progress. The numerical computations in Chapter 5 support this idea.

Time dependent discount factors like those in Chapter 7 create, under certain conditions, time inconsistency problems, i.e. when one recalculates the optimal solution after some period of time has elapsed, the original path will no longer be optimal. This may have important intergenerational consequences. Say that society consists of two types of individuals: one with a positive discount factor (utilitarian), and a second who does not discount the future (conservationist), but both having the same within-period utility functions. Moreover, assume that society at time zero maximizes a weighted sum of the utility of the two types of individuals. Regardless of the weight given to the utilitarians, their influence will disappear as time goes to infinity, since their discount factor goes to zero, and the conservationists will dominate the objective function. It is, therefore, conceivable that the economy, if it is possible to make a commitment to the open loop solution, will asymptotically approach the green golden rule.

However, if at a point in time along the growth path the solution is recalculated with the utilitarians being given the same weight as at time zero, the new solution will certainly differ from the original one; and we shall have a time inconsistency. This particular time inconsistency means that, if a new plan is made every year, the solution will eventually approach a steady state which is less conservationist than the green golden rule. Consumption may approach zero rather than a positive sustainable level. More details on this particular example are available in Li and Löfgren (1996).

The treatment of greenhouse gases in Chapter 7 is also incomplete, in the sense that it is more natural to approach the global warming problem from a game theoretical perspective, where each country participates in, say, an n country Nash game. The interested reader is referred to papers by Mäler (1991) and Tahvonen (1994, 1995), where such games are analysed. The concept of sustainability also has an international dimension. To what extent is it meaningful to approach sustainability in a regional rather than a global setting? Given that the global context is the more reasonable one, we must explicitly acknowledge the fact that many countries with conflicting objectives are involved. The implementation problem will certainly become much more difficult, and it will, as usual, contain political as well as economic aspects.

The importance of firm behaviour is also underdeveloped in an analysis which deals with principles rather than details. However, to adhere to one market form – perfect competition – throughout the book is perhaps to become too much of a slave to principle. However, this is the way things are usually done within the economics profession.

The crux of the matter is that although by writing this book we may have contributed to the clarification of certain aspects of welfare measurement in a dynamic setting, and even deepened understanding of the intricacies of sustainable development, we have a strong feeling that the number of new questions which have surfaced during the journey far exceeds those we have been able to answer.

References

Ahlroth, S., A. Björklund and A. Forslund (1994), 'The Output of the Swedish Education Sector', *Working paper* no. 43, The Economic Council, Stockholm.

Åkerman, J., F.R. Johnson and L. Bergman (1991), 'Paying for Safety: Voluntary Reduction of Residential Radon Risks', *Land Economics*, **67**, 435–46.

Aronsson, T., K. Backlund and K.G. Löfgren (1996), 'Nuclear Power, Externalities and Pigouvian Taxes – A Dynamic Analysis under Uncertainty', Department of Economics, *Umeå Economic Studies* no. 399, University of Umeå.

Aronsson, T., P.O. Johansson and K.G. Löfgren (1994), 'Welfare Measurement and the Health Environment', *Annals of Operations Research*, **54**, 203–15.

Aronsson, T., P.O. Johansson and K.G. Löfgren (1995), 'Investment Decisions, Future Consumption and Sustainability under Optimal Growth', *Working Paper Series in Economics and Finance* no. 49, Stockholm School of Economics.

Aronsson, T. and K.G. Löfgren (1993), 'Welfare Consequences of Technological and Environmental Externalities in the Ramsey Growth Model', *Natural Resource Modeling*, **7**(1), 1–14.

Aronsson, T. and K.G. Löfgren (1995a), 'National Product Related Welfare Measures in the Presence of Technological Change, Externalities and Uncertainty', *Environmental and Resource Economics*, **5**, 321–32.

Aronsson, T. and K.G. Löfgren (1995b), 'Social Accounting and Welfare Measurement in a Growth Model with Human Capital', *The Scandinavian Journal of Economics* (forthcoming).

Asheim, G.B. (1994a), 'Net National Product as an Indicator of Sustainability', *The Scandinavian Journal of Economics*, **96**, 257–65.

Asheim, G.B. (1994b), 'Capital Gains and "Net National Product" in Open Economies', mimeo, Department of Economics, University of Oslo.

Asheim, G.B. (1995), 'The Weitzman Foundation of NNP with Non-Constant Interest Rates', mimeo, Department of Economics, University of Oslo.

Asheim, G.B. and K.A. Brekke (1993), 'Sustainability when Resource Management has Stochastic Consequences', mimeo, The Norwegian School of Economics and Business Administration, Bergen.

Åström, K. (1970), *Introduction to Stochastic Control Theory*, New York: Academic Press.

Bachelier, L. (1900), 'Théorie de la Spéculation', *Annales de l'École Normale Supérieure*, **17**, 21–86. Translated in P.H. Cootner, (ed.) (1964), *The Random Character of Stock Market Prices*, Cambridge, Mass.: MIT Press.

Backlund, K., B. Kriström, K.G. Löfgren and E. Polbring (1995), 'Global Warming and Dynamic Cost–Benefit Analysis under Uncertainty', Department of Economics, *Umeå Economic Studies* no. 395, University of Umeå.

Barro, R.J. and X. Sala-I-Martin (1995), *Economic Growth*, New York: McGraw-Hill.

Becker, G.S. (1964), *Human Capital*, New York: Columbia University Press; 2nd ed. 1975.

Blanchard, O.J. and S. Fisher (1989), *Lectures on Macroeconomics*, Cambridge, Mass.: MIT Press.

Blinder, A.S. and Y. Weiss (1976), 'Human Capital and Labor Supply: A Synthesis', *Journal of Political Economy*, **84**, 449–72.

Blomquist, G. (1979), 'Value of Life Savings: Implications of Consumption Activity', *Journal of Political Economy*, **87**, 540–58.

Brock, W.A. (1977), 'A Polluted Golden Age', in V.L. Smith (ed.), *Economics of Natural and Environmental Resources*, New York: Gordon and Breach.

Brock, W.A. and M.J.P. Magill (1979), 'Dynamics under Uncertainty', *Econometrica*, **47**, 843–68.

Brock, W.A. and L. Mirman (1972), 'Optimal Economic Growth under Uncertainty: The Discounted Case', *Journal of Economic Theory*, **4**, 479–513.

Browning, M., A. Deaton and M. Irish (1985), 'A Profitable Approach to Labor supply and Commodity Demand over the Life-cycle', *Econometrica*, **53**, 503–43.

Caputo, M.R. (1989), 'The Qualitative Content of Renewable Resource Models', *Natural Resource Modeling*, **3**(2), 241–59.

Caputo, M.R. (1990a), 'Comparative Dynamics via Envelope Methods in Variational Calculus', *Review of Economic Studies*, **57**, 689–97.

Caputo, M.R. (1990b), 'How to do Comparative Dynamics on the Back of an Envelope in Optimal Control Theory', *Journal of Economic Dynamics and Control*, **14**, 655–83.

Cass, D. and T. Mitra (1991), 'Indefinitely Sustained Consumption Despite Exhaustible Natural Resources', *Economic Theory*, **1**, 119–46.

Chamley, C. (1993), 'Externalities and Dynamics in Models of "Learning by Doing"', *International Economic Review*, **34**, 583–609.

Chichilnisky, G. (1993), 'What is Sustainable Development?' *Stanford Institute of Theoretical Economics* (mimeo).

Clarke, F.H. (1983), *Optimization and Nonsmooth Analysis*, Philadelphia, Pa: SIAM.

Conrad, K. (1992), 'Comment on D.W. Jorgenson and B.M. Fraumeni "Investment in Education and U.S. Economic Growth"', *The Scandinavian Journal of Economics*, **94**, Supplement, 71–4.

Daly, H. (1984), 'Alternative Strategies for Integrating Economics and Ecology', in A. M. Jansson, *Integration of Economy and Ecology: An Outlook for the Eighties*, Proceedings from the Wallenberg Symposium, Stockholm, 1982.

Daly, H. (1992), 'Allocation, Distribution and Scale: Towards an Economics that is Efficient, Just and Sustainable', *Ecological Economics*, **6**, 185–94.

Dardis, R. (1980), 'The Value of a Life: New Evidence from the Marketplace', *American Economic Review*, **70**, 1077–1082.

Dasgupta, P. and G. M. Heal (1974), 'The Optimal Depletion of Exhaustible Resources', *Review of Economic Studies*, symposium issue.

Dasgupta, P. and G.M. Heal (1979), *The Economics of Exhaustible Resources*, Cambridge Economic Handbooks, Cambridge.

Dasgupta, P., B. Kriström and K.G. Mäler (1995), 'Current Issues in Resource Accounting', in P.O. Johansson, B. Kriström and K.G. Mäler (eds), *Current Issues in Environmental Economics*, Manchester: Manchester University Press.

Dasgupta, P. and K.G. Mäler (1991), 'The Environment and Emerging Development Issues', *Beijer Reprint Series*, no. 1, The Royal Swedish Academy of Science.

Dasgupta, S. and T. Mitra (1983), 'Intergenerational Equity and Efficient Allocation of Exhaustible Resources', *International Economic Review*, **24**, 133–53.

Dixit, A., P. Hammond and M. Hoel (1980), 'On Hartwick's Rule for Regular Maximin Paths of Capital Accumulation', *Review of Economic Studies*, **47**, 551–6.

Dixit, A. and R.S. Pindyck (1994), *Investment under Uncertainty*, Princeton, NJ: Princeton University Press.

Duffie, D. (1992), *Dynamic Asset Pricing Theory*, Princeton, NJ: Princeton University Press.

Ehrlich, P.R. and A. Ehrlich (1992), 'The Value of Biodiversity', *Ambio*, **21**, 219–26.

Einstein, A. (1956), *Investigations on the Theory of Brownian Motion*, New York: Dover (contains Einstein's papers on Brownian motion).

Fisher, I. (1906), *The Nature of Capital and Income*, New York: Macmillan.

Frisch, R. (1932), *New Methods of Measuring Marginal Utility*, Tübingen: J.C.B. Mohr.

Hahn, F.H. (1970), 'Savings under Uncertainty', *Review of Economic Studies*, **37**, 21–31.

Harcourt, G.C. and N.F. Laing (eds) (1971), *Capital and Growth*, Harmondsworth, Middlesex: Penguin.

Hartwick, J. (1977), 'Intergenerational Equity and the Investing of Rents from Exhaustible Resources', *American Economic Review*, **66**, 972–4.

Hartwick, J. (1990), 'Natural Resources, National Accounting and Economic Depreciation', *Journal of Public Economics*, **43**, 291–304.

Hartwick, J. (1992), 'Deforestation and National Accounting', *Environmental and Resource Economics*, **2**, 513–21.

Hartwick, J. (1994), 'National Wealth and Net National Product', *The Scandinavian Journal of Economics*, **96**(2), 253–6.

Hartwick, J. and N. van Long (1995), 'Constant Consumption and Economic Depreciation of Natural Capital: The Non-Autonomous Case', mimeo, Department of Economics, Queens University.

Heal, G. (1995), 'Lecture Notes on Sustainability', Memorandum from Department of Economics, University of Oslo, no. 16.

Herbertsson, T.T. (1994), 'Growth Accounting: An Alternative Approach', *Iceland Economic Papers* no. 25, Faculty of Economics and Business Administration, University of Iceland.

Hicks, J.R. (1939), *Value and Capital* (2nd ed.), Oxford: Clarendon Press.

Howarth, R.B. and R.B. Norgaard (1992), 'Economics of Sustainability or the Sustainability of Economics: Different Paradigms', *Ecological Economics*, **4**, 93–116.

Hulten, C. (1992), 'Accounting for the Wealth of Nations: The Net Versus Gross Output Controversy and its Ramifications', *Scandinavian Journal of Economics*, supplement, 9–24.

Hultkrantz, L. (1992), 'National Account of Timber and Forest Environmental Resources in Sweden', *Environmental and Resource Economics*, **2**, 283–305.

Ito, K. (1944), 'Stochastic Integral', Proceedings of the Imperial Academy, Tokyo, 20, 519–24.

Johansson, P.O. and K.G. Löfgren (1994), 'Comparative Dynamics in Health Economics: Some Useful Results', *Working Paper Series in Economics and Finance* no. 17, Stockholm School of Economics.

Jorgenson, D.W. and B.M. Fraumeni (1992a), 'Investment in Education and U.S. Economic Growth', *The Scandinavian Journal of Economics*, **94**, supplement, 51–70.

Jorgenson, D.W. and B.M. Fraumeni (1992b), *Investeringar i utbildning och ekonomisk tillväxt i U.S.A.*, Ekonomisa rådets årsbok.

Kemp, M.C. and N. van Long (1982), 'On the Evolution of Social Income in a Dynamic Economy: Variations on the Samuelsonian Theme' in G.R. Feiwel (ed.), *Samuelson and Neoclassical Economics*, Boston, Mass.: Kluwer–Nijhoff.

Koopmans, T.C. (1960), 'Stationary Ordinal Utility and Impatience', *Econometrica*, **28**, 287–309.

La France, J.T. and L.D. Barney (1991), 'The Envelope Theorem in Dynamic Optimization', *Journal of Economic Dynamics Control*, **15**, 355–85.

Leland, H.E. (1968), *Dynamic Portfolio Theory*, PhD dissertation, Department of Economics, Harvard University.

Leonard, D. and N. van Long (1992), *Optimal Control Theory and Static Optimization in Economics*, New York: Cambridge University Press.

Levhari, D. and T. N. Srinivasan (1969), 'Optimal Savings under Uncertainty', *Review of Economic Studies*, **36**, 153–63.

Li, C. and K.G. Löfgren (1996), 'Renewable Resources and Economic Sustainability: A Dynamic Analysis with Heterogeneous Time Preferences', mimeo, Department of Economics, University of Umeå.

Lindahl, E. (1933), 'The Concept of Income', in G. Bagge (ed.), *Economic Essays in Honor of Gustaf Cassel*, London: George Allen & Unwin.

Löfgren, K.G. (1992a), 'Comments on C.R. Hulten, "Accounting for the Wealth of Nations: The Net versus Gross Output Controversy and its Ramifications"', *The Scandinavian Journal of Economics*, **94**, supplement, 25–8.

Löfgren, K.G. (1992b), 'A Note on the Welfare Gains from Genetic Progress in Forestry: What can the Market Tell Us?', *Forest Science*, **38**, 479–83.

Löfgren, K.G. and P. Markland (1996), 'The Regional Output from Human Capital: Do Universities Matter?', mimeo, Department of Economics, University of Umeå.

Lucas, Jr, R. E. (1988), 'On the Mechanics of Economic Development', *Journal of Monetary Economics*, **22**, 3–42.

Lucas, R.E. and E.C. Prescott (1971), 'Investment under Uncertainty', *Econometrica*, **39**, 659–81.

Magill, M.J.P. (1977), 'Some New Results on the Local Stability of the Process of Capital Accumulation', *Journal of Economic Theory*, **15**, 174–210.

Mäler, K.G. (1991), 'National Accounts and Environmental Resources', *Environmental and Resource Economics*, **1**, 1–15.

Malliaris, A.G. and W.A. Brock (1991), *Stochastic Methods in Economics and Finance*, Amsterdam: North-Holland.

Merton, R. (1975), 'An Asymptotic Theory of Growth under Uncertainty', *Review of Economic Studies*, **42**, 375–93.

Michel, P. (1982), 'On the Transversality Condition in Infinite Horizon Optimal Control Problems', *Econometrica*, **50**, 975–85.

Mincer, J. (1974), *Schooling, Experience, and Earnings*, New York: Columbia University Press.

Mirman, L. (1973), 'Steady State Behavior of One Class of One Sector Growth Models with Uncertain Technology', *Journal of Economic Theory*, **6**, 219–42.

Mirrlees, J.A. (1965), 'Optimum Accumulation under Uncertainty', mimeo.

Mirrlees, J.A. (1971), *Optimum Growth and Uncertainty*, IEA-Workshop in Economic Theory, Bergen.

Nordhaus, W.D. (1993), 'Rolling the Dice: An Optimal Transition Path for Controlling Greenhouse Gases', *Resource and Energy Economics*, **15**, 27–50.

Nordhaus, W.D. (1995), 'How Should We Measure Sustainable Income?' *Cowles Foundation Working Paper*, Yale University.

Nordhaus, W.D. and J. Tobin (1972), 'Is Growth Obsolete?' in *Economic Growth*, New York: National Bureau of Economic Research.

Oniki, H. (1973), 'Comparative Dynamics in Optimal Control Theory', *Journal of Economic Theory*, **6**, 265–83.

Pezzey, J. (1995), 'Non-declining Wealth is not Equivalent to Sustainability', mimeo, Department of Economics, University College, London.

Pezzey, J. and C. Withagen (1995), 'Single-Peakedness and Initial Sustainability in Capital-Resource Economics', mimeo, Department of Economics, University College, London.

Phelps, E.S. (1961), 'Accumulation and the Golden Rule', *American Economic Review*, **51**, 638–43.

Phelps, E.S. (1962), 'The Accumulation of Risky Capital: A Sequential Utility Analysis', *Econometrica*, **30**, 729–43.

Radner, R. (1967), 'Efficient Prices for Infinite Horizon Production Programmes', *Review of Economic Studies*, **34**, 51–66.

Ramsey, F.P. (1928), 'A Mathematical Theory of Saving', *Economic Journal*, **38**, 543–59.

Rawls J. (1971), *A Theory of Justice*, Cambridge, Mass.: Harvard University Press.

Razin, A. (1972), 'Optimum Investment in Human Capital', *Review of Economic Studies*, **39**, 455–60.

Repetto, R., W. Magrath, M. Wells, C. Beer and F. Rossini (1989), *Wasting Assets: Natural Resources in the National Income Accounts*, Washington, DC: World Resources Institute.

Romer, P.M. (1986a), 'Increasing Returns and Long Run Growth', *Journal of Political Economy*, **94**, 1002–37.

Romer, P.M. (1986b), 'Cake Eating, Chattering, and Jumps: Existence Results for Variational problems', *Econometrica*, **54**(4), 897–908.

Romer, P.M. (1990), 'Endogenous Technical Change', *Journal of Political Economy*, **98**, 71–102.

Samuelson, P.A. (1961), 'The Evaluation of Social Income: Capital Formation and Wealth', in F. Lutz and R.C. Hague (eds), *The Theory of Capital*, Proceedings from the IEA Conference, New York: St Martin's Press.

Samuelson, P.A. (1965), 'Proof that Properly Anticipated Prices Fluctuate Randomly', *Industrial Management Review*, **6**, 41–9.

Schultz, T.W. (1961), 'Investment in Human Capital', *American Economic Review*, **51**, 1–17.

Seierstad, A. (1981), 'Derivatives and Subderivatives of the Optimal Value Function in Control Theory', memorandum from Institute of Economics, University of Oslo.

Seierstad, A. and K. Sydsæter (1987), *Optimal Control Theory with Economic Applications*, Amsterdam: North-Holland.

Sen, A. (ed.) (1970), *Growth Economics*, Harmondsworth, Middlesex: Penguin.

Solow, R. (1957), 'Technological Progress and Productivity Change', *Review of Economics and Statistics*, **39**, 312–20.

Solow, R.M. (1974), 'Intergenerational Equity and Exhaustible Resources', *The Review of Economic Studies*, symposium, 29–46.

Solow, R.M. (1986), 'On the Intergenerational Allocation of Natural Resources', *Scandinavian Journal of Economics*, **88**, 141–9.

Solow, R.M. (1992), 'An Almost Practical Step Towards Sustainability', Resources for the Future Invited Lecture, Washington, DC.

Stiglitz, J.E. (1974), 'Growth with Exhaustible Natural Resources: Efficient and Optimal Growth Paths', *Review of Economic Studies*, symposium, 123–38.

Stokey, N.L. (1991), 'Human Capital, Product Quality and Growth', *The Quarterly Journal of Economics*, **106**, 587–616.

Tahvonen, O. (1994), 'Carbon Dioxide Abatement as a Differential Game', *European Journal of Political Economy*, **10**, 685–705.

Tahvonen, O. (1995), 'International CO_2 Taxation and the Dynamics of Fossil Fuel Markets', *International Tax and Public Finance*, **2**, 261–78.

Tahvonen, O. and J. Kuuluvainen (1993), 'Economic Growth, Pollution, and Renewable Resources', *Journal of Environmental Economics and Management*, **24**, 101–18.

Toman, M.A. (1994), 'Economics of Sustainability: Balancing Trade offs and Imperatives', *Land Economics*, **70**, 399–413.

Turner, R.K. (ed.) (1993), *Sustainable Environmental Economics and Management: Principles and Practice*, London: Belhaven Press.

US Commerce Department (1994), 'Integrated Economic and Environmental Satellite Accounts', *Survey of Current Business*, April, 33–49.

Uzawa, H. (1965), 'Optimum Technical Change in an Aggregate Model of Economic Growth', *International Economic Review*, **6**, 18–31.

Varian, H. (1992), *Microeconomic Analysis*, New York: Norton.

Von Weizsäcker, C.C. (1965), 'Existence of Optimal Programmes of Accumulation for an Infinite Time Horizon', *Review of Economic Studies*, **32**, 85–104.

Weitzman, M.L. (1976), 'On the Welfare Significance of National Product in a Dynamic Economy', *The Quarterly Journal of Economics*, **90**, 156–62.

Weitzman, M.L. (1996), 'Sustainability and the Welfare Significance of National Product Revisited', mimeo, Department of Economics, Harvard University.

World Commission on Environment and Development (1987), *Our Common Future*, Oxford: Oxford University Press.

Index